Linda Weber
2004

D0779614

Llewellyn's
Herbal
Almanac
2004

© 2003 Llewellyn Worldwide
Editing/Design: Michael Fallon
Interior Art: © Mary Azarian
Cover Design: Lisa Novak
Cover Photos © Digital Vision,
and © Digital Stock.

You can order Llewellyn annuals
and books from *New Worlds*,
Llewellyn's magazine catalog. To
request a free copy of the catalog call
toll-free: 1-877-NEW WRLD, or
visit our website at
http://subscriptions.llewellyn.com.

ISBN 0-7387-0127-0
Llewellyn Worldwide
P.O. Box 64383, Dept. 0-7387-0127-0
St. Paul, MN 55164

Table of Contents

Growing and Gathering Herbs

Culinary Herbs

Herbs for Health

Herbs for Beauty

Herb Crafts

Herb History, Myth, and Magic

Introduction to Llewellyn's
Herbal Almanac

What is old is new again, wrote the poet. In the case of the 2004 edition of Llewellyn's *Herbal Almanac*, the sentiment is entirely appropriate. In this, the fifth edition of a now-old book, we are taking some new approaches in looking at the wide range of current research on, and expanding use of, herbs as medicine, as culinary spice, as beautifying cosmetic, and as magical item. This year in particular we tap into some of the world's most ancient knowledge—the magic and healing power of Latin American herb lore, for instance, as well as the lore regarding the rose, the buckeye nut, and garlic. And we bring to these pages some of the most innovative and original thinkers and writers on herbs.

This focus on the old ways—on times when men and women around the world knew and understood the power of herbs—is important today, as it seems the balance of the world has been thrown off kilter. Terrorists, water shortages, hatred, internecine battles, militant religious fervor, war, all seem to be holding sway over the good things in life—beauty, good food, health, love, and friendship. While we don't want to assign blame or cast any other aspersions, this state of affairs perhaps is not surprising considering so many of us—each one of us—is out of touch with the beauty, magic, and health-giving properties inherent in the natural world. Many of us spend too much of our lives rushing about in a technological bubble—striving to make money, being everywhere but here, living life in fast-forward. We forget to focus on the parts of life that can bring us back into balance and harmony.

Still, the news is not all bad. People are still fighting to make us all more aware of the magical, beautiful things in the world. In January 2001, for instance, Vermont became the first U.S.

state to pass a "Complementary and Alternative Health Care Act," and thus regulate the age-old techniques of herbal healers. Llewellyn's own home state of Minnesota signed a similar bill into law in July 2001. No doubt other states are bound to follow suit in coming years as society evolves and grows.

In the 2004 edition of the *Herbal Almanac*, we pay tribute to the ideals of magic and beauty and balance as they relate to the health-giving and beautifying properties of herbs. This may sound a bit far-fetched, but after all it does not take much imagination to see that a moonlight herb garden is a beautiful and magical thing, that natural herbal wines and liqueurs will bring joy to our lives, and that making herbal bookmarks and herbal brooms will bring the magic of nature to our daily lives.

Herbs are the perfect complement to the power of the mind, an ancient tool whose time has come back around to help us restore balance in our lives. More and more people are using them, growing and gathering them, and studying them for their beautifying and healing properties. We, the editors and authors of this volume, encourage the treatment of the whole organism—of the person and of the planet—with herbal magic. One person at a time, using ancient wisdom, we can make a new world.

Note: The old-fashioned remedies in this book are historical references used for teaching purposes only. The recipes are not for commercial use or profit. The contents are not meant to diagnose, treat, prescribe, or substitute consultation with a licensed health care professional. Of course you must take care not to replace regular medical treatment through the use of herbs. Herbal treatment is intended primarily to complement modern health care. Always seek professional help if you suffer from illness. Also, take care to read all warning labels before taking any herbs or starting on an extended herbal regimen. Always consult an herbal professional before beginning any sort of medical treatment—this is particularly true for pregnant women. Herbs are powerful things; be sure you are using that power to achieve balance.

Growing
and
Gathering
Herbs

Gardens by Moonlight

⤞ by Carrie Moss ⤝

I n exploring herb garden design books, new and old, one may come across the enchanting idea of planting a garden to be enjoyed particularly by the light of the Moon. This is an appealing idea, of course, though before going any further it must be said that in the modern world, this project is sadly not open for everyone to enjoy. That is, those who live in many urban areas will suffer too much light pollution from street lamps and buildings to see the wonderful effect of natural moonlight upon carefully chosen plants and herbs. They will never know the natural patterns and moods of night and day that are lost to Edison's dream. That said, a moonlight herb garden will be a good herb garden that everyone can enjoy either by daylight or by artificial illumination.

So what exactly is a moonlight herb garden? It is simply the idea of choosing those herbs that sport blooms and foliage which respond particularly well to being lit by the Moon. These plants generally have bright, white flowers, and light gray or silvery leaves. A herb garden is appreciated through all the senses, and you can choose herbs for their fragrance on warm, still evenings. And you can even bring sound into your garden by choosing plants with seed pods that rattle or leaves that swish in summer breezes, or that attract the soothing hum of bees on a warm day. In times when so many of us spend most of our days away from home or cooped up in a home office and have no access to a garden, a nighttime garden is a great treat. Not to mention the sheer romance of the moonlight itself . . .

To get cracking on your moonlight plot, you will need to think about aspects common to all garden design—though you can rest assured that herb gardens are more forgiving than most other sorts of gardens.

Weather

To start planning your garden, you will need to consider the weather and temperature in your particular locale (or growing zone in the United States—see the chart on the next page for more information on this). Some plants will simply not be possible for you to grow if you experience seasonal or year-round extremes of heat or cold. Other plants will be possible only if you are careful to nurture them and bring them inside at the peak of summer or winter. The seed packets or plant tags of your chosen varieties will have information on this, or else you can simply ask your supplier—they are always willing to help.

In England where I have my garden, there are no great extremes to contend with other than occasional relatively light frost. I can grow most things if I judiciously use a greenhouse in winter. When I lived in Canada, however, the winters were so long and harsh that, despite the wonderful summers many plants simply could not survive outdoors.

United States Department of Agriculture (USDA) Hardiness Zones

USDA Zone 1:	Below 50°F
USDA Zone 2:	-50°F to -40°F
USDA Zone 3:	-40°F to -30°F
USDA Zone 4:	-30°F to -20°F
USDA Zone 5:	-20°F to -10°F
USDA Zone 6:	-10°F to 0°F
USDA Zone 7:	0°F to 10°F
USDA Zone 8:	10°F to 20°F
USDA Zone 9:	20°F to 30°F
USDA Zone 10:	30°F to 40°F
USDA Zone 11:	Above 40°F

Soil

Along with examining your local weather patterns and determining your geographical zone, you should consider the state of your local planting medium, or soil. Your indigenous soil will affect what you can grow, and, unless your plant everything in containers or are willing to ship in tremendous amounts of earth, you will have to learn to work with what you have.

That said, you should know any soil will need periodic feeding by compost or fertilizer. You can either purchase this material or produce it yourself.

To begin to understand what help your soil will need, first examine your garden space. Is you garden area very dry and well drained, or waterlogged and clay-like? Your local garden center or a professional gardener will be able to test your earth if you are not sure, but it is important to have an idea of these technical factors to avoid the disappointment of planting the wrong types of plants in the wrong sorts of soil.

Space

A moonlight garden needs at least a small bed to be effective. This is not the sort of herb garden that will fit well into a container or window box, as the plants most conducive to night gardening need a good-sized patch to grow. Ideally, of course, you should give over your entire garden space or yard to this worthwhile project.

You will also need to consider the space available in terms of specific plants (garden books will help you with this). In general, you should avoid planting giants in a small tub, and you should avoid throttling delicate and miniature blossom by planting them next to species that will outgrow and choke them. For instance, a six-inch cutting of angelica *(Angelica archangelica)* or lovage *(Levisticum officinale)* may look perfectly innocent, even beautiful, but both will grow to more than seven feet in height in their second year.

As well as growing upward, some plants—for example the mint family *(Mentha)* or the comfrey family *(Symphytum)*—will stretch their roots and spread wildly. You need to be aware of how to position plants in relation to each other, and in relation to barriers. You may need to contain some species in pots or in their own delineated beds, or you may need to forgo certain species altogether. For example, I would recommend you plant the aforementioned comfrey *(Symphytum officinale)*, only if you have a fairly large garden.

Time

It is important to consider the time you are willing to spend tending your plot. Personally, I am a great lover of the hardy perennial that needs little more than the occasional trim. But other gardeners find their pleasure in growing their plants from seed each year and in nurturing tender cuttings and specimens through the winter. Again, before purchasing plants and seeds, check on the requirements and have a realistic view of how much time you will need to work on garden maintenance. That is, be honest about how much time and skill you have, and scale down your garden plan to account for this—or else all your initial hard work will be for naught after a few short months of unchecked growth and lack of maintenance.

Design

Herb garden design is a complicated matter. It is so complicated, in fact, that it can amount to a lifelong interest and hobby. There are endless possibilities for gardens ranging from formal to more rural, and including only plants or incorporating other materials such as stones or wood.

However small your plot, it is both worthwhile and a great pleasure to sit down with pencil and paper and to sketch out, whether in great detail or more broadly, what you want. If starting from scratch, make a list of possible plants, taking into account the factors mentioned above (growing conditions, space, soil, and so on). Also think about edging and pattern aids. Some things that might be incorporated into your garden include low wooden fencing, terra cotta border tiles, bricks, logs, large stones, pebbles, statues, bark chips, containers, and larger ready-made structures such as wooden ladders and cartwheels.

The one design constraint I would suggest is that the moonlight garden is, as I have already mentioned, best enjoyed when you have rather substantial amounts of each plant you wish to see. You should keep this in mind as you arrange your bed patterns—more simple and spacious plots of plants are to be preferred over small and intricate planting designs.

These ideas are a basic introduction to the main factors you should consider in planning your moonlight garden—they are necessarily incomplete due to so space constraints. It would be wise to consult a good gardening or herb book on growing basics and further garden design ideas. What follows are some suggestions for wonderful plants available for your moonlight project.

Broadly speaking, you need to look for flowers with gray or silvery foliage, or startling white flowers. This white flower theme is well-known and was popularized by the great writer and gardener Vita Sackville-West (1892–1962), who had a garden at Sissinghurst in Kent, England. Exceptions to this rule-of-white are listed below. This includes such plants as the evening primrose (*Oenothera erythrosepala*), whose large and bright yellow blooms appear almost fluorescent at twilight.

Night Herbs

Artemisia

Southernwood–*Artemisia arbrotanum*
Wormwood–*Artemisia absinthium*, "Lambrook Silver"
Sagebrush–*Artemisia ludoviciana*, "Silver King"

Artemisia is a lovely herb group that, incidentally, includes French tarragon (*Artemisia dracunculus*, "Sativa"). The family name derives from the Greek Moon goddess Artemis. These plants grow into a wonderful scented herb of three feet or so. Most artemisias are easy to grow. Its strong scent led to its use as a strewing herb—that is, a herb spread on the floor to repel insects, give off fragrance, and attract dust before being swept up (see page 233 for more information on this subject in Lynne Smythe's article "Medieval and Renaissance Strewing Herbs"). All varieties of artemisia are used by medical herbalists for a number of ills. The chemical extracted from the wormwood root (*Artemisia absinthium*) formed the base of the notorious addictive French liqueur, absinthe, which was outlawed because of its toxicity in 1915.

The three artemisia varieties named above have a particularly good silver-gray foliage useful for your moonlight gardens. If you are interested, you will be able to seek out many more varieties of this plant in nurseries and catalogs.

Clary Sage

Salvia sclarea

Although still in the sage family, clary sage deserves a separate entry as it is so different in form from the standard culinary sage detailed below. It has a large leaf and grows to between three and four feet in height. However, the beauty of clary sage for our purposes is in its dramatic flower stems. It comes in several colors so you should take care to seek out the white form. Look out also for silver clary (*Salvia argentia*), which has large silver gray leaves—although its flowers are less white than they might be. Clary sage is used medicinally and has also been used in the past to adulterate wine and beer. It allegedly enhanced both the flavor and intoxicating qualities of the brews. Although the flower might look tempting to cut, be warned that the strong fragrance can be overpowering indoors.

Cotton Lavender

Santolina chaemaecyparissus

This plant, with its very gray leaves, is ideal for a moonlight garden. Don't be confused, however; cotton lavender is not related to ordinary lavender (*Lavandula angustifolia*). Ordinary cotton lavender has bright yellow flowers, but the *Santolina neapolitana*, "Edward Bowles," variety has small, tight, pompom-shaped, cream-colored flowers. Cotton lavender reaches a height of about twenty inches or so, and, being strongly aromatic, it has insect-repelling qualities. If required, smaller dwarf forms (such as *Santolina chamaecyparissus nana*) can be found.

A note that may be of interest: Many varieties of garden plants carry the name "Edward Bowles" or "E A Bowles" after the great early twentieth-century English gardener Edward Augustus Bowles (1865–1954). He was, in case you were wondering, distantly related to Camilla Parker Bowles, Prince Charles' long-time friend.

Foxglove
Digitalis purpurea, "Alba"

The foxglove is a good plant to include in your moonlight garden, as it has tall flower spikes that reach up to around five feet in height. Common foxglove (*Digitalis purpurea*) has, as its Latin names indicates, purple flowers, but for our current project we need to look out for the excellent white varieties (i.e. "Alba"). The foxglove does not have a medicinal use suitable for home treatment, but as a herbal remedy developed for use in standard medicine it has been extremely effective for heart problems. In 1795, a Dr. Withering wrote, in "An Account of the Foxglove," of receiving a herbal recipe from a village herbalist in Shropshire, England, for the cure of dropsy. Although Withering noted that the great power and strength of the plant probably meant that it killed as many as it cured in less than expert hands, in his case it was a help. During the Second World War, foxglove leaves were gathered in large quantities in England by County Herb Committees run by the Women's Institutes.

Lamb's Ears
Stachys byzantina

Lamb's ears are another great moonlight garden choice. This appealing little plant has downy silvery leaves with an almost furry texture, and it grows to around two feet tall. The flowers are small and bright magenta-pink, and they grow on tall spikes (as signified by the Latin name *Stachys*, meaning "spike-like"). Often thought of as a garden plant rather than a herb, this lovely specimen has reputed medicinal qualities as a natural bandage beneficial for minor wounds (an ancient name for the plant is woundwort). It is also a useful plant for flower arranging. A circlet of larger leaves make an especially attractive border for a herbal tussie-mussie, or a knot of flowers, both for their soft coloring and tactile quality. For an even better moonlight effect from larger leaves, look for the cultivar "Silver Carpet."

Lavender

Lavandula angustifolia

Lavender is must for any herb garden I have ever planted. Another Mediterranean native, lavender likes dry, well-drained soil, and lots of Sun. As well as having a wonderful scent, lavender has gray leaves that are good for catching moonlight. You may also want to look out for white- *(Lavandula angustifolia,* "Alba") or pale-pink- ("Loddon Pink') flowered varieties, though these tend to be less robust and less heavily flowered than the more standard mauve-flowered varieties. In the end, you may be more tempted to enjoy the gray foliage of plain old lavender and just forget the flowers by night (they are lovely by day).

Lavender has useful sedative and soothing medicinal qualities and can be seen in many aromatherapy oils, candles, and sleep pillows. It can also be used to charming effect in the kitchen as an additive to sponge cakes and ice creams—just so long as a it is added with a very sparing hand; otherwise you might imagine you are eating a mouthful of cologne. For cakes, just infuse four flower heads per cup of sugar for two or three days before adding the sugar to your batter. For ice cream, add a few flower heads to some warm liquid (cream or sugar syrup) and strain before use.

Lily of the Valley

Convallaria majalis

This is another charming little plant to be grown for its delightful and startling white flowers. The flower has a wonderful perfume, and is often used in commercial soaps, bath preparations, and perfumes. It is said, in legend, that the scent lured the nightingale away from the fields and hedgerows to the forests and woodlands where lily of the valley likes to grow. As it favors woodlands, so too does the plant like a shady spot. But it should not be too damp. Like the foxglove, lily of the valley has properties beneficial to some heart conditions, but it is not suitable for home administration and should only be prescribed by a qualified medical herbalist. The Latin *majalis* refers to the month of May, the time it blooms in Europe. The French name for this plant is *muguet de mai*, and in German it is called *Maiblume*. In Britain, however, lily of the valley rarely flowers before June.

Rose

Rosa

No garden looking for strong white colors should be without at least one beautiful rose, climate permitting. The first true herb rose was the Apothecary's Rose or *Rosa gallica "Officinalis."* This flower was called the Queen of the Flowers by the Greek poetess Sappho in 600 BC. Known generally for its powerful fragrance, rose varieties are too various to enumerate, but this means you can go exploring and find one to suit your needs. This may include a modern hybrid tea rose, or, my favorite, an old-fashioned variety or a moss rose.

You will also have many options in terms of planting design, as you can opt for a climber, a standard, a bush or a hedge-forming wild rose, or a dog rose *(Rosa canina)*. Roses are easy and robust once established, though they do need certain conditions and pruning—so seek advice if you are new to these lovely blooms. Try to visit a specialist garden or nursery to get an idea of the wonderful selection available.

Shakespeare noted the wonderful romance and scent of the wild sweet briar rose *(Rosa rubiginosa)*, which he referred to as the eglantine:

> *I know a bank whereon the wild thyme blows*
> *Where oxlips and the nodding violets grows,*
> *Quite over-canopied with luscious woodbine*
> *With sweet musk roses and with eglantine.*
> *Midsummer Night's Dream, Act 2, Scene 2*

Rosemary

Rosmarinus officinalis

As with lavender, I find it hard to be satisfied with a herb garden that lacks rosemary. Fortunately, this plant fits into many garden themes, including culinary, medicinal, or, as now, moonlight. The upright growth of rosemary and its gray-green leaves make this an excellent choice for our moonlight design, and although common rosemary has nondescript mauve flowers, the white-flowered "Alba" cultivar is relatively easy to find. This cultivar is a far more robust specimen than white lavender. It will grow, as will all rosemary, to a good four or five feet high, and it will last many years. Legend has it that rosemary can grow to a maximum of six feet in height and can have a life-span of thirty-three years, and that these are the height and life span of Christ. As another Mediterranean native, rosemary likes dry, warm conditions, but it will live happily through light frost once it is established.

The Latin name comes from *ros marinus*, or "dew of the sea," and the plant particularly enjoys salty sea air. As Shakespeare knew, it is the herb of love, fidelity, and remembrance, hence its traditional inclusion in bridal sprays:

Here's rosemary for remembrance,
Pray you love remember.

Hamlet, Act 4, Scene 5

Rue

Ruta graveolens

Rue has an unusual rounded, three-lobed leaf and forms a lovely gray-green bush. The plant does, however, have a bitter scent and can given an extremely unpleasant blistering rash to those with sensitive skin. It is advised that you avoid handling it if possible, and that you particularly do not handle it on hot days as perspiration on the skin can set off a reaction. Rue has been called the "herb of grace," as branches were used to sprinkle holy water many hundreds of years ago in Europe. For garden design purposes, an even better effect might be achieved with the variegated form (*Ruta graveolens*, "Variegata"), which has a good proportion of cream in its leaf coloring along with the usual gray-green. Rue needs a well-drained soil and full Sun to thrive.

Sage

Salvia officinalis

Another common herb, *Salvia officinalis* is the common, or garden, sage. With its grayish green leaves, sage fits well into our moonlight garden. It forms a satisfying patch of foliage that grows to about three feet in height. For still better effect, however, seek out species, such as *Saliva officinalis*, "Albiflora," with bright white flowers.

As a general rule, sage enjoys a dry spot with plenty of Sun and will overwinter outside through moderate frost. Although a perennial, sage does have a habit of getting an open, woody center after a time, so plan on taking cuttings and replacing it every four or five years. A popular culinary herb, particularly in its native Mediterranean and England, the name sage derives from the Latin *salvere*, meaning "to cure," an indication of its strong healing properties. Indeed, the botanical name *officinalis* (which includes several other plants in this short moonlight garden list) indicates that the plant was used medicinally in ancient times.

Sweet Woodruff

Galium odoratum

One of my favorite little plants, sweet woodruff is a treasure despite that it does not have the gray leaves we are seeking. In fact, its leaves are a fresh, bright green, and they grow in attractive whorls around upright stems. However, sweet woodruff forms a low (up to a six inch-high) carpet of green topped with a mass of tiny, bright, chalk-white flowers that look lovely by moonlight. This plant can not only stand the shade, it actually requires it. Its natural habitat is the European and British forest floor, and it will lose its greenness in the Sun.

When fresh, sweet woodruff is scentless, but it has the unusual quality that when dried the hitherto dormant chemical coumarin is released. This gives off the powerful and not unpleasant fragrance of new-mown hay. This scent will be retained for many months, and woodruff, along with its close relative lady's bedstraw *(Gallium verum)*, was widely used in cupboards to freshen linens and deter insects. In Germany, sweet woodruff was traditionally used to scent the festive drink *Maiwein* or *Maibowl*. To enjoy this ritual, put a few dried sprigs of sweet woodruff into a bottle of sweet white wine a few days before May 1. Drink your Maiwein with some freshly sliced strawberries floating atop. To allow children to join in the fun, infuse apple juice in the same way.

Thyme

Thymus

There are literally dozens of different varieties of thyme in this family *(thymus)*, and in fact common garden thyme *(Thymus officinalis)*, with its green leaves and pinkish-mauve flowers, is not the best choice for your moonlight garden. Some of the lemon thymes (such as *Thymus x citriodorus*, "Silver Posie") have graywhite leaves, and many varieties (such as *Thymus praecox* sub. *Articus*, "Alba," and *Thymus serpyllum*, "Snow Drift") have pretty white flowers.

You probably know that thyme is a low-growing, robust herb, and that most of the ornamental varieties have the same strong scent that derives from the oil thymol, and thus the same culinary value, as garden thyme. Being of Mediterranean origin, thyme likes a sunny, well-drained location. The strong fragrance has led to thyme often being included in the posies that were carried in Europe some hundreds of years ago. These were intended to offer protection from disease.

Yarrow

Achillea millefolium

Yarrow is a strong background herb that grows to around three feet in height and has clusters of flower heads. Wild yarrow has dull white flowers, and of the domesticated varieties some have wonderfully colored flowers ("Cerise Queen" is vibrant pink, and "Sulphur" and "Cloth of Gold" are bright yellow). For our moonlight garden we want a really good white, so, although the common specimen would do at a pinch, look for cultivars such as "White Beauty" and "The Pearl."

Yarrow is named botanically for Achilles, whose only weak spot was on his heel. Yarrow has the property of staunching blood flow and was used in the American Civil War for such purpose. It has also been known as staunchweed, bloodwort, and carpenter's weed—all of which, as the names indicate, were used as wound dressing. As with the botanical name *officinalis,* the Old English suffix *wort* indicates medicinal usage. The name *millefolium* means "a thousand leaves" and accounts for the many tiny leaf divisions of the plant.

Closely related to yarrow is the self-explanatorily named sneezewort *(Achillea ptarmica).* This plant has good white flowers, though it is not as handsome as yarrow. It gained its name from being dried, powdered, and taken as snuff to clear the head of "tough slimy humours," according to the great herbalist, Nicholas Culpeper (1616–1654).

The above is but a short selection of plants that will bring the right touches of color to your moonlight garden. This is a wonderful and romantic project, and I hope that some readers take up the challenge to plant up a wonderful herb patch to enjoy by the light of the Moon.

Natural Pest Control

❧ by Laurel Reufner ❧

Got the proverbial aphids in your roses? Thrips in your peach trees? Or, as in my case, scale claiming your sweet laurel? While a few pests aren't necessarily a bad thing, no one wants to let them get out of hand and destroy the beauty, hard work, and enjoyment that make up a garden. When dangerous numbers of pests do make their presence known, try some of the techniques included in this article to bring them back under control while still being kind to the environment.

It's been said that the best defense is a good offense, and in this case, the best offense is good prevention in the first place. To keep the majority of pests out of the garden to begin with, there is little need for pesticides and other methods of eradication. To start, take a weekly walk through your garden just to look for signs of bad bugs going wild in your herbs, fruits, and vegetables. Oh, and learn to tell the difference between good bugs and bad bugs. (Yes, Virginia, there are good bugs.) Then try putting the following measures in place instead that repel pests and attract beneficial bugs to help out.

Companion Planting

Companion planting has a long history among gardeners. As soon as mankind had the time to pay attention to the details of their little plots of plants, they also started noticing that some plants did better with certain other plant neighbors, and worse with others. Some plants attracted beneficial bugs and others repelled the pests. What follows is just a partial listing of the many wondrous plant combinations that send the bad bugs packing or that kill them outright. This should be enough to get you started, but please, feel free to further explore this organic gardening option.

Artemisia/wormwood will control or repel ants, black flea beetles, cabbage moths, maggots, loopers, carrot flies, flea beetles, fleas, Japanese beetles, mice, moths, snails and slugs, and whiteflies. When used in insecticidal sprays (see below) do not let it come in contact with the parts of your vegetables, fruits, or herbs that you eat—as wormwood is poisonous.

Basil controls asparagus beetles, flies, mosquitoes, thrips, tomato worms, and whiteflies. Don't plant it near rue, as they to are antagonistic to one another.

Chrysanthemums, dried, crushed and scattered about, will help with aphids and leafhoppers. The living plant will also kill nematodes.

Dill helps control aphids, imported cabbageworms, spider mites, squash bugs, and tomato worms. Since dill controls tomato worms by attracting them to itself, do not plant dill near your tomatoes.

Fennel will help control aphids, snails, and slugs.

Feverfew will attract aphids away from to roses, making it a good trap crop.

Garlic helps with aphids, cabbage looper, cabbage maggots, flea beetles, imported cabbageworms, Japanese beetles, mites, mosquitoes, peach borer, onion fly, rabbits, snails, slugs, and ticks.

Geraniums will control corn earworms, imported cabbage-worms, leafhoppers, and mosquitoes. The leaves of white geraniums are poisonous to Japanese beetles.

Marigolds help control populations of aphids, cabbage maggots, Colorado potato beetles, corn earworm, cucumber beetle, Mexican bean beetles, mosquitoes, nematodes, rabbits, and whitefly. Pot marigold will help with asparagus beetle and tomato worms. However, marigolds do not like beans, and they may attract slugs.

Mints, in general, help keep down ants, aphids, imported cabbageworm, and white cabbage moths. Here are some specific mints and their uses: **Peppermint** controls ants, cabbage looper, and whitefly; **spearmint** controls ants and cabbage loopers, and **catnip** helps with ants, aphids, Colorado potato beetle, flea beetle, cucumber beetle, Japanese beetle, and squash bug.

Pennyroyal repels ants, cabbage loopers, fleas, flies, imported cabbageworms, and mosquitoes.

Nasturtium controls aphids, cabbage loopers, Colorado potato beetle, cucumber beetle, imported cabbageworm, squash bugs, and striped pumpkin beetles. Plant it as a barrier around plants you wish to protect. Nasturtium also make a nice trap crop for black aphids.

Rosemary helps keep out bean beetles, cabbage moths, carrot flies, Mexican bean beetles, snails, and slugs.

Rue repels cucumber beetles, flies, slugs, and moles. This herb will also help repel cats from your garden. Keep it clear of basil, cabbage, and sage.

Sage repels black flea beetles, cabbage maggots and moths, flea beetles, imported cabbageworms, and slugs. However, sage does not agree with cucumbers or rue.

Savory will help with bean beetles, cabbage moths, and Mexican bean beetles.

Tansy will help contain ants, Colorado potato beetles, flea beetles, flies, imported cabbageworm, Japanese beetles, mice, squash bugs, and striped cucumber beetles. Be careful where you plant tansy, as it is toxic to many animals, and to people.

Thyme helps control cabbage loopers, moths, worms, imported cabbageworms, and whiteflies.

The Good Bugs

You'll want most of these guys in your garden. All of the following bugs are the good guys, helping you keep down the level of pests. Attracting these to your garden to live and dine is a great way of keeping the destructive tendencies of the bad guys in check, so this is another good preventative measure for a healthy garden. Further, many true insects feed on pests during one stage of their life and then help pollinate the flowers during another.

If you're out walking in your garden and see one of these bugs, cheer them on and pat yourself on the back. It means these guys were traveling along and happened to see an oasis—and buffet—in your yard.

Lacewings are odd, delicate-looking insects. With the open lacework of their wings and their solid bodies, they look like something out of science fiction or the land of fairy.

Don't let their delicate appearance throw you, though, these little guys chow down on aphids, thrips, mites, mealybugs, scales, moth and other insect eggs, small caterpillars, and any other soft-bodied slow-moving insect. Attract them to your garden with pollen and nectar plants, and water when it is hot out.

Ladybird beetles, or **ladybugs,** are considered sacred to the Virgin Mary, having arrived en masse, once upon a time, in answer to some distraught farmers' prayers. And they truly are an answer to the gardener's prayers for pest relief. These little ladies feed on aphids by the dozens, eating up to forty per hour when on a spree. They also go after other small, soft-bodied insects and insect eggs. Some species will eat mealybugs, others prefer spider mites, and still others enjoy a good meal of soft scale. If you want ladybugs in your garden, attract them with pollen and nectar plants. They especially enjoy angelica, dill, Queen Anne's lace, dandelion, and yarrow. If you plan on purchasing ladybugs to release into your garden, make sure to let them loose at night when they will stick around rather than flying off to other areas.

Praying mantids, or **mantises,** take the prize for dramatic-looking insects. They look a bit like praying aliens and are a lot of fun to watch. The praying mantis is also an incredible garden warrior who eats anyone and everyone who doesn't move fast enough, including other mantises. But hey, what can you expect from a species where the female bites the head off the male after mating?

Soldier beetles have leathery-looking wings and come spotted (yellow with black spots) or gray (with orange heads). They love to eat aphids, caterpillars, corn rootworms, grasshopper eggs, and beetle larvae. These warriors also chow down on other insects, including beneficial ones, but they really are good bugs to have in your garden.

Attract them there by planting goldenrod, hydrangea bushes, and catnip. They will also come for pollen and nectar plants, especially milkweed and wild parsley.

Tachnid flies are nasty little beneficials. While the adults feed exclusively on nectar and honeydew, their larvae are parasitic fellows who will pupate in and consume some of the garden's worst caterpillars. Their menu includes cutworms, codling moths, hornworms, cabbage loopers, armyworms, tent caterpillars, earworms, and gypsy moth larva. Some tachnids will target sawflies, squash bugs, stinkbugs, and grasshoppers. Get these guys into your garden by offering dill, parsley, sweet clover, Queen Anne's lace, and yarrow.

Ground beetles are one of my favorite critters. They are voracious in their eating, and they go after many ground-dwelling pests—including horrid slugs. This common beetle will also feast on snails, cutworms, cabbage maggots, codling moth pupae, and other pests. If it spends part of its life cycle in the dirt, it is fair game for the ground beetle. Some species will hunt pests living in plants, while others take to the trees to hunt, among other things, tent caterpillars. Attract these beetles by offering them a habitat they can call home by planting perennials and other permanent bedding plants in your garden. Cover pathways with stones, clover, or sod, so they have a place to hide during the day.

Fireflies may not show up in many books concerning beneficial bugs, but they certainly deserve to be there. Remember my least favorite bug, the slug? Well, these guys love to dine on them, along with snails. Who knew? And they put on such a lovely light show during the height of summer.

Other Beneficial Critters

While some spiders do cause damage in the garden, most arachnids are great to have around outside. To bring more spiders into your garden, offer them flowering plants wherein they may lie in wait for their prey. Also, permanent bedding plants and perennials will offer spiders a good year-round habitat.

Toads are just cool. As a small child I always got excited whenever I found a toad hopping around near the rosebushes. Of course, as a child there was always the danger of the toad peeing on you and giving you warts. Mere superstition, of course, but it did add to the thrill and excitement of picking one up. If you can attract a toad to live in your garden, you will have an invaluable partner in your quest for pest control. Try making a toad villa by turning a broken terra cotta pot on its side and partially burying it in the soil. Also, they need water, both for drinking and reproducing, so if you can offer a shallow pool, even if just a sunken birdbath, your toads will be happier.

Bats are one of the most understood, and yet most helpful, of all animal species. Coming out only after dark, bats consume thousands of flying insects per night—including mosquitoes and many of the critters that hurt your garden. All they ask in return is a place to nest and fresh water to drink. If you want to attract bats to your garden or yard, hang some bat boxes in shady, protected areas and maybe install a small pool. If you're lucky, the pool will attract bats and toads.

Insecticides

Organic insecticides should be your last line of defense when it comes to pest control. These sprays and dusts do not give you as much control over which bugs and other critters you invite into your garden, and which you want to exclude. That is, insecticide tends to kill indiscriminately. That said, use insecticides only in the late evening or at night, when there are fewer beneficial insects out that might be harmed by drifting spray. And try not to spray too close to ponds and other bodies of waters, as cold-blooded creatures may also be affected.

Two of the most commercially popular organic sprays are rotenone, from the roots of *Derris elliptica*, and pyrethrum, from the chrysanthemum family. They should be available at organic garden suppliers if you can't find them elsewhere. However, you can also make your own herbal insecticides quite easily at home. The bonus in making your own is that you can better tailor the solution for a particular troubled area. A good general formula when making sprays is four cups of boiling water to a healthy handful of the fresh herb (or two tablespoons dried herb.) Add a teaspoon or so of dishwashing detergent—I use a Castile soap available at health food stores. This will allow the insecticide to stick more easily to the leaves.

For aphids, place about 8 ounces of either elder or rhubarb leaves in 4 cups of water and simmer for a half hour. Cool and strain, then add 1½ cups of cold water in which a teaspoon of detergent has been dissolved. Other herbs for aphids include basil leaves and garlic. With garlic, use 4 cloves for every 4 to 5 cups of water.

To make a general-use insecticide, for when there are no other insecticides for the job, use leaves from either costmary or great fleabane. Wormwood will also do the job, as well as tackle bigger bugs such as caterpillars.

Coriander works well as a spray against spider mites.

Try a spray of kelp infused in water to feed your plants and get rid of pesky bugs. Kelp is beneficial enough just as a plant food, but it will also repel aphids and Japanese beetles.

A good insecticidal dust can be made of crushed and ground bay leaves, peppermint, tansy, and cayenne pepper. Sprinkle it around troubled plants in the garden as a pest deterrent.

Lemon balm makes another good insect-repelling dust for the garden.

Other Pest Control Tricks

As you may have guessed by now, slugs are one of my least favorite creatures. Our house is a huge slug magnet. I've seen huge masses of them, usually crawling all over the cat food (yuck!). And just try stepping on one slithering across your floor in the dark while you're barefoot!

While applying salt does indeed work to kill slugs, the results are plainly disgusting and I just don't have the heart, or stomach, for the job. Another method of killing slugs, which isn't nearly as messy, drowns the little leaf-eaters. Get a wide-mouthed bottle or dish and sink it into the ground up to the opening. Buy a bottle or can of cheap beer, and fill your container up to about the halfway mark. Slugs love the booze and will come over to take a drink, whereupon they will fall in and drown. Simply clean out the dish or bottle after a few days, and repeat.

There are two slug-deterring methods that will not kill the creatures. Sprinkling ashes around targeted plants will repel slugs, as they don't like the feel of the stuff. Also, you can lay down copper strips in select areas. Slugs really don't like them as they get a good chemical jolt when their mucus comes into contact with the metal.

Ants not only eat in your garden, but also build colonies all over the place. Ants deserve some credit, though, as they are smart pests who "farm" other insects the way we do cattle. They love the honeydew that aphids and scale produce, and have been known to herd colonies of said critters. However, by sprinkling bone meal, wood ash, or crushed and powdered charcoal around your garden area, you can deter ants from entering and building their colonies. They can also be talked into moving by pouring lemon juice on their homes.

One last suggestion is to plant a wildflower garden. All those beautiful flowers are sure to attract enough good bugs to more than contain any serious troubles from the bad bugs. And you'll have the added benefit of all that wild, natural beauty.

These are just a few suggestions for controlling pesky bug problems in your garden. There are numerous books and websites out there that provide far more information on the topic than I have. Oh, and to get rid of the scale on my sweet laurel plant, I give it a scrubbing with a soft cloth or nailbrush and some soapy water. You may have to remove some of the tougher scale with your fingernail, but it does take care of the problem.

For More Information

I collected information from all over, but found the following sources entertaining, knowledgeable, and fun:

Allison Mia Starcher's *Good Bugs for Your Garden* (Algonquin Books, New York: 1995) provides lovely botanical drawings of beneficial garden bugs and critters. Along with the drawings are commentaries on each insect—including its habitat, size, and ways to attract it to your garden.

A nice, thorough book on garden pests and diseases is Rodale Press's *Controlling Pests and Diseases*, part of their Successful Organic Gardening series (by Patricia S. Michalak and Linda A. Gilkeson, 1994). I highly recommend this book. It offers tons of tips, tricks, and information on protecting your garden organically and safely.

On the Internet, check out *Golden Harvest Organics* for more information on companion planting in general. Yes, this is a store site, but they offer some great information. It's located at: http://www.ghorganics.com/.

Another site is *Garden's Ablaze*, which offers a fantastic chart for looking up which plants repel which bug. It is located at: http://www.gardensablaze.com/.

A Child's Herb Garden

❧ by Dallas Jennifer Cobb ❧

When children enter our lives, many things change. As a mother and avid gardener, I have changed my herb garden to accommodate my daughter Terra.

During her baby and toddler years, for instance, my challenge was to identify and then remove potentially toxic herbs from the garden. Now that she is old enough to understand, my gardening tasks have changed. I am now trying to engage my daughter in the garden, and to teach her what I can about growing and harvesting herbs. That is, I have given her a small gardening space where she can learn, makes decision and mistakes, and muse about herbs.

In my larger section of the garden, I am cultivating only herbs I know to be nontoxic, and that are primarily beneficial and bountiful. These herbs provide relief and remedy to my daughter's ills, and they are culinary, cosmetic, and healing resources for our family.

As Terra grows, I will gently lessen my protective watch over her, and expect her to identify herbs herself. I hope to instill an awareness of toxicity and potential danger, without overwhelming her with fear. By teaching the uses and powers of herbs, I seek to enable her to approach herbs with a deep respect rooted in knowledge. Only then can I safely reintroduce potentially toxic plants to my garden.

Like me, you may want to share the magic of herbs with your children. In this article, you will find ideas for involving children in herb gardening, suggestions for the best herbs to include in a child's own herbal garden, and the most versatile healing herbs for treatment of some of the common ailments of childhood. To help you organize your garden so it is safe for your children, I have also listed potentially toxic herbs you should be wary of.

I am focusing on herbs that are generally beneficial to toddlers and children. For more information on herbs for babies and infants, see my article "Herbal Care for Expecting Mothers & for Infants" in Llewellyn's 2002 edition of the *Herbal Almanac*.

The Garden of Life

Parents and grandparents often struggle to protect their children from danger and teach them values and ways that will aid them through life. We have profound wishes for our youngers— abundance, love, peace, and well-being. We have dreams for them that we only hope they can fulfill. But the world today is filled with violence and unrest. Our lives are overshadowed by images of destruction, and the media brings us constant coverage of the atrocities committed around the world. Every day our children are exposed to information, ideas, and images that we have no control over.

While we cannot isolate our children and grandchildren from the world, we can offer a quiet, contemplative space where they may find calm and reward. That is to say, we can take our children to our gardens.

A Peaceful Practice

Gardening is a remarkable and blessed thing. Many people find meditative calm and reflection through the practice of gardening, and through a connection to the cycles of the seasons. By bringing our children into the garden, and by teaching them about plants, soil, and the cycles of growth through the various activities of gardening, we can impart spiritual and ecological values to our children. It is here that we plant the seeds of peace, cultivate respect for all living entities, and grow ecological awareness. The Earth is a living entity, and all life is an intricate part of the flow. The garden is a microcosm that can be used to teach lessons about the macrocosm of life. However vague and uncertain life can seem at times, gardens can teach us the magic of life.

But there are dangers in the garden too—namely, toxic plants and poisonous substances. This article focuses specifically on herbs, and is by no means fully conclusive. I urge you to research potentially toxic vegetables, flowers, trees, shrubs, and house plants. It is said that "an ounce of prevention is worth a pound of cure." By knowing what plants are toxic, we can avoid potential danger and practice priceless prevention.

Practical Methods for Involving Children in the Garden

Cultivating herbal interest and teaching the properties of herbs to children can be done easily and most immediately by creating a garden for your child. That is, plan to teach gardening to your child in a real garden plot that belongs to the child. By designing and designating an area of my garden as my daughter's own herbal garden, I have given her a sense of ownership in the garden, and a subsequent sense of belonging. I am teaching her how to grow and care for herbs, and she is learning larger lessons about the cycle of life.

Start by designating an area of your garden or yard as the child's own. Create a special little spot where your child can plant. Choose an area that is blessed with good soil and has adequate sunlight. Give the child and the garden a head start by adding compost to the soil. Make a learning trip to the family composter, then till the soil as you teach the goodness of natural fertilizing. With four pieces of wood you can build a frame for a raised bed. The garden is now at a perfect height for a child. The wooden edges make a great spot for sitting to weed, plant, or contemplate.

Children learn through watching, mimicking, and copying. When they are in the garden with us, children copy our behaviors and actions. Get your child some good-quality garden tools to use. You can buy "toy" plastic garden tools, but there are quality trowels and weeding claws that are just the right size for children and made from durable wood and metal. These tools will last until the child outgrows them. For raking and hoeing, many garden centers sell telescoping tools with interchangeable heads. For very little money you can buy a lightweight alloy set that can adjust to suit your child, or to suit you.

Dig together. Shovel and turn soil, harvest the composter, and spread compost together. Let your child watch you rake and hoe, learning the movements and techniques. As you garden together, continue an ongoing chatter of explanation. Speak aloud what you are doing, and why. While it is necessary to chose words that your child will understand, you can still cover the complexities of gardening: "All this compost will feed the garden, and make the plants grow big and strong. Let's spread it all over, so all of the plants are nourished." And so on.

Choose seeds that are viable and easy to sprout, and choose plants that are nontoxic and safe for a small child. Show your child pictures of the plants that will grow, perhaps using a gardening catalog or magazine, and give them some decision-making authority. Allowing your children some choice in the plants they will grow cultivates ownership of and connection to the garden from the beginning. Just be sure to promote herbs that will be beneficial and bountiful. This way you limit their choices to nontoxic and versatile healing herbs.

Each day, teach a little bit. Make the lesson both fun and informational. Don't overwhelm your child with words, lectures, or details. They don't need to know everything at once—you are trying to instill a lesson for life here. Give them activities that they can easily perform; briefly discuss the reasons for doing it, and examine the effects. When the weather is dry, talk about the plants' need for water and soak the roots with water. Spend a little time each day weeding, and talk about the importance of removing some of the obstacles that get in the way of the growing plants. You'll be amazed how quickly children learn to recognize weeds and correctly cull them.

Life Lessons

Watering, feeding, and weeding are gardening lessons that are transferable to other areas of life. While you undertake these activities think about how you approach your life: How do you feed your soul; what do you thirst for; how do you deal with the minor annoyances and obstructions of everyday living? What do you when something thwarts your growth? Let the garden be a metaphor for imparting your deepest spiritual and philosophical beliefs to your children.

Talk about these things with your kids in simple and clear words. Where appropriate, use the metaphors from the garden: feeding, watering, sowing, growing, and weeding. As children work in the garden, they hone and refine their coordination, learn the names of plants, recognize the flowers, and learn to stoop and look, smell, and touch. And they bring these skills eventually to areas outside of the garden. They learn life lessons by learning the ancient growing crafts.

Lessons will be taught, not just by us, their parents, but by Mother Nature too. Lessons about time, cycles, biology, and the miracle of growth and change. The cycles of nature are expansive and wise. Daily gardening provides a focused time to observe and learn from the cycles of seeding, sprouting, rooting, shooting, flowering, fruiting, seeding anew, dying, and composting. Every aspect of life is reflected here.

Cultivating Herbal Interest

In your daily routines, start to point out the herbs contained in the cosmetic, culinary, and healing products that you use. Say for instance: "Ahhh, it's tea time. Shall we have some mint tea, from our garden mint? It's so refreshing." Or say: "Let's put some calendula salve on your itchy skin. It will it feel better." Or: "I know your tooth hurts. Here's some chamomile tea to soothe the pain." Using herbs and herbal products, and identifying them for our children, cultivates interest in herbs for life.

As we connect the herbs to the products, we introduce the child to the herbs at work. It is also important to name the herb, and talk about what it looks like, feels like, or smells like. If you can take your child to your garden and show them the herb, all the better. Children generally are kinesthetic, or experiential, learners. This means they like to see, taste, touch, smell, and feel things in order to learn about them. Use this fact to enliven your teachings. Don't rely just on words to teach them about herbs. Break off a sprig of fresh lavender, and let them look at the individual flowers that make up the blossom. Lightly crush a leaf of lemon balm, and let them smell it.

Teaching Herbal Properties to Children

The properties of herbs can be taught both as you use the herbs or herbal products, and as you grow and tend herbs. You may be surprised by how much your children already know about herbs that have been used in your household. The exact words we use may be parroted back to us, because our children reflect back to us what we do. One day I saw my daughter, who was then only fifteen months old, call to our cat with a sprig of catnip in her hand. She had seen me offer the herb to Kali many times, and she was a tiny reflection of me.

Plan to start slowly with this teaching. Focus on one or two herbs that you use regularly. Whenever you use the herb, tell your child what you are doing. Again, speak simply, and thoroughly, about what you are using the herbs for: "Let's gather some oregano to make pasta sauce"; "Pick some chives to put in our eggs"; "Add some sage to the tea to bring us peace." As time passes, build the repertoire to include a larger variety of herbs.

The Six Best Herbs for a Child's Herb Garden

When you are designing a child's herb garden, choose plants that are easy to grow, and that are hardy, bountiful, and beautiful. It is also best for your child to grow herbs that he or she may later use. They can then connect what they grow with the remedy that has helped them or brought relief.

Start small, and choose just a few herbs. My six suggested starter herbs are: calendula *(Calendula officinalis)*, catnip *(Nepeta cataria)*, chamomile *(Chamaemelum nobile)*, lavender *(Lavandula angustifolia)*, lemon balm *(Melissa officinalis)*, and peppermint *(Mentha x piperita)*.

A word of warning. Mint needs to be contained so that it doesn't send its shoots underground, and end up taking over the garden. Catnip and lemon balm should be harvested before they flower, so that they do not self-seed at too prolific a rate. Calendula should be harvested at the height of flowering to prevent the development of its fertile seed heads.

Other Herbs Safe for Children

Aside from establishing a child's herb garden, you need to make your larger garden child-safe. Though little comprehensive research has been done on herb ingestion, the following herbs are considered nontoxic in small amounts, and safe to have in a garden that children visit.

Anise *(Pimpinella anisum)*
Basil *(Ocimum basilicum)*
Borage *(Borago officinalis)*
Caraway *(Carum carvi)*
Chives *(Allium schoenoprasum)*
Coriander *(Coriandrum satibum)*
Cumin *(Cuminum cyminum)*
Dandelion *(Taraxacum officinale)*
Dill *(Anethum graveolens)*
Fennel *(Foeniculum vulgore)*
Garlic *(Allium sativum)*
Hyssop *(Hysoppus officinalis)*
Lovage *(Levisticum officinale)*
Marjoram *(Origanum majorana)*
Meadowsweet *(Filipendula ulmaria)*
Nasturtium *(Tropaeolum majus)*
Oregano *(Origanum vulgare)*
Parsley *(Petroselinum crispa)*
Rosemary *(Rosmarinus officinalis)*
Sage *(Salvia officinalis)*
Sorrel *(Rumex scutatus)*
Spearmint *(Mentha spicata)*
Sweet Basil *(Ocimum basilicum)*
Tarragon *(Artemesia dracunculus)*
Thyme *(Thymus vulgaris)*
Yarrow *(Achillea millefolium)*

This list is not comprehensive. If you have favorite herbs in your garden that are not listed here, take the time to research the herb, its toxicity, and its safety before you use it.

While it is not a common herb in North American gardens, I was convinced that the stevia *(Stevia rebaudiana)* growing in my garden was probably nontoxic if ingested. After all, we were drying it and using it as a sweetener in culinary preparations. But, safe for adult consumption and safe for child consumption are two very different issues. I chose to research it more carefully, to be certain that it was entirely nontoxic for children. I figured that if my daughter tasted a small piece of it, the pleasing sweet taste would compel her to eat much more. I needed to make sure that the ingestion of large amounts of stevia wouldn't cause adverse effects for her.

My Internet research led me to public statements made by the American Herbal Products Association and The Herb Research Foundation, attesting to the safety of stevia for consumption. I knew these organizations and felt secure that they had done legitimate research. Then, I found a statement by the Thomas J. Lipton Company citing the results of their literature and research reviews. In over 900 articles written about stevia, they found no references to, or documentation of, incidences of any adverse human health consequences associated with ingesting stevia.

Oddly enough, it was the review of research by this for-profit company that made me feel most secure in having stevia in the garden. They had literally spent millions of dollars researching the herb to protect themselves from future lawsuits. Their money and time has paid off for me. I have stevia in the garden, growing abundantly and providing sweetness for the snacks I prepare for my daughter.

Herbal Remedies for Common Childhood Ailments

For brevity sake, I am restricting this section to profiling only the six starter herbs that I suggested as the best, and most versatile, to include in a child's herbal garden. There are many herbal remedies suitable for use with children. Consult previous issues of Llewellyn's *Herbal Almanac* for further information.

Calendula

Calendula can be used as an eye bath for minor eye irritations. Steep the petals into a tea, dilute with distilled water, and bathe the eyes. With its antiseptic, antibacterial, antiviral, and antifungal properties, calendula is also useful for all kinds of skin ailments—including eczema, acne, psoriasis, fungal infections, and seborrheic dermatitis (also known as dandruff or cradle cap). For acne and black heads, wash the face with a warm calendula infusion. For other skin conditions, regularly apply calendula ointment to the affected areas. For minor burns, apply a cool compress of infused calendula. For cuts and scrapes, calendula ointment guards against infection and promotes rapid healing.

Catnip

Catnip, taken as a tea or tisane, reduces fever, calms gastric distress and nausea, and promotes sleep. It is also an effective bug repellent. In a study done at Iowa State University, nepetalactone, the chemical compound contained in catnip, was found to be ten times more effective than DEET (a highly toxic chemical commonly used in bug sprays) in repelling mosquitoes. For best results, grow catnip in your yard, and as you are leaving the house, grab a few leaves of catnip, crush them slightly in your hands, and rub them on your arms, legs, and other exposed skin. You may have to ward off cats who will want to lick and rub against you, but mosquitoes should no longer be a problem. For children who are more adversely affected by toxic chemicals because of their small size and weight, using catnip as a repellent can keep them safe from the adverse effects of DEET (which include everything from rashes to seizures).

Chamomile

Chamomile has antifungal, antibacterial, anti-inflammatory and anti-allergenic properties, and it is a versatile skin remedy for children. It is also a sedative, carminative, and antispasmodic that remedies gas, nausea or upset stomachs, sleeplessness, and the symptoms of nervousness. It calms children, promotes sleepy relaxation, and combined with lavender and infused in almond oil for six weeks makes a soothing "Sleepy Time Relaxing Rub" that can be massaged into the back for a peaceful sleep.

For teething children, chamomile is a gift to both child and parent. The sedative and antispasmodic qualities soothe the nerves and swollen gums associated with teething, easing pain and promoting sleep. A cup consumed by the parents will calm their frazzled nerves and allow them to rest.

Use chamomile to treat eye irritations such as conjunctivitis. Make a tea or tisane from the herb, cool it, and bathe the eyes in it. In the case of a minor burn, cold chamomile tea can be applied as a cooling compress, or swabbed on to ease the skin. As your child grows into the teen years, a chamomile tea is a good treatment for acne as a face wash.

Lavender

Lavender can be used as a soothing mouthwash in the case of sore gums, toothache, and foot, hand, and mouth disease (a blister-like rash on the feet, hands, and mouth). Make an infusion with the flowers, cool, and swish it around the mouth. Lavender is also useful in treating earache. Massage lavender oil diluted in a carrier oil around the outer ear to reduce the risk of infection.

Lavender is also excellent for calming the nerves and relieving headaches. It helps to lower blood pressure, ease nervous tension, and bring a sense of calm. For children, try making lavender shortbread, or adding lavender to their favorite tea.

Lemon Balm

Lemon balm is an excellent remedy for a nervous stomach, nausea or flatulence, frayed nerves, and disrupted digestion. Lemon balm acts very subtly on the nervous system, and remedies sleeplessness, headaches, and depression. It is known to "brighten" and lighten the temperament, and can be useful for children in times of transition and change.

Peppermint

Peppermint contains flavonoids that stimulate the liver and gall bladder, increasing the flow of bile. It calms nausea, indigestion, flatulence, stomach ache, and spasms. It is an good remedy for children experiencing travel or motion sickness.

Peppermint can also be used to treat headaches. Infused in oil, it can be rubbed on the temples and scalp to facilitate blood vessel relaxation. A cloth can be saturated with either the infused oil, or a strong tea, and laid gently over the face for some aromatherapy. Peppermint is a great breath freshener. Just pick a leaf or two in the garden, and chew on them. At snack time, place a few sprigs of mint in with the snack foods to discourage flies. They are a beautiful and useful inclusion on the table.

Toxic Herbs to Avoid

The following list contains some potentially dangerous herbs that are commonly found in gardens and used for herbal remedies. Some, like lungwort and digitalis, are better known as the flowers pulmonaria and foxglove. Though they are bright and beautiful and possibly useful, they should not be included in a garden that children visit often.

The toxicity level of a plant varies with the location of the plant, its age, the season, and the weather conditions. Some plants are only toxic in parts (for example the berries), but are listed here because they are best avoided until the children no longer taste things out of curiosity and can identify and differentiate between the parts of a plant.

For the safety of younger children, avoid cultivating:

Aloe *(Aloe vera)*
Arnica *(Arnica montana)*
Black cohosh *(Cimicifuga racemosa)*
Bloodroot *(Sanguinaria canadensis)*
Blue cohosh *(Caulophyllum thalictroides)*
Castor oil plant *(Ricinus communis)*

Columbine *(Aquilegia vulgaris)*
Comfrey *(Symphytum officinalis)*
Deadly nightshade *(Atropa beladonna)*
Foxglove *(Digitalis purpurea)*
Jimsonweed *(Datura stramonium)*
Licorice *(Glycyrrhiza glabra)*
Lobelia *(Lobelia siphilitica)*
Lungwort *(Pulmonaria offinalis)*
Mistletoe *(Phoradendron serotinum* or *Phoradendron flavescens)*
Monkshood *(Aconitum napellus)*
Pennyroyal *(Hedeoma pulegiodes)*
Peony *(Paenoia officinalis)*
Pokeweed *(Phytolacca americana)*
Poppy *(Papaver* spp.*)*
Rue *(Ruta graveolens)*
Tansy *(Tanacetum vulgare)*
Vervain *(Verbena officinalis)*
Wormwood *(Artemisia vulgaris)*

This list is not comprehensive, but it is a starting place for identifying toxic plants and is meant to be used as a guide when you choose and place plants in your garden. When you purchase plants, make sure they are properly identified and labeled. If you can, keep them labeled when they are placed in your garden.

For your peace of mind and your children's safety, remove all the toxic plants from your garden while the children are young. Teach children not to put anything in their mouth without checking with a responsible adult. This includes seeds, fruits, bulbs, leaves, stems, bark, berries, nuts, flowers, mushrooms, and the nectar sometimes contained in flowers.

As children grow older, teach them the dangers of plants, and how to recognize and identify them by name. Let your shared time in the garden, and shared herbal knowledge, grow as your child grows. Retreat often to the garden with your older child or teenager, and learn and grow together.

Other Things to Consider

Herbicides, pesticides, and other chemicals are also toxic to children. Plants that are nontoxic become toxic when they have been treated with chemicals. Consider making the effort to go organic in your garden, if only for the safety of your children and the long-term well-being of the entire family.

There are no magic tips for easy parenting and no surefire methods for easy herb gardening. Growing healthy children, like growing bountiful herbs, is a daily practice of care. Time spent together in the garden may inspire your child to become a herb lover, and it may cultivate the spiritual practices of gardening in your child-parent relationship. Whether in the garden, or in your family, may your harvest be bountiful and beautiful.

For Further Study

Cunningham, Scott. *Cunningham's Encyclopedia of Magical Herbs.* St. Paul, Minn.: Llewellyn Publications, 1987.

Kowalchik, Clair, and William H. *Rodale's illustrated Encyclopedia of Herbs.* Emmaus, Pa.: Rodale Press, 1987.

McHoy, Peter, and Pamela Westland. *The Herb Bible.* New York: Barnes & Noble, 1994.

Ody, Penelope. *The Complete Medicinal Herbal.* London, New York: Dorling Kindersley, 1993.

Growing a Protective Garden

⪼ by Ember ⪻

C hances are you have a magical garden growing right now in your yard, and you don't even realize it. Whether you're growing flowers, vegetables, or herbs, these plants put magical properties right at your fingertips. And plants that have been labeled as "weeds" are often some of the most powerful magical herbs you can find.

Start Seeking the Magic

When people consider their homes, one of the most important issues they examine is safety. We make certain our locks are in good working order, and we sometimes install security systems and outdoor lighting. But magical folks also consider something else: What kind of plants can I grow here that will protect my house magically?

There are far too many plants with protective qualities to list in a brief article, so I will discuss a few that I have grown successfully at my home and that are easily obtained and grown in a variety of locations. You can use this article as a basis for your further researches. Many of these plants can be grown on the smallest patio and in containers—so you need not let your location limit what magic you can grow.

Some Protective Plants

Flowering Plants

There are protective plants for every area, for shade or Sun. Violets, foxgloves, and alyssum are wonderful protective plants that thrive in shade or partial Sun. These plants are available at most nurseries. Violets can often be used as a ground cover, and many varieties have lovely, heart-shaped leaves. There are many of species of violets—you can probably find one that is native to your area and will thrive in your garden.

Alyssum, which most commonly appears in white or pastel shades, looks beautiful in containers spilling over the sides in a cascade of tiny flowers. This is an excellent choice to pair with other container flowers as an accent plant. Foxglove is tall and elegant, and one of my personal favorite plants, but use caution—it is not only protective but poisonous.

Protective flowers that need full Sun include the ever-popular marigolds and the classic rose. Roses are not just symbols of love, but their feisty thorns represent their strongly protective nature. And they're not as difficult to grow as you may think. Marigolds grow quickly and easily from seed, and you can save the dry seed heads to propagate new plants year after year. Other flowering plants of note are chrysanthemums and heliotrope, which bears fragrant purple flowers that butterflies adore. And, if you have the space, lilac is one of the loveliest of protective plants.

Protective Herbs

Herbs such as basil, rosemary, mint, and sage are excellent protective choices and can handle full Sun. And they are well-known for their uses in cooking. All of these grow very well in containers. When planted in the ground, mint will spread very rapidly—so you should only grow them in containers away from your regular garden.

Protective Vegetables

Don't forget to explore the protective qualities of vegetables as well. Tomatoes are probably one of the most popular garden vegetable that offers magical protection. They can be grown in patio pots—provided they have full Sun exposure.

Protective "Weeds"

This list wouldn't be complete without mentioning nature's own very protective green things—thistle and dandelion. Although considered by many to be noxious weeds—and indeed, in the state where I live thistle is actually controlled by law—these are wonderful wildflowers. The dandelion is considered by many to be a valuable herb and is beginning to earn the respect it deserves for its variety of uses. If these plants grow near you naturally, consider yourself fortunate, and try to encourage them to grow in your space.

Protective Trees

There are also many trees with protective qualities. You may have some of these growing near your home already. If not, planting trees is a wonderful way to mark a special occasion and express your love of your favorite planet, Earth. Look to plant some of the native trees that traditionally thrive in your area, along with more ornamental ones. A few of the most popular protective tree species are the rowan (or European mountain ash), the many varieties of oak, and the various varieties of the linden family, which are also often used as ornamental trees in suburban areas. At the very least, planting a tree near your house will encourage a new tree spirit to come and cast its watchful eye over you.

Tapping the Natural Protective Properties of Your Garden

So how can you utilize your magical garden's protective properties? There are countless ways. One is simply to save some bits of stem and leaf while pruning your plants, and scatter these around the perimeter of your home. Be sure these plants are healthy and free of disease and pests, otherwise you'll be spreading a problem!

You can also keep dried herbs for use in spells and amulets, and you can dry lovely flowers and even leaves, stems, acorns, and bits of bark for this purpose. The flowers and petals aren't the only part of the rose you can use. You can save pieces of the thorny stems or pick off the thorns individually for use in protection charms—just remember to wear gloves when handling any potentially prickly plant bit.

You can create a chant using the names of the protective plants you're growing, and then request that they use their energy to protect your home. This can take the form of a ritual or spell, such as the one at the end of this article, and it can be a simple list or even a poem. And you can create an amulet to carry with you, or make a spell jar or bottle to keep near the entrance of your home.

Use your plants to make wreaths and decorations for your home. An idea that has worked well for me is to use small branches, such as from a lilac bush, and fasten them together with hot glue in the shape of a protective symbol—such as a star, pentacle, or shield. Decorate your protective branches with dried flowers, leaves, and herb stalks from plants such as rosemary. This makes a lovely decoration for your home—and it's very powerful as well.

Finally, don't forget about the most practical things you can do—eating your herbs and vegetables, bringing cut flowers indoors and giving them as gifts. Also, take care to always think of Mother Earth when planting your garden. Organic gardening is important for our environment. This includes using organic fertilizers. There are many safe ways to handle pests and diseases. Books are widely available on these topics. (You can get a good start by reading Laurel Reufner's article "Natural Pest Control" on page 23 of this edition.) It's simple to create a magnificent, magical protective garden whether your home is in the wooded countryside, a house in the suburbs, or a city apartment.

Thyme Protection Ritual

To perform a protective ritual using a common herb—thyme—gather the following materials: some red cloth and ribbon; any combination of the following stones—carnelian, bloodstone, ruby, garnet, jasper, obsidian; a pinch of dried thyme; some rose thorns; some patchouli oil; and a red or white candle.

Carve the protection symbol of your choice into the candle, and anoint it with oil. Combine the stones, herbs, and thorns, and wrap them in the cloth. Visualize being enclosed in a protective shield of white light as you prepare your protective herb amulet. Light the candle, and place the amulet nearby. Focus on the energy of the burning candle infusing the amulet with power. Say the following words:

Mars, breathe your fire into these stones and herbs,
Wrap me in the warmth of your protection.
Shield me from harm.

Allow the candle to burn completely, and then carry the amulet with you for protection.

Sun Dance to Increase Protective Strength

For a dose of protective strength from the light of the Sun, choose several white and yellow candles, and place them in a circle around your sacred space. Imagine dancing around a huge fire. Visualize its warmth on your skin. Choose your favorite music, or imagine music in your mind. You can play recorded music or use any handheld instrument, such as a rattle.

Focus on those parts of your body, mind, or spirit, that feel weak or in need of energy. Concentrate on them as you dance, imagining the energy of the Sun flowing through you and giving you its protection and strength. Imagine your body glowing with sunlight; as you move, feel your body heat increase and your blood moving. Your strength has returned. You are shielded from any darkness.

Gardening for Fairies

❧ by Vivian Ashcraft ❧

G arden fairies have been around at least as long as humans have. Thanks to various cartoons and children's stories, though, many people think of fairies as nubile little girls with wings. But in fact the fairy world includes all manner of beings—elves, sprites, gnomes, trolls, dryads, sylphs, mermaids, and leprechauns. And though most Americans associate fairy-folk with England or Ireland, almost all cultures have fairy lore concerning creatures of many names and shapes. In Iceland, there are guardian fairies known as *fylgiars*. In Africa, there are the *abatwa*; in Japan the *tengu*, and in Denmark the king of elves is Ellerkonge.

Still, it is Great Britain that has the richest tradition of gardening for fairies. In this country, it has been known for centuries that when fairies are treated with respect and appreciation, they are a rich source of wisdom and protection for your home and family.

There are many reasons to cultivate a fairy garden. It could be that you want fairies to come live in or around your property—bringing all their traits, tricks, and favors into your life. Or you might like a little bit of whimsy in your yard. With a little planning, the fairies will come.

The interest in fairy gardening has grown almost hand-in-hand with the increase in gardening as a hobby. When you love to dig in the earth, when you can't wait until spring so you can get dirt under your fingernails and grass stains on your knees, you begin to learn that each plant has its own spirit. The fairies embody these spirits, and bring the attributes of plants and flowers into your life. Fairies come in all sizes, but flower fairies are generally tiny beings.

Providing Space for the Fairies

Fairy gardens can be planted in your yard or in containers. They can be as large or as small as you wish. My first fairy garden was a just a one-foot-round and eight-inch-deep container. Eventually I outgrew my terrarium and planted my first outdoor fairy garden, and now I have little fairy hiding places in most of my outdoor gardens.

In my herb garden, I have placed a tea set and a picnic basket. In my butterfly garden I have a ceramic Victorian fairy house, with a garden bench outside. In my woodlands garden, I have a rosemary tree, and the ground is softly carpeted with patches of moss, thyme, and Corsican mint. There are paths made of smooth river stones, and tiny wind chimes hang in a nearby fir tree. There are ferns and other plants that provide hiding places for the shy creatures.

Many other plants in my yard are beneficial for the fairies, but too large for the fairy garden. Hollyhocks and foxglove grow by my creek, and the fairies use the flowers to make dresses and gloves for special occasions. Lamb's ears grow with forget-me-nots in a garden by my back door. And my butterfly and herb gardens are filled with plants that are beneficial and appreciated by my fairy friends.

Plan to Start with Plants

When you make your fairy garden plans, it's important to remember that fairies love herbs and aromatic plants. You will find that most of what you plant for your fairies is also attractive to butterflies, so in time your garden will become a moving picture-show of color. I have tansy, Mexican heather, yarrow, and clematis in my woodlands garden. There are plenty of books and websites from which you can learn about plants you want to include in your garden. I have included examples of such plants in this article, but you are not limited to what I suggest.

Fairy gardening is a great family activity. Children are true believers in fairy folk, so it is a way to encourage not only their interest in gardening, but also their respect for plants. Because of its versatility, fairy gardening can be enjoyed by anyone. If you are limited in movement, or are housebound, you can make a raised bed or container garden. This can be as simple as a single fairy ornament or as extravagant as a yard-sized village. No matter how you approach the planning of your fairy garden, and whatever you put into the process, you will find it a captivating and joyful place to visit and to tend.

Beginning to Build Your Fairy Garden

In addition to the usual gardening supplies (trowels, dirt, plants), and various fairy-friendly plants and other garden elements (rocks, ferns, moss), you will need a number of trinkets and shiny appealing items to lure the wee folk to your garden. This may include tinsel, little bells, smooth river pebbles, wind chimes, gazing globes, pieces of old glass, ribbons, and any small and shiny items you think may be appealing.

First, shape your garden into a mini-landscape of hills and valleys. If you would like a pond, you can sink a pot into the ground at this point. If you have a fairy house, this would be the time to decide where the fairies would like it to be placed. Keep in mind that fairies are very private, so if you put their living quarters out on a main walkway they likely will not use it.

If you don't have a fairy house, consider building one. It does not have to be terribly fancy. Use natural materials: bark, twigs, dry moss, grass for thatch. Or purchase a small birdhouse if you do not have the time to build one. With all the birdhouse collectors around, some very pretty and unusual houses have become available. You will also find that your friends and family, once they discover your passion, will start giving you tiny items for your garden.

As a philosophical entry-point, it may help you to start small and let the garden evolve. Put in a few herbs and a path, and let it rest. Nothing has to be final in a fairy garden. Next year is always another year to try new things. And in fact, the fairies will sometimes move things around for you. Plan in your first years to spend some quiet time with your garden, and it will tell you what it needs.

Adding Plants

Once you have a basic garden layout, add your plants. Take care to notice where the fairy trails are. Use lots of moss and thyme, as these make soft places for the delicate feet of the little ones to fall. A small rosemary plant makes a beautiful fairy tree, and if it's the right shape you can hang a little swing on it. Thyme is a wonderful ground cover, and you can use several varieties: elfin, pink chintz, woolly.

The plants do not necessarily have to be miniatures. You can keep them small by pruning them. A plant that is small by human standards can make a lovely shade tree in a fairy's world. And again, you can start small and add plants over time. You can replace plants that become too large, or take them out altogether if they do not feel right for the space. Most gardeners know that plants can be and usually are moved around often until the right spot is found.

The Language of Plants

Certain plants suggest certain things to the fairy world. By planting certain plants, you can help determine which types of fairies will explore your garden. Also, I have included some basic gardening instructions to help make your garden work.

Bee Balm: Sympathy and consolation. This plant is perennial, and prefers moist, rich soil. It can be invasive; cut back to two inches after blooming and you may get a second flower.

Coreopsis: Always cheerful. This plant is perennial and prefers full Sun or partial shade. Remove old blossoms and you will have a blooming plant for the whole season.

Daisy: Innocence. Perennial. Plant in full Sun, and keep moist.

Larkspur: Lightness and laughter. Perennial. Plant in rich soil in partial shade.

Lupine: Imagination. Perennial. Needs cool night temperatures for optimal performance.

Mint: Virtue. A perennial wildflower. All varieties are extremely invasive, but also very useful in teas, cooking, poultices, potpourris, and toiletries.

Ranunculus: Radiant with charm. Perennial, but may need tubers dug up in autumn to survive colder winters.

Rosemary: Remembrance. Perennial, but the plant does not survive colder winters. If you take it in for the cold season, it needs daily water. Prune after flowering to ensure bushiness.

Sage: Long and healthy life. Perennial. Plant in soil that is not too rich, and mulch in winter. Prune heavily in spring.

Thyme: Thriftiness and activity. Perennial. Many varieties can be used as ground cover that can be walked on. They release a wonderful aroma. Use soil that is not too rich or wet.

Verbena: Enchantment. Perennial. Needs full Sun and well-drained soil.

Other plants that are fairy-friendly include:

Bluebells or **cowslip:** Fairies hide in these plants when they are frightened. The morning dew you see is actually the pearls the fairies hang on the flowers in gratitude. This is a perennial wildflower. It thrives in acidic soil with lots of water, and needs full Sun to partial shade.

Boxwood: This plant can be trimmed into topiary and decorated for special events. It is a shrub, and likes alkaline soil with good drainage.

Foxgloves: Fairies use the flowers to make petticoats and gloves. It is a perennial that can be invasive. Plant in partial shade, though it will tolerate full Sun if watered frequently. Remove old flower stems for a second blooming.

Lady's Mantle: The dew drops from this plant are used to soften the fairies' skin. (When you're as old as the fairies, this is important.) Plant in light shade to full Sun.

Lamb's Ears: These plants function as the fairies' pets, as most animals are just too big for such a purpose. Perennial. Can be invasive. Plant in light shade to full Sun. Also known as betony.

Lavender: Fairies hang their clothes on this plant to dry. A perennial, lavender can be grown as a shrub or hedgerow. Plant in full Sun in alkaline, well-drained soil.

Ragwort: Leprechauns bury their treasure under this plant. It is a perennial wildflower. Plant in acidic, moist soil in full Sun to partial shade.

Toadstools: These are handy seats for visitors.

Accessorizing

Once you have invited fairies into your garden space and your plants are beginning to grow and thrive, now you can begin to add accessories to your garden. Craft stores have a number of great miniature items. If you've been an alert shopper, you probably already have found little fairy furniture and wind chimes. If you don't want a pond, you can simulate one with a mirror or with blue pebbles. Fashion a tiny nest, and put it in your rosemary tree. Set out a tiny tea set or picnic basket. Make a table from a piece of log that looks like a tree stump. The ideas are endless. You may even put out "fake" fairies if you like. The real ones don't mind this, because it helps them to stay even more hidden in your garden.

Last, but definitely not least, you have to sprinkle your garden all over with fairy dust. This can be just plain glitter if you like, but you can make a special fairy dust by drying rose petals and herbs, powdering them, and then mixing that with the glitter. The fairies will like this blend much better because you will have put your heart into it.

Fairies are generally sweet, loving creatures, but they do love to play tricks on humans. They may hide your keys, or steal your spices. If you see fleeting shadows at the corners of your eyes, it's usually them, flitting about. They will also plant beneficial herbs near your home, and keep an eye on your children.

Like all mythology, fairy lore is prevalent in all cultures in every area of the world. Remember there is always a note of truth in every myth. So enjoy your garden and enjoy your fairies. And if you find things moved around . . . don't ask who did it.

For Further Study

Gannon, Linda K. *Creating Fairy Garden Fragrances*. North Adams, Mass: Storey Books, 1998.

Mager, Marcia Zina. *Believing in Fairies*. Essex, U.K.: C.W. Daniel Company Ltd, 2000.

McCann, Michelle Roehm. *Finding Fairies: Secrets for Attracting Little People from around the World*. Hillsboro, Ore.: Beyond Words Publishing, 2001.

Morrison, Dorothy. *Bud, Blossom & Leaf: The Magical Herb Gardener's Handbook*. St. Paul, Minn.: Llewellyn Publications, 2001.

Moura, Ann (Aoumiel). *Green Witchcraft: Folk Magic, Fairy Lore & Herb Craft*. St. Paul, Minn.: Llewellyn Publications, 1996.

Culinary Herbs

The Herbal Flavors of Greece

❧ by James Kambos ❧

I was introduced to Greek cuisine, and its many flavorful herbs, in my grandmother's garden at an early age. Greece was my grandmother's homeland. After settling in America in the earlier part of last century, she continued to follow her native eastern Mediterranean cooking traditions. She was very different from many of the other women around her.

For one, gardening was my grandmother's passion. Early in May each year she would prepare her kitchen garden for planting. As the tiller churned the soil, I'd watch with excitement as the scent of earth rose in brown waves. It smelled of spring and life renewed. Soon, she would plant, in her plot, the vegetables that are essential to Greek cooking. This included slender green-speckled zucchinis,

shiny purple–black eggplants, and an endless array of summer squash, bell peppers, and, of course, garlic.

The plants which captured my imagination the most, however, were the herbs. These give Greek cooking its robust flavor. My grandmother planted these along the edge of the garden's border or in terra cotta pots on the patio. I remember the feathery plumes of dill, rising in the back of the border and capped with their brilliant yellow-green seed heads. Basil, considered by Greeks to be one of the most sacred of all herbs, would overflow in pots on the patio. And the varieties of mint—I'll never forget the fragrant clumps of mint, tucked here and there in a shady corner of the garden. Their crinkled foliage would release a heady fragrance each time I rubbed them—and I did this often.

That was many years ago, but I carry on the same tradition and try to preserve my heritage. On hot and dry July mornings, as I tend my own herb garden, I find I am again surrounded by many of the same herbs I loved in my grandmother's garden. In the early morning stillness, I'm greeted by the perfume of oregano, thyme, savory, dill, and mint. And I think how important these plants are to Greek cooking.

As my hoe unearths a rock, I smile, because it reminds me of the folk story about how Greece was created. The tale goes something like this: After the council of gods and goddesses created the Earth, and all of the other great nations, they noticed that a few rocks remained unused. These last rocks were tossed into the Mediterranean Ocean, and as the legend goes, became Greece. This is only a folktale, but like most folktales it does contain a kernel of truth.

A Brief History of Greek Cooking

Greece is indeed a dry, rocky country with little fertile soil. It is Sun-drenched and has very little good farm or grazing land. Despite all these shortcomings, Greece has produced such an abundance of flavorings in its cuisines that the country has influenced cooks and bakers for centuries.

The inspiration for Greek food has always come from the East. Greece is located in the southeastern corner of Europe. It is surrounded by the aquamarine waters of the Ionian Sea to the west, the Aegean Sea to the east, and the Mediterranean Sea to the south. To the north, Greece is cut off from the rest of Europe by remote rugged mountains. This unique geographic position has influenced Greek cooking since ancient times.

Being more accessible by sea, Greece has always looked to eastern and southern trade routes for goods, food, and spices. This left Greece open to the herbs and spices from the Middle East and North Africa. Also, Greece has always fallen under the influence of Eastern empires. Briefly, the Persians ruled. Then, the Byzantine Empire, based in Constantinople (present–day Istanbul), controlled Greece for about eleven centuries. When the Byzantine Empire fell to the Ottoman Turks, Greece became part of the Ottoman Empire, and it stayed so for nearly four hundred years until independence in 1830.

As empires were won and lost, the cuisine of Greece took shape. The herbs and spices used in the Greek kitchen today have ancient beginnings. Some may have been brought to Greece by invaders, others may have been discovered by the conquerors in Greece and then taken back to their homeland. The Ottoman Turks were a good example. The rulers of the Ottoman Empire had great respect for the cuisines they encountered as their empire spread. Some of the Greek flavorings were discovered by the Turks and then spread throughout their great empire. Then again, some of the Turkish herbs and foods were later incorporated into the native Hellenic cooking style. No matter how it occurred, the flavor of Greek food will always been linked to the culinary pool of the Middle East.

Taste of Greece

Greece is an herbalist's delight. Blue skies, even bluer seas and wind–swept rocky hillsides, impress even the most jaded traveler.

Many of the herbs I struggle to grow in my American garden grow wild or can be cultivated year-round in Greece's dry healthy climate. In Greece, meat is a luxury food, and is seldom the primary focus of a meal. So to expand the flavor of any recipe, or to add extra zip to vegetarian dishes, Greek cooks rely heavily on the use of herbs.

The following is a list of herbs, spices, seeds, and other flavorings used in Greek cooking. Some of these ingredients are not herbs at all, but are included in case you are interested in some of the nonherb natural flavorings from Greek cuisine. Many of these herbs and spices are well-known to you, but others may be new. All items listed can be found at any Greek or Middle Eastern grocer in your town. Where possible, I have also included magical uses and folklore information along with the culinary uses of these herbs.

Anise: The seeds, extract, and oil of this herb are sometimes used in Greek pastries such as *paxemathia*, a sort of Greek biscotti that are great to dunk into coffee. Anise is also used to flavor the national drink of Greece, ouzo. Ouzo is a clear powerful aperitif and should be drunk with *mezze*, an appetizer. It is a strong drink, but may be drunk straight or poured over ice. Mixed with water, it becomes cloudy, hence its nickname "lion's milk." If you travel in Greece, you may come across homemade ouzo. Watch out; it may just knock your socks off. During a trip to Greece, I was invited to take part in a village celebration. The gentlemen in the town square handed me a bottle of the bootleg stuff. All eyes were on me as I took a sip. It burned all the way down, but I managed to choke out in Greek, *na kalo*—meaning, "it is good." Their eyes sparkled, and they smiled and slapped me on the back. Just remember, ouzo deserves respect.

Basil: This beautiful herb is held in great esteem by the Greeks. It is the traditional flower of the Orthodox church. As a food element, basil is delicious combined with tomatoes and in tomato-based sauces. It may have been used in the earliest forms of aromatherapy. Greek men would frequently carry a sprig tucked behind their ear or in a shirt pocket, taking it out occasionally to savor its scent. Traditional Greek basil is a small annual plant and grows nicely in pots or a window box. In folk magic, use basil to clear and protect a sacred space.

Cinnamon: Greeks use cinnamon in many pastries. However, unlike in America, cinnamon is used in Greece as a subtle flavor for some white sauces and meat dishes. It adds an extra depth of flavor.

Clove: Cloves are used in sweets and in Greek folk magic. The flavor of cloves is frequently added to the famous Middle Eastern pastry, baklava. Near the Christmas holiday, Greek bakers will garnish certain pastries with whole cloves. This has a deep religious meaning, because the clove symbolizes the spices brought to the Christ child as gifts. In Greek folk magic, the scent of clove aids in purification.

Dill: Dill grows all over Greece. Magically, it is used to protect a home against evil. Dill is used in meatballs, in filling for stuffed grape leaves, and in salads and some bean dishes.

Garlic: People around the world use garlic to protect against evil. In Greece, garlic is used to repel the dreaded evil eye. The word for "garlic" in Greek is *skortha*, and people frequently whisper this word as magic to protect themselves from the evil. In the Greek kitchen, garlic finds its way into many sauces and dips. To impart a subtle garlic flavor to an old standard dish, try tucking a clove or two of garlic into a roast or leg of lamb prior to cooking it. This is simply delicious.

Lemon: Lemons grow in Greece, and the cooks of Greece would be lost without them. The juice of lemons is frequently combined with olive oil and oregano to make a zesty marinade for chicken. Straight lemon juice can also be sprinkled over meatballs, before and after baking or broiling. The best-known Greek soup, *avgolemono*, receives much of its flavor from lemon juice. Also, if you are preparing lamb, try rubbing the meat first with half a lemon. This removes any of the strong gamey flavor that some people find objectionable in lamb.

Mahlepi *(mahleb* in Arabic): This unusual flavoring was brought to Greece by the Persians. It is the ground seed of a tree that similar to a cherry tree. It is used in making breads. I have used it to make Orthodox Easter bread.

Mastic *(mastika* in Greek): Mastic is not an herb, but a dried sap. Few Americans have ever heard of it, and the stories surrounding it are fascinating. First of all, mastic is derived from the sap of the mastic tree. The only place in the world where mastic trees grow are on the Greek island of Chios, my ancestral home. The trees are small and planted in groves. Late each summer the bark is cut, and the trees then "cry." The sap drips, then hardens after the harvest into yellowish amber-like crystals. These crystals may be pulverized into a powder and used to flavor liqueurs, candies, puddings, and gum. At confectioner shops in Athens, I have seen mouth-watering displays of the mastic-flavored Greek candy called *lokum* (or more commonly, Turkish Delight), piled high on fancy trays. Much of the mastic is exported around the Middle East. Some of the mastic is left in its crystal form as a natural chewing gum. Above the sink in my grandmother's kitchen, we always kept a terra cotta jar filled with natural mastic. I was encouraged to chew it as a child, because it was an oral cleanser and teeth whitener.

Westerners probably wouldn't care for it in this natural form, but I learned to like it. During the Ottoman Empire, much mastic was sent to Topkopi Palace, the sultan's home in Istanbul. There it was used as an aphrodisiac by the ladies in the sultan's harem. At sunset, they would chew a bit of mastic to sweeten their breath in case they were chosen for a night of passion with the sultan. If you are magically inclined, a pinch of mastic added to a love charm can add an extra punch. Modern science, it seems, has recently discovered mastic. I learned in my research that mastic, taken in capsule form, can aid in the treatment of stomach ulcers. You should check with a licensed health care professional before you try this. To learn more, log on to your favorite search engine on the Internet, and simply key in the word "mastic."

Mint: Mint is actually used a great deal in the cuisines of the eastern Mediterranean. Unlike the Western world, where mint is relegated to the role of garnish, tea, or jelly, cooks from Greece eastward love the fresh taste it adds to salads, stuffings, and meatballs. For a quick sauce, combine one-half teaspoon crushed dried mint to one cup cold plain yogurt. Spoon over plain rice pilaf for a touch of Greek flavor.

Olives and olive oil: According to Greek mythology, the goddess Athena created the first olive tree. No Greek kitchen is complete without olives and golden olive oil. Olive oil was so cherished by the ancients, it was given as prizes to athletes. The modern medical community has proven what the ancient Greeks may have known: Olive oil, used in moderation, is healthy. It helps lower bad blood cholesterol levels. One of my favorite olive varieties available in America is the Kalamata olive. These olives are dark purple, oblong, and come in jars. They are packed in vinegar and olive oil and are the best all-purpose Greek olive. Kalamatas can add a splash of Mediterranean color and flavor to salads or a plate of appetizers.

Oregano: This mountain-grown herb is indispensable to Mediterranean food. I like it fresh or dried in chicken, pasta sauces, or lentils. It is slightly bitter and earthy.

Rosemary: Instead of adding this herb directly to food, on many occasions Greeks add rosemary to hot cooking coals, which lets the smoke penetrate the meat—usually lamb—with a supremely delicate flavor. I have prepared a Turkish chicken stew that calls for rosemary and found that the flavor marries quite well with poultry also.

Savory: Savory is one of the finest, but one of the least used, herbs this region of the world offers. Winter savory thrives in my garden and air-dries beautifully for winter use. I add it to lentils and other bean soups. It also blends well with eggplant and is great sprinkled on pizza. When you use it, and I hope you do, combine it with a pinch of dried oregano.

Sesame seeds: In Greece, sesame seeds are used to garnish numerous breads and cookies. More than just a garnish, sesame seeds are a high-energy food. They are frequently combined with honey to make a crispy and light health food bar. Such bars are easily found in American health food stores.

Other herbs: Parsley, sage, and thyme must also be mentioned on this list. Parsley grows year-round and is blended into cheeses and used as fillings for appetizers. Sage, as in America, is added to pork dishes. Thyme grows wild in the region. I like to combine thyme with chopped parsley and add it to boiling water or broth before preparing rice. Combined they blend to make an easy herbal rice pilaf.

Flower Waters

Among the most exotic flavorings used in the Greek kitchen are the flower waters. There are two kinds: rose water and orange blossom water. These fragrant waters are made by distilling water over rose petals or orange blossoms. They are mostly used in sweets or syrups, and they are exquisite. You can purchase them bottled from middle eastern grocers or some health food stores. I always refrigerate them after opening. Flower waters are delicate and should never be added to a boiling syrup. Always let the syrup cool slightly, then add the flower water. (Later in this article I have included a recipe containing flower water, so you will better understand this.) Flower waters were probably developed by the Persians, whose sophisticated cuisine dates back a bit earlier than the Greeks'.

Greek Herbal Recipes

I don't have the space to share with you all the recipes I'd like to. What follows are three recipes that can be put together to form a meal, and that allow you to try out some of the herbs and flavors I have explained above.

I have not mentioned that the Greeks love tomatoes and pasta. Traveling in Greece, I encountered a tomato sauce similar to the following and, after much trial and error, eventually duplicated it at home. The tomatoes should be left chunky. This dish freezes well.

Greek Tomato Sauce

1   small onion, finely chopped

1   Tbl. olive oil

2   cloves of garlic minced

¼   cup finely chopped fresh parsley

2   Tbls. chopped fresh basil or 1 tsp. dried basil

1   tsp. dried oregano

8   Italian plum tomatoes peeled and coarsely chopped

1   8-oz. can of tomato sauce

1   Tbl. of tomato paste

1   tsp. brown sugar

Salt and pepper to taste

In a medium saucepan, sauté the onion in oil until soft. Add the rest of the ingredients, stirring to break up the tomatoes. Bring to a boil; turn down, and simmer, uncovered, for 30 minutes. Stir occasionally. Serve by tossing with cooked spaghetti or penne pasta. Serves 4.

Greek Salad

The Greek salad served in America rarely exists in Greece. If you order a salad in a Greek village cafe, you'll likely be served sliced tomatoes and a few slices of cucumber splashed with a little olive oil. Simple but delicious. Here's a recipe for a more traditional Greek salad.

1   head curly endive

1   head iceberg lettuce

1   cucumber, peeled and sliced

2   tomatoes sliced into wedges

12   Kalamata olives

1   small thinly sliced red onion

¼   lb. feta cheese, cubed

½   tsp. dried oregano

6 or 8   anchovy filets

Dressing

½   cup olive oil

3   Tbls. red wine vinegar

Dash of fresh ground pepper

Tear the endive and lettuce into small pieces, and place these into a salad bowl. Add the cucumber, tomatoes, olives, and onion. Separately, roll the cubed feta in the oregano and set aside. Whisk together the dressing ingredients in a small bowl until foamy. Pour over salad ingredients and toss. Garnish salad with feta and anchovy filets. Serve this pasta and salad with hard rolls or garlic bread and red wine. The dessert which follows can be made a day or two ahead.

Walnut–Honey Cookies

This walnut–honey cookie recipe is not well-known outside of Greece, but my guests always love them. In Greek they are called *Phoenekia* [Fe–neek–ya]. As a boy, I remember them always being on the table at parties.

½   cup butter or margarine

¼   cup olive oil

¼   cup sugar

1   egg

¼   cup orange juice

½   tsp. grated orange peel

½   tsp. cinnamon

2½ cups unsifted all–purpose flour

1½ tsps. baking powder

Dash of salt

½   cup regular cream of wheat cereal

½   cup ground walnuts (¼ cup reserved for garnish)

Beat the butter until creamy. Add olive oil and sugar, and beat until smooth. Blend in egg, juice, orange peel, and cinnamon. In a separate bowl, stir together the flour, baking powder, and salt, and add gradually to the batter. Mix until smooth. With your hands, knead in cream of wheat cereal and only ¼ cup of the walnuts. Pinch off walnut-size pieces of dough and shape into ovals. Place on a greased cookie tray, one inch apart. Bake at 350°F for 20 minutes or until golden. Let cool. Make the syrup below.

Syrup

¼ cup sugar

¼ cup water

¾ cup honey

1 Tbl. orange blossom water (optional)

In a small saucepan, boil together the sugar and water until clear. Remove from heat and cool slightly. Stir in honey and orange blossom water. Place a few cookies at a time in the saucepan and coat with syrup. Transfer the cookies, using a slotted spoon, to a clean tray. Garnish with the remaining ¼ cup walnuts. To serve, place each cookie in a paper baking cup to catch any excess syrup; arrange on a platter. Or, pack in an airtight container until ready to serve. They keep well. Yield: about 30 cookies.

Learning More About Greek Food

Many people embrace a more wholesome lifestyle and are discovering the simple and healthy food of Greece. This article has served as a short introduction to the herbs and flavorings used to enhance this very ancient cuisine. Remember, Greek cooking is just one segment of the much larger realm of Middle Eastern food. And it is my wish that your interest in Greek food will open the door, leading you to explore the other fascinating cooking traditions of the region—including Arabian, Armenian, Iranian, Jewish, Kurdish, North African, and Turkish.

In general, most of the ingredients and herbs used in Greek recipes will be found in the spice and gourmet food sections of major supermarkets. To obtain the more exotic ingredients, try health food stores, Greek, or Middle Eastern grocers.

Yarrow Beer

⁓ by Chandra Moira Beal ⁓

Y ears before hops became the predominate flavoring and bittering agent in beer, yarrow was often used by brewers. The herb provided pleasant flavors and acted as a preservative, and medicinally it had astringent and pungent qualities that drinkers found pleasant. In fact, during the Middle Ages, adding herbs such as rosemary, valerian, and yarrow to beer was quite popular. Such concoctions were called "gruit," and the herbs were believed to increase beer's intoxicating effects.

Yarrow Today

Yarrow today lives on as a hardy, prolific herb with many applications. It grows wild in many parts of the world and is easy to grow in the garden. The plant is a perennial that usually grows in bushy clusters. The stalks can grow as high as two feet and has white or pink flowers that bloom from summer to fall.

White-flowered yarrow has the most potent flavor of all the varieties of the plant. Its the leaves are rich in vitamins and minerals. In general, yarrow has a strong aromatic fragrance reminiscent of sage. If you are gathering your own, the leaves are most pungent in the spring. Dried yarrow flowers are fairly common at health food stores and can be used in place of the fresh flowers.

Ruled by Venus, yarrow promotes love and courage, and enhances psychic powers. The Navajos used yarrow as an aphrodisiac, so you may want to explore the herb's potential uses in this realm with your loved one.

Yarrow beer makes a good summertime brew with its light, herbal flavors, but it is also delicious anytime of year.

How to Make Yarrow Beer

Homebrewing is a fun hobby. There are many volumes of books devoted to its crafting. The beer recipe included below is designed for the beginning home brewer and uses a minimum of specialized equipment. You'll find many of these implements in your kitchen, though you should visit a homebrewing supply store for specialized equipment.

Homebrewing supplies are now available online, too. It is worth investing in a few time-saving brewing devices if you plan to brew more than once. You will also find malt extract and cane sugar at brewing supply stores as well as at your better gourmet grocery stores.

Equipment

A large stainless-steel cooking pot

Measuring spoons and cups

A long handled spoon or paddle

A cooking thermometer

Five-gallon glass jug

Plastic siphon tubing

Airlock and rubber cork

Sanitizing agent (idophor or bleach)

48 glass beer bottles and caps

Bottle capper

Optional: outdoor propane cooker, wort chiller, ice

Yarrow Beer

5 gallons cold fresh water

2 ozs. dried yarrow leaves or flowers

2 ozs. dried chamomile flowers

2 ozs. dried raspberry leaf

1 oz. dried agrimony leaf

½ oz. crushed fennel seed

½ lb. malt extract

2 lbs. sugar

Juice of 2 lemons

1 package liquid ale yeast or dry bread yeast

1 oz. cane sugar

To brew your own beer, you need to set aside several hours to devote to the process. Before you begin, be sure that you have all the equipment and ingredients you need.

If you're using liquid yeast, the package must be brought to room temperature before you begin brewing. If you're using dry yeast, make a starter just before you begin to brew. Using a starter gives the yeast a head start and helps prevent weak fermentation.

Put 1 cup of warm (90°F) water that has been boiled for at least fifteen minutes into a sterile jar and stir in the yeast. Cover with plastic wrap, and wait 10 minutes. Stir in 1 teaspoon of sugar.

Cover and place in a warm area out of direct sunlight. After about thirty minutes or so, the yeast should be actively churning and foaming. It will now be ready to pitch.

Sanitizing

The next thing you need to do is sanitize everything that will come in contact with your unfermented beer. To do this you'll need a sanitizer such as idophor or chlorine bleach. Immerse everything in a solution of 1 tablespoon bleach to 5 gallons of water, or follow the directions that come with your sanitizer. A large plastic bucket makes a good container for this, or a large kitchen sink. It takes time for the sanitizer to do its job, so allow your equipment to soak in the sanitizing solution for at least thirty minutes. If you use bleach, you must next rinse everything thoroughly to remove the odor. A solution of idophor does not need to be rinsed away.

Note on Water

The water you use is very important to this process. After all, beer is mostly water. If your tap water tastes good at room temperature, it should make good beer. It will just need to be boiled for a few minutes to remove the chlorine and kill any bacteria. Do not use water from a salt-based water softener, and don't use distilled (deionized) water. Beer needs the minerals for flavor, and the yeast needs the minerals for proper growth. A good bet is the bottled water sold in most supermarkets as "drinking water." Real spring or aquafer water is even better if you can get it.

Add 5 gallons of cold water to your brew pot and bring it to a boil. *Note:* If you're using a five-gallon pot on the stove, it may cover two burners and take awhile to heat. If you have an outdoor propane cooker, it can save you a lot of time.

While the water is boiling, mix together the dried herbs and fennel seeds. You can add them loose when you add the malt, or tie them in a muslin bag for easier clean-up.

The Wort

When the water boils, add your malt syrup and the sugar. Stir it well, making sure the syrup and sugar dissolves and does not stick to the bottom of the pot. (You don't want your beer to taste like burnt sugar.) Now you've got what is called "wort." Make sure the wort keeps up a good rolling boil, and that it does not boil over onto the stove. Not only is it a mess, but this boil-over can negatively affect the flavor of your beer as certain compounds turn bitter when overheated. Set your timer to 1 hour, and let the wort boil.

After an hour has passed, turn off the heat and stir in the lemon juice.

Let the wort cool to less than 80°F. While it is above 130°F, bacteria and wild yeasts are inhibited, which is good. However, it is very susceptible to oxygen damage as it cools, which is bad. There are also sulfur compounds that evolve while the wort is hot. If the wort is cooled slowly, these can dissolve back into the wort, causing cabbage or cooked vegetable flavors in the final beer. The objective is to rapidly cool the wort before oxidation or contamination can occur. Also, if the liquid is too hot it will kill the yeast.

If you have a wort chiller (usually a copper coil with connections to a garden hose on either end so cool water flows through), use it now. To cool the wort quickly without a wort chiller, place the pot in a sink or tub filled with ice water that can be circulated around the hot pot. Take great care because wort is heavy and very hot. While the cold water is flowing around the pot, gently stir the wort in a circular pattern so the maximum amount of wort is moving against the sides of the pot. If the water gets warm, replace it with cold water. The wort will cool in about twenty minutes. Do not add commercial ice to the wort itself. Commercial ice harbors lots of dormant bacteria that would love a chance to work on the new beer.

When the wort is cool enough, transfer it from the cooking pot to the glass jug using the siphon tube. Put the jug on the floor so it is lower than the cooking pot. Sanitize the siphon first, then place one end of the tube in the cool wort and the other in the jug. Gravity will start the flow, and the beer will follow the water into the new vessel. Monitor the transfer closely, and when you see the thick, sludgy sediment at the bottom pull the end of the siphon out of the jug. This is mostly dead yeast. You should try to leave this behind by not allowing the suction end of the tubing to touch it, as it can add undesirable flavors to your beer. The sediment, or "trub," can be composted or thrown away.

Pitching the Yeast and Waiting

Now, open your sanitized yeast package or yeast starter, and add the contents to the jug. This is called "pitching" the yeast. Gently rock the jug to aerate the wort, splashing it around. This provides oxygen to the yeast so it will do its job.

Now assemble your airlock and cork, fill it the jug with water, and insert it into the top of your jug.

In about twelve to twenty-four hours some signs of yeast activity should be present. That is, you should see bubbles rising through your airlock, and if you sniff the gas coming from the airlock it should smell yeasty or beer-like.

After a few days, the vigorous fermentation should subside. The surface of the beer will become clear of foam. When the bubbles in your airlock appear only once a minute or so, their production will have stopped. Your beer is now ready to move to the next stage. Reaching this stage takes about a week.

Conditioning with Sugar

Dissolve the cane sugar in 1 quart of water and bring it to a boil. Add this mixture to the contents of the jug. The yeast will feed on this new sugar and continue to produce carbon dioxide, causing carbonation and pressurization in the bottles. This is a process called "conditioning."

You could drink your beer at this stage when it's still "green," or weaker than it will be in a couple of weeks. But most people prefer the stronger alcohol content and the carbonation that comes with conditioning.

Bottling

You will need at least forty-eight bottles (two cases) and the same number of caps to bottle a five-gallon batch of beer. Don't use the screw-top kind of bottle, as the caps will not adhere properly. It is fine to reuse pop-top bottles that have been thoroughly washed and sanitized. If you want to avoid capping altogether, the flip-top Grolsch-style bottles work well. Again, be sure that anything you use has been fully cleaned and sterilized.

Using the siphon process again, fill each bottle, leaving about an inch of headroom. This headroom allows the carbon dioxide to expand and create a proper seal. When your bottles are filled, cap them and place them in a cool, dark place for at least ten days to condition, or become carbonated. The flavor of your beer will be best after about three weeks.

Chill and Enjoy

When it's time to enjoy your first homemade beer, chill it upright for several hours. There will be some sediment at the bottom of each bottle. This is mostly spent yeast, and you should avoid mixing it into your beer as it will cloud it and add a bitter, yeasty flavor. Pour your beer slowly, in one smooth motion, and stop before you pour any of the yeasty dregs into your glass.

Say a toast to your fresh yarrow beer before you drink it.

Kegging

If you prefer, you may keg your beer instead of bottling it. Kegging does require additional equipment, but it offers added convenience over bottling.

You must, of course, sanitize your keg and anything else that will come in contact with your beer. If you are using a plastic keg, then follow the sanitizing procedures outlined above. If you are using a metal keg, use iodine to sterilize your keg as bleach and other oxidizing sanitizers may react with the metal. This is extra work, of course, but it is better to be safe rather than sorry.

Prepare your priming sugar as before by dissolving it in water and bringing it to a boil. Siphon your beer into the keg, and add the dissolved sugar as you go. Seal the keg, and place it in a cool place for two weeks.

When it seems ready, tap your keg and enjoy a few glasses of your homebrew.

The Story of the Edible Herbal Flower

⤫ by Lynne Smythe ⤫

The history of edible flowers can be traced back thousands of years. For instance, capers *(Capparis spinosa)* are the flower buds of a Mediterranean evergreen shrub and have been used as a condiment for more than two thousand years in Europe. Dandelions were one of the bitter herbs referred to in the Old Testament of the Bible. Edible flowers such as daylilies and chrysanthemums have been used by the Chinese and Greeks for centuries.

A Brief Survey of the History of Flower-Eating

The practice of eating flowers has a long and varied history that spans across the globe. The Romans used edible flowers such as mallows, roses, and violets in numerous dishes. The

English learned to use edible flowers such as borage and roses through their contact with the Romans. Anglo-Norman cuisine of the thirteenth and fourteenth centuries utilized a variety of edible flowers—including as roses, hawthorn blossoms, and elder flowers. Hugh Platt's 1602 book *Delights for Ladies* includes recipes for candying flowers. Violets, cowslips, pinks, roses, and marigolds were used as natural food colorings during the Renaissance. The Portuguese first used the safflower *(Carthamus tinctorius)* in the 1700s as a substitute for the more expensive saffron. Saffron comes from the dried stigmas of the crocus flower *(Crocus sativus)* and is very expensive to produce. It takes approximately 4,000 flowers to make one ounce of saffron. Necessity is the mother of a lot of food innovation.

Europeans continued to use edible flowers after colonizing the New World. Colonists arriving in America from Europe brought with them the seeds of a variety of plants to grow in their gardens. Among the seeds were a number of edible flowers, including pot marigold and dandelions, that were used for making candied flowers, flower jelly, flower wine, salads, and syrups.

Native Americans have used a variety of flowers in their cooking throughout the years. American colonists were exposed to the uses of these plants and their flowers through contact with various tribes. Among the flowers used by Native peoples are cattails *(Typha latifolia)*, century plant *(Agave americana)*, bee balm *(Monarda didyma)*, red clover *(Trifolium pratense)*, yucca *(Yucca* spp.), and squash blossoms *(Cucurbita* spp.).

Edible flowers were very popular during the Victorian era (1837 to 1890), especially in salads. The Victorians added a variety of items to their salads, including violets, borage, primroses, gilly flowers (clove pinks), and nasturtiums. Many of these flowers could also be pickled for storage during the winter months when fresh flowers were not available. Victorians also candied violets and other flowers to garnish baked goods such as wedding cakes. After the Victorian era, the use of edible flowers fell out of favor for a time.

But in the past ten or twelve years there has been a resurgence of interest in and use of edible flowers as part of the organic health food movement. Upscale restaurants and home cooks are now using edible flowers in their recipes, and magazines such as *Country Living* and *Gourmet* have featured edible flower recipes in recent issues.

Modern-Day Uses of Edible Flowers

You probably have already consumed a number of edible flowers without even realizing it. When you consume cauliflower and broccoli you are eating the unopened flower buds of those plants. Artichoke lovers are eating the unopened flower bud of the plant *Cynara scolymus.* The flower receptacles of Carolina thistle *(Calina acaulis)* can be used as a substitute for artichoke hearts. Cloves *(Syzgium aromaticum)* are the dried, unopened flower buds of an evergreen tree from the myrtle family.

Cloves are commonly used to flavor baked goods and holiday hams. Saffron *(Crocus sativus)*, which was also used in medieval European cooking, is currently used to impart a regal color and subtle flavor to rice and other dishes. Do not confuse the edible saffron crocus with the poisonous autumn crocus *(Colchicum autumnale).*

This article will inform the budding chef and history buff about some of the more interesting flowers and flower petals that can be safely used for consumption.

Obtaining Edible Flowers

Flowers obtained from nursery and garden centers and florists are probably not safe to eat. The flowers you use must be free from any harmful chemicals such as are found in many commercially applied pesticides and fertilizers. You should always only eat organically grown flowers.

Check out your local health food store and farmer's market to see if they offer edible flowers for sale. Flowers intended for consumption should only be purchased from businesses that label their produce regarding as to whether they are organic and free of chemical pesticides and fertilizers.

Another option would be to grow your own organically raised flowers, or to obtain them from a friend who has an organic garden.

Safety Precautions for Today's Flowers

Always make sure you know what you are eating. Do not begin to use flowers in your cooking unless you are positive of their identification. Consult a good reference book for a comprehensive list of edible flowers. It can get tricky—for instance, day lilies (*Hemerocallis species*) are edible, while all other lilies (Asiatic, Oriental) are not. The flowers from garden peas are edible; however, sweet pea flowers (*Lathyrus* spp.) are not edible. Tuberous begonia flowers are edible; however, wax begonia flowers (*Begonia semperflorens*) are not safe to consume.

Make sure you know the Latin name of the flower you want to consume. Many plants share the same common name, but the Latin name is unique for each plant.

Moderation and thoughtfulness are key. Something as mild as lettuce can cause you to have an upset stomach if eaten in abnormally large quantities. If you are interested in incorporating edible flowers into your cuisine, first start off with small amounts to see how your body handles them.

Perform a taste test. Even if a flower is edible and your digestion can handle them without any problems, you may not like the taste of certain flowers. Taste a few before adding them to any of your recipes to be certain you will enjoy the flavor.

Avoid harvesting edible flowers from the side of the road. They may be contaminated from harmful car and truck exhausts.

Do not harvest flowers in the wild unless you have permission from the land owner and are absolutely certain of their identification.

Certain flowers in the composite family (chamomile, chrysanthemum, daisies, sunflowers) should be avoided by people with asthma, allergies, and hayfever problems. The presence of large amounts of pollen on these types of flowers may produce an allergic reaction in sensitive individuals.

The following edible flower varieties should be approached with caution. I probably wouldn't eat them myself since it is not 100-percent certain that they are safe to consume. There are so many other safe choices when choosing edible flowers, why take chances?

Apple blossoms *(Pyrus malus):* May contain cyanide precursors.

Bachelor buttons *(Centurea cyanus):* Some references say these are edible, while others say they are not.

Linden *(Tilia* **spp.):** Frequent consumption of linden flower tea may cause heart damage.

Snapdragons *(Antirrhinum majus):* As with bachelor buttons, some references claim these are safe to eat while others say that they are not.

Sweet woodruff *(Galium odoratum):* These flowers may have a blood-thinning effect if eaten in large quantities.

Tulips *(Tulipa* **spp.):** These flowers may cause certain people to develop a rash or upset stomach.

Types of Edible Flowers

Most culinary herbs produce edible flowers. They usually taste like a milder version of the herb; that is, rosemary flowers have a lighter tasting herb flavor than do the leaves. Some of the more palatable herbs with edible flowers include the following: basil *(Ocimum* spp.), borage *(Borago officinalis),* chervil *(Anthriscus cerefolium),* cilantro *(Coriandrum sativum),* common chives *(Allium schoenoprasum),* dandelion *(Taraxacum officinalis),* dill *(Anethum graveolens),* English lavender *(Lavandula angustifolia),* fennel *(Foeniculum vulgare),* garlic chives *(Allium tuberosum),* hyssop

(Hyssopus officinalis), lovage *(Levisticum officinale)*, lemon verbena *(Aloysia triphylla)*, marjoram *(Origanum majorana)*, Mexican tarragon *(Tagetes lucida)*, mint *(Mentha* spp.), oregano *(Origanum vulgare)*, rosemary *(Rosmarinus* spp.), common sage *(Salvia officinalis)*, society garlic *(Tulbaghia violacea)*, summer savory *(Satureja hortensis)*, thyme *(Thymus* spp.), *and* winter savory *(Satureja montana)*.

Many vegetables and fruits also produce edible flowers. When you harvest the flower of many of these fruits and vegetables, you sacrifice the blossom that would have turned into the fruit or vegetable. In some cases the plant would have produced more fruits or vegetables than you could normally use, so sacrificing a few flowers should not adversely affect your harvest. Here are some examples of fruits and vegetables which have edible flowers: arugula *(Eruca vesicaria sativa)*, chicory *(Cichorium intybus)*, garden peas *(Pisum* spp.), lemon flowers *(Citrus limon)*, mustard *(Brassica* spp.), okra *(Abelmoschus aesculentus)*, orange flowers *(Citrus sinensis)*, pineapple guava *(Feijoa sellowiana)*, radish *(Raphanus sativus)*, runner bean *(Phaseolus coccineus)*, squash blossoms *(Curcubita* spp.), and strawberry *(Fragaria ananassa)*.

Many ornamental flowers are also edible. Here is a brief listing of some of the specimens that are safe to consume: bee balm *(Monarda didyma)*, garland chrysanthemum *(Chrysanthemum coronarium)*, cowslips *(Primula veris)*, day lilies *(Hemerocallis* spp.), English daisy *(Bellis perennis)*, evening primrose *(Oenothera biennis)*, fuchsia *(Fuchsia arborescens)*, gardenia *(Gardenia jasminoides)*, hibiscus *(Hibiscus rosa-sinensis)*, hollyhock *(Alcea rosea)*, jasmine *(Jasminum sambac)*, Johnny jump-ups *(Viola tricolor)*, lilac *(Syringa vulgaris)*, mallows *(Malva* spp.), moss rose *(Portulaca grandiflora)*, nasturtium *(Trapaeolum majus)*, pansy *(Viola wittrockiana)*, pot marigold *(Calendula officinalis)*, redbud *(Cercis canadensis)*, rose *(Rosa* spp.), signet marigold *(Tagetes signata)*, and sweet violets *(Viola odorata)*.

Some Particularly Tasty Flowers

The following flowers have particularly marked or distinctive flavors that you can work into you regular dishes if you choose. A little experimentation goes a long way.

Anise hyssop *(Agastache foeniculum):* Mild licorice or root beer flavor.

Clove pinks *(Dianthus caryophyllus):* Sweet clove flavor.

Dame's rocket *(Hesperis matronalis):* Mild lettuce flavor.

Japanese honeysuckle *(Lonicera japonica):* Sweet honey flavor.

Lavender *(Lavandula* spp.): A lemony perfume flavor.

Redbud *(Cercis canadensis):* A tart apple flavor.

Rose of Sharon *(Hibiscus syriacus):* Sweet and mild flavor.

Sweet violet *(Viola odorata):* Sweet and perfumed in flavor.

Tuberous begonia *(Begonia x tuberhybrida):* A tangy citrus flavor.

Yucca *(Yucca* spp.): A delicately sweet flavor.

Preparing and Storing Flowers

As a general rule, you should use only the flower petals of edible flowers. Certain flowers such as violets, pansies, and Johnny jump-ups, however, can be consumed whole. Here are a few rules to live by in using your own flowers.

Pick flowers early in the morning after the dew has dried on them or in the early evening. Flowers that are picked during the heat of midday will quickly wilt or dry out before you have a chance to use them.

Remove pistils and stamens, and gently remove any residual pollen with a soft brush. Also remove the sepals unless using pansies, violas, and Johnny jump-ups—in which case you will want to consume the sepals along with the rest of the flowers.

Remove the white heel that is present at the base of some flowers petals—such as in chrysanthemums, daisies, marigolds, pinks, roses, and tulips. This heel imparts a bitter flavor to the petals.

Gently wash the flowers if any dirt or bugs are present.

Pat the flowers dry with a paper towel, or use a salad spinner to remove excess water.

Use the flowers immediately or store them in one of two ways:

1. Place the flowers in a plastic bag or other air-tight plastic container, along with one or two moist paper towels, and store them in the vegetable bin of your refrigerator.

2. Flowers with longer stems can be placed in a bowl or vase of water, which can then be placed in the refrigerator.

The General Culinary Uses of Flowers

Among the various uses for flowers, below I've listed a number of possible recipes so you can enjoy this unusual culinary treat in the following: salads, both fruit salad or green salad; hot or iced teas; baked goods, such as cakes, cookies, and muffins; jams and jellies; vinegar, oils, and butters; ice cubes and punches; and soups and sauces.

Edible Flowers in Salads

My husband (a.k.a. Mr. Meat & Potatoes) has eaten a variety of edible flowers in salads that I prepare from organic ingredients picked from our garden. This is true testimony to the natural appeal of flowers. To make a salad, hold off adding any dressing until you are ready to eat the salad. Otherwise, the acids from vinegar and lemon juice may affect the color of certain flowers.

Various mixed greens (lettuce, spinach, kale, etc.)

1–2   tomatoes, chopped

1–2   orange or yellow sweet peppers

A handful of edible flowers petals

Various herbs (both the leaves and flowers). Try basil, thyme, and Mexican tarragon to start.

Add the first three ingredients to a large bowl, and toss to mix well. Sprinkle the petals of the edible flowers and herbs on top of the salad prior to serving. My favorite flowers to use in green salads are borage, calendula, chives, garlic chives, and nasturtium. When using chive and garlic chive flowers be sure to pull apart the individual florets prior to adding them to your salad or other dishes.

Floral Tea Blends

One of my favorite store-bought tea blends includes cactus flowers, sunflower petals, and blue bottle flowers among its ingredients. Certain edible flowers can be dried to preserve for later use such as in your own tea blends.

To preserve flowers and flower petals for later use, pick bunches of flowers in the early morning. Gently rinse the flowers in water to remove any dirt or insects that may be present. Pat the flowers dry with paper towels. Place the flowers still attached to their stems in a bundle, and secure them with a rubber band.

Hang these bundles upside down, and store them in a dark, well-ventilated area. For best results, dry one type of flower per bundle. When the flowers are dry, the individual flower petals may be removed from their stems and stored in an airtight glass container away from direct sunlight. I like to make up a mixture of herbs and flower petals chosen from the lists below. I like to use 1 teaspoon dried tea blend or 3 teaspoons fresh herbs or flowers infused in 1 cup boiling water. Let the the tea steep for five to ten minutes, then strain and pour into a cup. Sweeten with honey or sugar if you desire. I sometimes add dried stevia leaves to the tea blend. *Stevia rebaudiana* is a natural, low-calorie sweetener I have growing in my garden.

Harvest these flowers for use in tea: cowslip *(Primula veris)*, elder *(Sambucus nigra)*, English lavender *(Lavandula angustifolia)*, florist's chrysanthemum *(Chrysanthemum morifolium)*, German chamomile *(Matricaria recutita)*, hibiscus *(Hibiscus rosa-sinensis)*, hollyhock *(Alcea rosea)*, Arabian jasmine *(Jasminum sambac)*, pot marigold *(Calendula officinalis)*, rose *(Rosa* spp.), and sunflower *(Helianthus annuus)*.

Harvest these flowers and their leaves for use in tea: basil *(Ocimum* spp.), bee balm *(Monarda didyma)*, clary sage *(Salvia sclarea)*, hyssop *(Hyssopus officinalis)*, Korean mint *(Agastache rugosa)*, lemon balm *(Melissa officinalis)*, mint *(Mentha* spp.), pineapple sage *(Salvia elegans)*, roselle *(Hibiscus sabdariffa)*, and scented geraniums *(Pelargonium* spp.).

Floral Ice Cubes

For a very clever and wholly artistic way to use edible flowers, place a whole flower (such as borage, Johnny Jump-ups, sweet violets, scented geraniums) or flower petals (such as daisy, nasturtium, roses) in the bottom of an ice cube tray. Fill the tray halfway with water and freeze overnight.

Remove the tray from the freezer, and fill to the top with water. Return the tray to the freezer until the entire ice cube has frozen. These floral delights can be used in iced teas and lemonades or floated on the top of punch bowls to impart a festive touch to any occasion.

Other Flower Recipes

Edible flowers can be incorporated into a variety of conventional culinary creations. Get creative and try adding edible flowers to your favorite recipes. I have included a few of my personal favorites to help get you started.

Garlic Cheese Biscuits

1¼   cups sifted all-purpose flour

½   tsp. salt

3   tsps. baking powder

6   Tbls. chilled butter

1   cup milk

2   Tbls. minced garlic chive leaves

1   Tbl. minced garlic chive flowers

⅓   cup shredded cheddar cheese

¼   cup melted butter

Preheat your oven to 450°F. Sift the flour, salt, and baking powder into a large mixing bowl. Add the chilled butter, and cut into the dry ingredients using a pastry blender or two knives, until it has the appearance of coarse corn meal. Add the milk, garlic chive leaves, garlic chive flowers, and cheddar cheese. Mix until well blended. Form the dough into 12 balls. Roll each ball in melted butter, and place it into a muffin pan. Place the pan in the oven, and cook for twelve to fifteen minutes or until the biscuits are lightly browned.

Roasted Rosemary Potatoes

6   large baking potatoes

6   flowering rosemary springs (each around 4 inches)

⅓   cup olive oil

Salt and pepper to taste

Finely chop the rosemary leaves and flowers after removing them from the tough, woody stems. Peel, wash, and cut the potatoes into ¼-inch slices. Brush the bottom of a large baking dish with some of the olive oil. Place a layer of potatoes on the bottom of the dish, brush the potatoes with olive oil, and sprinkle with salt, pepper, and part of the rosemary. Continue layering the potatoes, olive oil, and seasonings until all of the potatoes have been used up. A 9½-by-13-inch pan will hold three layers of potatoes. Bake in a 400°F oven for 1 to 1¼ hours. For even browning of the potatoes, remove the pan from the oven after ½ hour, and flip the potatoes over with a spatula. Return the pan to the oven and continue baking.

I like my potatoes on the crispy side so I leave them in for a bit longer. If you like moister, less-crispy potatoes, take the dish out after an hour.

Floral Icing

    4   oz. cream cheese, at room temperature

    2   Tbls. pineapple juice

    2   cups confectioners sugar

    2   Tbls. pineapple sage flowers, finely chopped

Place the softened cream cheese into a mixing bowl. Mix in the pineapple juice, and stir until well blended. Sift the confectioners sugar into another bowl. Gradually add the sifted confectioners sugar into the cream cheese and juice mix. When the desired consistency has been reached, stir in the pineapple sage flowers. This icing can be served on top of your favorite cake (angel food cake, pound cake, and so on). The cake can then be garnished with candied flower petals for a truly festive look (see below for more details).

Other Uses of Edible Flowers

Edible flowers can be used to add a creative touch to a variety of beverages and food dishes. They work great as garnishes on your dinner plate or floating in a bowl of your favorite soup.

Candied Flowers

Candied flowers look elegant garnishing a variety of items such as fruit salads, puddings, and wedding cakes. Prepare the flowers as mentioned in the preparation and storage section above. Candy the flowers using one of two methods.

Method one: Brush the petals of the flowers with beaten egg white using a very small artist's paint brush, and sprinkle with fine granulated sugar.

Method two: Mix ¼ cup of corn syrup with 1 teaspoon of vanilla, almond, or peppermint extract, depending upon your personal preference. Brush the petals and flowers with this mixture using an artist's paint brush. Sprinkle them with powdered confectioners sugar.

With either method you may want to use a pair of tweezers to help you hold on to the flowers and petals. Place the candied flowers and flower petals on a wire rack that has been covered with waxed paper to dry for a day or two. If you are not using the candied flowers right away, you can store them for up to two months in the refrigerator, or in the freezer for up to six months. Place them in an airtight container in single layers with a piece of waxed paper between each layer. Don't place more than three layers of candied flowers per container. The following flowers work especially well for candying, as they have the best taste and appearance: borage, clove pink, cowslip, Johnny jump-up, lavender, lilac, pansy, rose, scented geranium, and sweet violet.

Chocolate Flowers

1   cup edible flowers and flower petals

1   12-oz. package semisweet chocolate chips

1   14-oz. can sweetened condensed milk

1   cup chopped pecans

     Confectioners sugar

Lightly spray a muffin pan with nonstick cooking spray. Evenly distribute the edible flowers and flower petals among the twelve muffin cups of a muffin pan. Melt the chocolate chips and sweetened condensed milk in a double boiler. Remove the chocolate mixture from the stove and stir in the chopped pecans.

Cover the flowers by dividing the chocolate mixture among the muffin cups. Let them chill until the chocolate has hardened. Remove the chocolate flowers from the muffin tin, and cut each one into 4 pieces. Place the chocolates onto a platter, and sprinkle them with sifted confectioners sugar.

Floral Spreads

Add two to three tablespoons of fresh chopped flower petals into one cup of any of the following: butter, cheese spreads, cream cheese, mayonnaise, sour cream, or yogurt.

Mix well, and use these spreads as you normally would on top of toast, bagels, crackers, fruits, vegetables, and so on.

Edible Flower Uses in Ethnic Cooking

Many Hispanic culinary creations utilize hibiscus flowers, linden flowers, coral-tree flowers, and squash blossoms as staple ingredients. These flowers are used in a variety of dishes such as squash blossom soup and hibiscus flower water. Canned squash blossoms are even available from one of the major Mexican food distributors. Squash blossoms are also chopped, sautéed, and served in tortillas.

Garland chrysanthemum *(Chrysanthemum coronarium)* is a traditional oriental chop suey ingredient with dainty orange-yellow flowers. The flowers have bright yellow petals that have a flavor similar to the leaves (spicy and aromatic). The petals can be sprinkled on top of salads, rice dishes, and stir fries prior to serving.

Dried daylily flowers (also known as golden needles) are used in Chinese hot and sour soup. The fresh petals and flower buds of this plant are used in stir fries in Asian cuisine. They have a fresh taste that is similar to asparagus or green beans. The flowers of gardenia *(Gardenia augusta)*, meanwhile, are used to flavor Chinese tea.

In Scotland, the dried flower heads of heather *(Calluna vulgaris)* are mixed with other herbs such as blackberry leaves, wild thyme, and wild strawberry leaves and brewed to create what is called Moorland tea.

The flowers of mock lime *(Aglaia odorata)*, which is also known as Chinese perfume plant, are used to scent Chinese tea. Mock lime flowers have a pleasant vanilla scent when they are dried. The flowers of the neem tree *(Azadirachta indica)*, meanwhile, are used along with its leaves to make a tasty tea in India. These flowers' sweet jasmine-like scent are utilized in chutney and other recipes.

Rose water (which is made from rose petals) is a popular flavoring in Indian, Middle Eastern, and Chinese cooking. Turkish delight is a Persian confection that includes rose water as one of its ingredients.

The flowers and leaves of wasabi *(Wasabia japonica)* are used to make *wasabi-zuke*, a type of Japanese pickle.

Water lily *(Nymphaea odorata)* flower buds are very fragrant, and they appear in oriental cooking both pickled or cooked as a vegetable.

The flower buds of the wax gourd *(Benincasa hispida)* are used in Chinese cooking, both steamed and stir-fried.

Winged beans *(Psophocarpus tetragonolobus)*, which are also known as gao beans, have been cultivated in Asia and India for centuries. The flowers are edible and used in numerous dishes.

Mail Order Sources

Here is a brief listing of garden catalogs that sell certified organic plants and seeds, should you be interested in growing your own edible flowers.

The Natural Gardening Company
P.O. Box 750776
Petaluma, CA 94975-0776

1-707-766-9303
www.naturalgardening.com

Ritcher's Herbs
P.O. Box 26
Goodwood, Ontario LOC 1AO
Canada
1-905-640-6677
www.richters.com

Seeds of Change
P.O. Box 15700
Santa Fe, NM 87506
1-888-762-7333
http://store.yahoo.com/seedsofchange

Sow Organic Seed
P.O. Box 527
Williams, OR 97544
1-888-709-7333
www.organicseed.com

Territorial Seed Company
P.O. Box 158
Cottage Grove, OR 97424-0061
1-888-657-3131
www.territorialseed.com

Internet Sources

The following companies offer fresh or dried edible flowers, flower petals, and floral-based condiments that are ready to add into your own culinary creations. This is a great way to incorporate edible flowers into your diet if you don't have the room or time to grow them yourself.

Earthy Delights
1161 E. Clark Road, Suite 260
DeWitt, Michigan 48820
1-800-367-4709
www.earthy.com

Edible Flowers
1934 Hano Road
Santa Fe, NM 87505
1-505-989-7341
www.edibleflowers.net

The McCluney Company
P.O. Box 26
Freedom, CA 95019-0026
1-888-677-8008
www.virtualvegetable.com

For Further Study

Barash, Cathy Wilkinson. *Edible Flowers: From Garden to Palate.* Golden, Colo.: Fulcrum Pub., 1993.

Brown, Deni. *New Encyclopedia of Herbs & Their Uses.* New York: Dorling Kindersley Publishing, 2001.

Brown, Kathy. *The Edible Flower Garden: From Garden to Kitchen: Choosing, Growing and Cooking Edible Flowers.* Lanham, Md.: Lorenz Books, 1999.

Creasy, Rosalind. *The Edible Flower Garden.* Boston: Periplus Editions, 1999.

McGee, Rose Marie Nichols. *McGee & Stuckey's The Bountiful Container: A Container Garden of Vegetables, Herbs, Fruits and*

Edible Flowers. Illustrations by Michael A. Hill. New York: Workman Pub., 2002.

Tenebaum, Frances, (ed.). *Taylor's Fifty Best Herbs and Edible Flowers: Easy Plants for More Beautiful Gardens.* New York: Houghton Mifflin Company, 1999.

Herbal Wines and Liqueurs

by Chandra Moira Beal

Grape growers don't have a monopoly on winemaking. Herbs, fruits, flowers, and even vegetables can be made into delectable wines and liqueurs.

Making your own herbal wines and liqueurs is fun and easy, and a great way to continue an ancient tradition. Wines and liqueurs can be used socially or medicinally, or can be incorporated into your magic rituals. These are time-tested recipes that are simple and economical, using ingredients found in gardens and fields. There is no end to the possible combinations of wines and herbs. Let your imagination lead you into new realms.

Getting Started

Before you attempt your first recipe, gather all the equipment you need to make wine. This includes one-gallon glass jugs, corks or screw-tops, strainers, large stainless-steel cooking pots, funnels, wooden spoons, and fermentation locks. A fermentation lock is a device that fits into the top of your jug and is filled with water. It allows the gases produced by the yeast to escape, but it prevents contaminants from sneaking into your wine. They are inexpensive and readily available at brewing supply stores. I highly recommend this simple but effective device.

Some Basic Starter Tips

When filling your bottles, leave as little headroom between the liquid and the cork as possible. This minimizes the chances of a sharp flavor invading your wine.

Sanitation is the key to successful brewing, so wash, in hot soapy water, anything and everything that will come into contact with your wine. Do not use bleach as it can leave an odor behind that will be absorbed by your wine. Other odor-free sanitizers such as idophor are available at homebrew shops.

Start with fresh, cool water in your brew pot. Use only the freshest ingredients available. More than anything, your wines will be as good as the ingredients that go into them. Use exact measurements, and follow instructions carefully. Always pick through your herbs, and remove any green stalks, leaves, or stems. These plant elements tend to contain bitter oils not welcome in your wine.

Because high temperatures will kill the yeast, it is important to let the hot liquid cool completely—to at least 75°F, before adding yeast to it.

Most of these wines will tend to improve with age. Let them sit for at least six months before tasting. Wines will also clarify as they age, so when you can read a sheet of paper held up to the glass through the liquid, your wines are probably ready.

Racking is another way to clarify your wine, but this is more time-consuming. It involves repeatedly pouring the liquid off the settled yeast wastes at the bottom of the jug into a clean jug.

You can also taste along the way and adjust the sweetness to your personal tastes.

The Basic Procedure

The procedure is basically the same for each of the following wines. First, heat the water to just below boiling so it will extract the herbs' essential oils but not their bitterness. Pour the hot water over the herbs and allow them to steep (the duration of steeping will vary by recipe). Strain out the herbs and add the sugar, any citrus element called for, and the yeast. Stir to dissolve the sugar. Stirring aerates the yeast and activates it. As the yeast bacteria eat the sugar, they produce carbon dioxide—thus causing the beverage to ferment.

You should see bubbles in your liquid within twenty-four hours as evidence of yeast activity. If fermentation is slow to start, shake your jug vigorously to aerate again. Make sure the ambient temperature where you are keeping your incipient wine is not too hot or too cold. Yeast prefers a temperature around 60–65°F to ferment—such temperatures are typical of a basement or garage. Place a fermentation lock over the top of the bottle, and place the bottle in a dark, cool place to age. It will keep for years until opened.

Herbal Wine Recipes

Coltsfoot Wine

Coltsfoot is best known for its expectorant qualities. A glass of this wine may help quiet a cough.

2 quarts coltsfoot flowers

1 gallon boiling water

1 lemon, cut into thin slices

½ lb. raisins

½ oz. yeast

3 lbs. sugar

Pick the flowers on a sunny day, and wash them well to remove any insects. Place the flowers in a large bowl and pour the boiling water over the top. Cover the bowl with a clean tea towel, and let it sit for 4 days. Strain the liquid into a large saucepan, and add the lemon slices and raisins. When the mixture begins to boil, turn off the heat. Pour the liquid into a large bowl, and let it cool. Stir in the yeast and sugar, and stir to completely dissolve these into the liquid. Cover the bowl again with a towel, and stir it once a day for three days. The wine is then ready to strain and bottle. Cork it loosely or use a fermentation lock. Let it age for 6 months.

Cowslip Wine

Cowslip flowers are said to help cure jaundice. The plant itself is associated with the Norse goddess of beauty and love, Freya. It is a good herb for protection, and it has strong maternal qualities.

2   quarts cowslip flowers

1   gallon boiling water

1   lemon, thinly sliced

3   lbs. sugar

½   oz. yeast

Pick the flowers on a sunny day, and wash them well to remove any insects. Use only the heads of the flowers. Place the flowers in a large bowl, and pour the boiling water over the top. Cover the bowl with a clean tea towel, and let it sit for 4 days. Strain the liquid into a large saucepan, and add the lemon slices. When the mixture begins to boil, turn off the heat. Pour it into a large bowl, and let it cool. Add the sugar, and stir to dissolve. Spread the yeast on a piece of toast, and float the toast on top of the liquid.

Cover the bowl again with a towel and stir it once a day for 3 days. Remove the toast, and strain the liquid and bottle. Cork it loosely, or use a fermentation lock. Let this wine age for at least six months. This wine may need to be sweetened with more sugar after a few weeks of aging.

Dandelion Wine

The dandelion is unfairly criticized as a weed. Dandelions are actually very rich in vitamins and minerals, and they are good for indigestion and kidney trouble. The plant also makes a very mean bottle of wine.

- 2 quarts fresh dandelion flowers
- 1 lemon, sliced thin
- 1 orange, sliced thin
- 1 gallon boiling water
- 3 lbs. sugar
- ½ oz. yeast

Pick the flowers on a sunny day when the flowers are fully open. Remove all green stems and stalks, and measure 2 quarts of loose, fresh flowers. Wash the flowers in cold water to remove any insects. Place the blossoms in a large bowl. Add the sliced lemon and orange, and pour the boiling water over the top. Cover the bowl with a clean tea towel, and let it sit for 10 days. Strain the liquid into another bowl, and add the sugar. Stir to completely dissolve the sugar into the liquid. Spread the yeast on a piece of toast, and float the toast on top of the bowl. Cover the bowl and let it sit for another three days. Remove the toast, and strain again. Bottle the wine with a loose cork or fermentation lock.

Elderflower Wine

Elder has long been associated with protection against disease, lightning, and it can assist in divination.

- 1 gallon elderflowers
- Zest from 1 lemon
- Zest from 1 orange

1   gallon boiling water

3   lbs. granulated sugar

1   oz. yeast

Cut the stalks from the flowers, and measure out a gallon of flowers. Wash them, and remove any insects. Place the elder-flowers in a large bowl with the lemon and orange zest. Pour the boiling water over the top. Cover the bowl with a clean tea towel, and let it sit for 4 days. Strain the liquid into a large saucepan, and bring it to a boil. Add the sugar, and stir well until it is dissolved in the liquid. Let the mixture cool, and add the yeast. Cover the bowl again for 6 days, stirring every day. Then strain, and bottle with a fermentation lock. Age for 6 months.

Ginger Wine

Ginger is excellent for indigestion, and this wine will warm you during cold winter nights.

2½   ozs. ginger root

3½   lbs. granulated sugar

      Juice of 3 lemons

2   Tbls. honey

2   gallons of water

Bruise the ginger, and put it in a saucepan with 3 pints of water. Bring the water to a boil, and simmer 30 minutes. Pour sugar into a large bowl. Add the lemon juice and honey. Pour the ginger and the hot liquid into the bowl, and stir well to dissolve the sugar. Boil the remaining water, and add it to the bowl. Let it sit for 24 hours. Strain and bottle.

Rosehips Wine

3½   lbs. rosehips

1   gallon boiling water

3½   lbs. sugar

This is an easy to make recipe that doesn't involve yeast. Wash the rosehips, and cut them in half. Place them in a large bowl, and pour the boiling water over the top. Cover the bowl with a clean tea towel, and let it sit for 2 weeks. Strain the liquid into a bowl, and add sugar. Stir until dissolved, then cover and let it sit for another 5 days, stirring daily. The wine is ready to bottle at this stage.

Marigold Wine

In Mexico, marigolds are used as visionary herbs and can be found in recipes for love divination.

4   quarts marigold flowers

1   lemon

1   orange

1   gallon boiling water

3   lbs. granulated sugar

½   oz. yeast

Pick the flowers on a sunny day, and wash them clean of insects. Place the flowers in a large bowl. Grate the orange and lemon rinds, and squeeze out the juice. Add the rind and juice to the flowers. Pour the boiling water over the top. Cover the bowl with a clean tea towel, and let it sit for 4 days. Strain the liquid into a large saucepan, and bring the mixture to a boil. Pour sugar into a bowl, and pour the hot liquid over the top. Stir the liquid until the sugar is dissolved, and then allow it to cool. Stir in the yeast. Cover the bowl again, and stir it for the first 3 days. Strain and bottle. Age for 6 months.

Herbal Liqueurs

Making your own liqueurs is somewhat easier than making wine or beer, and the results are rewarding. Liqueurs make dazzling gifts with their bright colors and decadent spirits. They are also great for personal and ritual use, or medicinally in small sips.

Don't limit yourself to just sipping these concoctions, though. Liqueurs are also delicious drizzled over ice cream, added to coffee, or brushed on foods as a glaze.

These recipes can all be adjusted to your tastes by adding more or less sugar. To sweeten, the general ratio is 1 ounce of sugar to 4 ounces of base liquid. If the liqueur is too sweet, and a bit of lemon juice and let it steep before using. If you like a more syrupy drink, add one or two teaspoons of glycerin.

Always let liqueurs mature for at least a week, and preferably for a month. Maturing mellows and balances the flavor. The process of steeping is what blends the base alcohol with the flavor of your additions. When straining to separate the liquid from the solids, press as much liquid as you can from fruit—as this liquid holds all the flavor. You may need to strain some things such as nuts more than once. To clarify the liquid even further, strain it through a paper filter, such as for making coffee. Be sure to taste your recipe at this stage and adjust the sugar or steep it longer if necessary. The shelf life for most liqueurs is about six months. It is helpful to keep a log of what you made and when, and to label all your creations.

When working with fruit, fresh is always best. Fresh fruit has the most potent flavor, though dried, canned, or frozen fruits will work in a pinch. Nuts and herbs should always be crushed first to release volatile oils. In recipes calling for herbs or spices, start with the minimum amount of ingredients listed. Herbs and spices are potent and can always be adjusted up for a stronger flavor, but not down.

You'll need a few pieces of equipment to start, most of which can be found in the common kitchen. Gather some glass jars (dark colors and quart-sized are best); a cooking pot; funnels; a blender or food processor; a strainer; cheesecloth; a hammer or rolling pin; a paring knife; and coffee filters.

Look for pretty bottles at garage sales and thrift stores, or at hobby supply shops. Decorative labels are easy to find, or you can make your own. You can find corks at homebrew shops, or seal your bottles with foil and brightly colored yarn or melted beeswax.

Before you begin, mix a batch of sugar syrup to use it in many of the recipes to follow. Each recipe below yields 1 quart of liqueur.

Base Recipe for Sugar Syrup

1   cup granulated white sugar

½   cup water

When making sugar syrup, the ratio is 1 part water to 2 parts sugar. Boil for 5 minutes, and be sure the sugar is dissolved. Cool completely before proceeding.

Licorice Liqueur

This liqueur is tasty iced or hot, and can help soothe sore throats and other upper respiratory ailments.

2½   Tbls. chopped licorice root

1½   cups vodka

½   cup sugar syrup

Wash the licorice root, and chop it into small pieces. Add to the vodka, and steep this for 1 week. Strain and filter. Add sugar syrup, and steep another week. Adjust to taste.

Cinnamon Liqueur

This liqueur is a stimulant and a popular ingredient in love potions.

1   cinnamon stick

2   cloves

1   tsp. ground coriander seed

1   cup vodka

½   cup sugar syrup

Steep all of the herbs in vodka for 2 weeks. Strain and filter until very clear. Add sugar syrup to taste. Let stand another week. Makes a nice hot toddy when added to hot water.

Peppermint Liqueur

Peppermint's menthol oil makes this liqueur a mild *anodyne* that anesthetizes nerve endings. The liqueur can quiet a nervous stomach as a tonic, help any nausea, and stimulate appetite. It is also quite tasty.

2–3   tsps. peppermint extract

3   cups vodka

1   cup sugar syrup

Combine all the ingredients and stir. Let stand for 2 weeks. If you don't want too strong a mint taste, use just 2 teaspoons of extract. Add more sugary syrup for a thicker liqueur.

Herbs for
Health

Growing the Medicinal Herbs of Latin America

❧ by Scott Appell ❧

B oth the endemic (native), and alien (nonnative) flora of Latin America—ranging from northern Mexico southward through Central and South America to the Amazon Basin and Tierra del Fuego, and eastward to the Caribbean—have provided millions of people with hundreds of cures for various maladies. Many of these herbs are familiar to us—perhaps as common greengrocer produce, as lovely tropical foliage encountered on a vacation, as common garden plants, or even as house plants.

A Selection of Latin American Medicinal Herbs

There are many herbs to choose from in this category, and given enough time and space I could write a book on the subject. For now, I will focus on some of the most useful, colorful, and interesting of the herbs of Latin America, at least so you can make a start in learning about the plants of this remarkable region.

Epasote or Mexican Tea (Chenopodium ambrosiodes)
(Family: Chenopodiaceae)

Also called epazote, aposote, pazote, or Yerba de Santa Maria, epasote's strong taste is characteristic of the Mayan cuisine in the South of Mexico (particularly in the Yucatán Peninsula) and Guatemala. This uncommon herb belongs to a plant family that contains some very important economic plants, namely the *Chenopodiaceae* family. Its members include such vegetable crops as spinach, beets, sugar beets, Swiss chard, lamb's quarters, and orache; such herbs as Good King Henry; and the increasingly popular South American grains known as quinoa, huauzontle, and cañihua.

The common name epasote is derived from Nahuatl, the tongue spoken by the Aztecs before the arrival of the Spanish. This is a minority language in Mexico, but it is still in use among the Indios living around Mexico City. The name is comprised of *epatle*, "skunk," and *tzotl*, or "sweat"—therefore, the plant is "skunk sweat," a reference to its strong and, to some, disagreeable smell. Naturally, *epazote*, *aposote*, and *pazote* are linguistic variations. The genus name *Chenopodium* is derived from the Greek *cheén*, "goose," and *poùs*, "foot"—making "goose-foot," a reference to the three-lobed leaf shape of several of the species. The species epithet, *ambrosiodes*, which translates as "ambrosia-like," probably refers to its copious production of seeds. Recollect from Greek and Roman mythology that ambrosia was the inexhaustible source of food of the gods and conferred eternal life to any mortal who ate it.

This herb is indigenous to Central and Southern Mexico, but it is now a common weed throughout Europe and the United States. Epasote may reach a height of forty inches under ideal conditions. The leaves may be oblong or lance-shaped, often with a toothed margin, and about two to four inches long. The entire plant is slightly resinous to the touch, a result of its inherent essential oils. The herb flowers from July to September, and the tiny yellowish flowers are borne on long, grainy clusters produced from the leaf axils. The miniscule black seeds ripen in October. The leaves, flowers, and sprigs of the unripe fruit have the strongest flavor.

Epasote couldn't be easier to cultivate. It self-sows remarkably quickly, and one purchased plant will multiply freely. In northern zones, the plants are killed by the first hard frost, but its seeds will survive hibernal freezes and germinate in the spring. Epasote needs full Sun and average garden soil to prosper. Once established, epasote is remarkably drought-resistant, though this herb will not tolerate constantly damp beds.

Pungent-tasting *Chenopodium ambrosiodes* is always used fresh (and therefore only available to those people who grow their own or have neighbors who do). The dried leaves are considered to be an inferior product. In general, it is used to flavor corn, black beans—particularly *frijoles refritos*—mushrooms, fish, soups, molé verde, stews, chili sauces, shellfish, and freshwater snails. An infusion of the foliage is used as a tea substitute. The tender young leaves are often consumed as a potherb. Cooking the leaves with beans is said to reduce flatulence. In the Himalayas, the seeds are ground into black flour that is mixed with warm water and eaten. They are also roasted and added to *chang* and *rakshi*, both alcoholic beverages.

Epasote is pharmaceutically known as *herba chenopodii ambrosiodis*, and the essential oil pressed from its seeds has long been understood as an effective treatment for round worms, hookworms, tapeworms, and other intestinal parasites. This oil contains about 70 percent ascaridol, and care should be taken when using this medicine internally, as differing amounts of the active principles—including limonese, p-cymene, and numerous monoterpenes—may cause poisoning. Use the refined oil only under the guidance of your general practitioner or homeopathic healer. Allegedly, ascaridol content is lower in epasote grown in Mexico than in epasote grown in Europe and Asia. *Materia Medica Mexicana* prescribes an infusion of the leaves and flowers of epazote for St. Vitus's dance (an archival term for chorea, a neurological symptom of rheumatic fever in young people), as an emmenogogue, and as an anthelmintic. As a tonic, it produces perspiration, promotes urination, and prevents flatulence.

Native Americans learned about the medicinal virtues of epasote from northward migrating Mexicans, and many tribes, including the Creek (from Georgia), Koasati (from the southeastern United States), Mahuna (from southwestern California), Miwok (from Sierra Nevada), Natchez (from the lower Mississippi River), and Rappahannock (from Virginia) employed it for its anthelmintic and tonic properties.

Broadleaf Coriander, Cat Claw, or Fitweed (Eryngium foetidum) *(Family:* Apiaceae)

This plant is also known as *recao* or *culantro* in Spanish. I am an avid cook and particularly enjoy emulating the ethnic recipes of cultures around the world. I scour the shops in New York's Spanish Harlem for the ingredients to recreate the cuisines of Puerto Rico, the Caribbean, and South America, and one of the most interesting fresh herbs I buy is broadleaf coriander, or *Eryngium foetidum*, an ingredient not included in Asian, Mediterranean, Middle Eastern, or European dishes. Its green, hairy, and somewhat spiny foliage supplies it the common name "cat claw." Its five- to six-inch leaves, have a coriander-like flavor, inspiring its common English name, broadleaf coriander. But the leaves are too tough to be eaten raw in salads and must be cooked in order to be palatable.

This herb's species name, *foetidum*, translates as "bad smelling," an allusion to the pungent fragrance of the crushed foliage. It is sold either as small bunches bound with rubber bands or "cello-packed" in plastic wrap. Bottled products abound, but I find the taste and texture are insipid and inferior, and are loaded with unwanted ingredients. I never the saw this herb actually in cultivation until I became a regular visitor to Puerto Rico, where I realized it was a common constituent of the local kitchen garden.

As a member of the *Apiaceae*, broadleaf coriander is a cousin to some of the best-known culinary and medicinal herbs, including true coriander *(Coriandrum sativum)*, parsley *(Petroselinum crispum)*, caraway *(Carum carvi)*, cumin *(Cuminum cyminum)*, angelica *(Angelica arachangelica)*, and fennel *(Foeniculum vulgare)*, to name a few. It is also related to some important vegetable crops, such as parsnips *(Pastinaca sativa)*, carrots *(Daucus carota)*, celery *(Apium graveolens)*, and the highly unusual and saline samphire *(Crithmum maritimum)*. In addition, broadleaf coriander is related to some very worthwhile perennial flower garden plants: sea holly *(Eryngium maritimum)*, masterwort *(Astrantia major)*, and variegated goutweed *(Aegopodium podograria*, "Variegata").

Once encountered, broadleaf coriander is easily recognized. Its leaves are toothed and spiny along the margins, and are held in a simple rosette about seven inches across. The inflorescences are thimble-shaped heads about a half inch in length, subtended by stiff leaf-like bracts held in a star-like pattern on an eight-inch stem with a prominent Y-shaped branching pattern.

Seeds can be procured from Hispanic markets. The broadleaf coriander requires plenty of moisture and a lightly shaded site to succeed. Shade is particularly important in areas with scorching summers. The flower stems should be removed in order to keep the plant producing foliage, but a few flower stems can be left on the plant to guarantee the production of seed, which readily germinates. Use this little herb as an edging subject in dappled beds and borders, or try an ornamental container strategically placed in a shady part of the garden. This plant can be grown outdoors year round in USDA Zones 10 and 11, but can be cultivated anywhere as a summer produce item.

Broadleaf coriander has multiple culinary aspects. Although the tough outer leaves must be cooked to be palatable, the tiniest foliage can be eaten raw in salads. The foliage in general is often steamed and eaten with rice, and it enhances grilled fish and meats, soups, sauces, and curries. The roots are frequently employed as a condiment for soups and meat dishes, to which they impart a savory flavor. The seeds are also used as an ingredient in the Puerto Rican flavoring mixture *sofrito*, along with true cilantro and small chilies called ajicitos (*Capsicum chinense*).

In Puerto Rican folk medicine, an infusion of recao, rue *(la ruda)*, *Ruta graveolens*, and fennel (*el hinojo* or *Foeniculum vulgare*) is employed to regulate menstrual cycles and alleviate cramps. There is an interesting recipe to aid sufferers of high blood pressure—every day, in a quart of fresh water, boil for fifteen minutes up to five leaves of recao along with the outer skins and ends of three heads of garlic, five leaves of common plantain (*el llantén* or *Plantago majus*), plus five leaves of the sour orange (*el naranjo* or *Citrus aurantium*). Drink this infusion, cold, warm, or hot instead of water or juice all day long. Infusions of recao are recommended to lower blood sugar.

Common Plantain (Plantago major)
(Family: Plantaginaceae)

Common plantain, called *lanten, llantén,* or *yantén* in Spanish, is a wayside plant familiar to walkers, hitchhikers, or stranded people waiting for automotive assistance. But who would imagine this lowly persistent weed of flower bed and lawn would be steeped in mythology, homeopathy, and religious significance?

Plantago is an invasive, non-native, herbaceous perennial endemic to Eurasia. In all likelihood, plantain was brought to the New World due to its medicinal properties (for treating coughs, cuts, and hemorrhoids), and escaped from cultivation. Alternately, its seed may have been introduced into North America transported in the mud on people's shoes or within the hay and feed for livestock—as is the case for the majority of American "weeds." Native Americans found it spreading wherever the European went, and called it "white man's foot."

The genus name *Plantago* may have been derived from a secondary meaning of the Latin word *planta*, meaning the "sole of the foot." The species name, *major*, refers to "bigger" or "larger"—therefore, "bigger sole of the foot." Plantain is easily recognizable. The foliage is broadly obovate ("reverse egg-shaped"), and may be as long as thirteen inches, and as wide as four inches. The plant grows in a rosette shape with the leaves held flat against the ground. The flower parts are not discernable with the naked eye (about .08 inches wide). They are borne on slender, stiffly upright spikes that grow up to twelve inches tall.

Surprisingly, this unusual herb is a common subject in medieval and Renaissance religious arts, in which it was referred to as "way bread," an allusion to its wayward habitat and existence. By virtue of its procumbent, or downward lying, growth habit, it became a symbol of the "well-trodden path" of the multitude that seeks the path of Jesus. It was prominently placed in several of the renowned Unicorn Tapestries on display at the Cloisters Museum in Fort Tryon Park, New York City. You can particularly see it in tapestry number three, "The Unicorn Leaps Out of the Stream," woven in the Netherlands between 1495 and 1505.

Henry Chaucer included plantain in his writings, and William Shakespeare recommends plantain leaves for "broken skin" in two of his plays: *Romeo and Juliet* (1597) and *Love's Labour's Lost* (1598). Also he alludes to it in *Troilus and Cressida*, written in 1609.

As true as steel, as plantage to the moon.

Troilus and Cressida, *Act III, Scene 2*

Within the *Materia Medica Mexicana*, a decoction of lanten is used against dysentery, burns, and mouth ulcers. An infusion mixed with rose water is used for inflammation of the eyes. Lanten has some intriguing applications in Puerto Rican folk medicine, as well. For stomach ulcers, take a couple of handfuls of common plantain and some black nightshade *(la mata gallina* or *Solanum americanum*), and toss it into a blender with two cups of water. Process, strain, and divide the mash in half. Drink morning and night on an empty stomach. To alleviate kidney pains, make a voluminous decoction of plantain using one part leaves to three parts water. Boil for twenty minutes and strain, then take a sitz bath in the warm liquid. For kidney stones, boil up common plantain with some monkey's hand (*la baquiña cerrada* or *Lepianthes peltatum*) and iron grass (*Juana la blanca* or *Borreria laevis*). Serve each morning with the water from a whole green coconut. Simple teas of lanten leaves lower fevers, relieve pains, aids bronchial distress, and stops hemorrhaging. To aid insect bites and stings, or heal small wounds or cuts, use an entire plantain leaf as a bandage.

Despite plantain's reputation as a pernicious weed, horticulturists have selected some remarkable cultivars that make beautiful additions to the garden. The selection "Atropupurea" has wonderful purple-tinged bronzy foliage. "Rosularis," which is called the "rose plantain," bears bizarrely magnificent green, crenelated, ruffled leaves that give the plant the overall look of a great green rose. The cultivar "Variegata" has foliage variegated with cream. Plantago major is not the least bit fussy about soil quality, although it does demand full Sun.

Penguin Bromeliad (Bromelia pinguin) *(Family:* Bromeliaceae)

Named in honor of prominent Swedish medical doctor and botanist, Olof Ole Bromel (1639–1705), the genus *Bromelia* contains about forty-seven species, but the plant family to which it belongs, the *Bromeliaceae*, contains about 2,110 species on the whole. The best-known cousins of *Bromelia pinguin*, also known as *pinguin, piñuela, maya,* or *piña de ratón* in Spanish, may be *Ananas comosus,* the beloved pineapple, and *Tillandsia usneoides,* or so-called Spanish moss (it is not from Spain, nor is it a moss, but a graceful, hanging, tree-dwelling bromeliad that grows in parts of Georgia, Alabama, Louisiana, and Mississippi).

Bromelia pinguin is native to a wide area of the New World—including the West Indies, parts of Mexico, Central America, and northern South America. It is a large plant—about four feet tall and as much as ten feet wide. The stiff, linear, long, attenuate (or long, narrow, and tapering) leaves may be six feet in length and two inches across, and are held in a compact rosette similar in appearance to the cluster of leaves on top of a pineapple fruit—only much more massive. The foliage is serrated, and armed with sharp, recurved prickles. Many of these spines point toward the tip of the leaf, but many curve inwardly, toward the base of the leaf, making this species of bromeliad well equipped to fend off herbivorous animals and clumsy wayfarers. In fact, it is widely used throughout the West Indies and Antilles as a living fence.

The penguin bromeliad spreads by means of vegetative side shoots that arise from the base of the plant in large clumps. The leaves gradually change from shiny-green to a reddish color with age. The white or pinkish flowers are produced on a dense inflorescence that arises several feet from the heart of the plant. It is an easy plant to cultivate in southern home gardens. It flourishes in full Sun or light shade, and needs a fertile but well-drained soil. It appreciates copious amounts of water during the summer (which, of course, is the hurricane season in the Caribbean), but needs no additional water in winter (its natural dry period). This bromeliad's large stature is both a boon and a bane in the home landscape, and it takes careful planning to incorporate it into the herb garden.

The well-armed foliage is best appreciated from a safe distance. Consider using this odd sacred herb to keep out unwanted intruders such as livestock or packs of stray dogs, or perhaps cultivate this plant in enormous, ornate Italian Della robbia urns. The architectural form of *Bromelia pinguin* is perfectly suited for a life in this decorative type of container. It works well as a specimen plant as well. This bromeliad is surprisingly salt-tolerant, and makes a great maritime screen planting or beach-side landscape subject. This tough tropical plant is hardy to the southern areas of USDA Zone 9 (where it can endure short periods of 28°F) through Zone 11. Although it is a bromeliad of easy conservatory or home greenhouse culture, its large size and spiny leaves can be quite prohibitive, and only very small specimens are suitable for windowsill culture.

When ripe, the pulp of the fruit is pleasantly acid in taste, and considered antiscorbutic, but it can cause irritation to the throat or mouth due to the presence of proteolytic enzymes. However, the juice extracted from the flesh of the fruit makes a refreshing drink. It is also employed to make vinegar. In El Salvador, the fried inflorescences are eaten as a vegetable. The young, tender, vegetative shoots found at the base of the plant are eaten raw or boiled as a vegetable, or are added to soups, stews, or egg dishes. The Mayan people employed the young leaves mashed up with salt as an effective poultice for bruises and sprains. The aboriginal female population of Costa Rica employ the young side shoots as a cure for menstrual cramps. The spiny leaves yield a strong fiber, *pinguin*, which can be used as a substitute for jute.

Black Nightshade (Solanum melanocerasum, *formerly* S. nigrum var. guineense) *(Family:* Solanaceae)

The black nightshade, or *yerba mora* in Spanish, is a herb that has a convoluted taxonomic background. Despite the fact it has undergone numerous name changes over the past few years, the most confounding aspect of this plant is its completely divergent qualities. All plant parts, including the leaves, shoots, and unripened fruit, are toxic and used in powerful homeopathic concoctions. Conversely, some varieties are cultivated for their nontoxic juicy berries and their edible leaves and shoots— giving this poisonous plant a lesser-known, confusing common name, the garden huckleberry.

Solanum melanocerasum (a name that translates as "black cherry," a reference to its black, shiny berries) was introduced into the New World from West Africa (thus the varietal name *guineense*, or "from Guinea"). It has become a familiar weed of gardens, borders, waste places, and roadsides in North America. Black nightshade is an annual herbaceous plant that may reach a height of forty inches. The ovate foliage is about four inches long and two inches wide, and may have irregularly toothed or wavy margins. The small flowers are white and greatly resemble those of the tomato or bell pepper—the black nightshade's edible cousins—and are borne in little drooping clusters of five or so blossoms. The fruit is a round berry about a third of an inch or so in size, green ripening to shiny black.

Recent clinical studies of the chemical makeup of the black nightshade are both interesting and enlightening. It appears the roots, shoots, leaves, and mature berries are low in (but not void of) poisonous alkaloids, while the unripened fruit contains solanine glycoalkaloids—lethally toxic compounds. Upon ingestion, these solanine glycoalkaloids affect the cardiovascular and central nervous systems and the gastrointestinal tract, and death may occur from cardiac arrhythmia and circulatory and respiratory failure. To compound the issue further, some phytotoxicologists believe the solanin glycoalkaloid content varies with the seasons.

Because of black nightshade's dual nature as poisonous herb and food item, never use portions of plants collected from the roadside for the dining table. Solely employ your home-cultivated varieties that were grown from seeds labeled "garden huckleberry"and procured from reputable seed sellers. When in doubt, cultivate this herb in a child-free zone, and consider it a dangerous but educational, "look-but-don't-touch" addition to your herb collection.

Solanum melanocerasum var. *guineense* has few cultivational needs. A soil of average fertility and plenty of Sun are its primary requirements. Although I have seen specimens growing under drought conditions, the best examples I have encountered received plenty of water. It is best to start new plants each year in spring, as with tomatoes or bell peppers. Fresh seed should be procured annually because collected seed may not produce the finest plants. Because black nightshade is an annual plant, it can be cultivated in any USDA Zone, but will of course, succumb to the first hard frost of autumn.

The young shoots and leaves are eaten as potherbs or added to soups. The ripe fruits are cooked with sugar and lemon, and they are eaten stewed or made into pies, pastries, jams, preserves, puddings, sauces, and spicy relishes. As mentioned above, the green, unripe fruits contain solanine glycoalkaloids, and should never be consumed.

In spite of (and thanks to) black nightshade's chemical constituents, it is a valuable medicinal herb. Many herbalists agree that one or two grains (a grain is the smallest unit of weight, equal to about .007 pound) of the dried leaves, infused in boiling water, is a strong sudorific (that is, sweat producer). The bruised fresh foliage, used externally, is said to ease pain and abate inflammation, and they are often applied to burns and ulcerations of the skin. The juice has been used for ringworm, gout, and earache, and when mixed with vinegar it is reported to be good as a gargle and mouthwash. Yerba mora has a cherished place in Puerto Rican folk medicine. To relieve diarrhea, patients should drink a strong green tea of the herb mixed with *sal de Eno*—a sodium bicarbonate-based digestive available at Hispanic *farmacias*. For indigestion, drink strong infusions of yerba mora and *tuatúa (Jatropha gossypifolia)*, the "bellyache bush."

Turkey Berry or Pea Eggplant (Solanum torvum)

The turkey berry or pea eggplant *(Solanum torvum)*, which is known as *berenjena cimarrona* in Spanish, is another interesting New World herb. One may encounter it on tropical vacations in the Caribbean, West Indies, and Antilles, though it has also spread throughout the tropical regions of the world, where it is considered a noxious weed species. Roughly speaking, this resident of moist, fertile fields and wet roadsides resembles a mutant eggplant, its Old World cousin. It may grow as tall as nine or ten feet in height, and its stems are densely tomentose (fuzzy) and armed with scattered prickles. The large leaves, which may also be irregularly prickled, can range from three to ten inches in length and five or so inches wide. The foliage may have large uneven lobes as well. The pretty five-petaled, white, star-shaped flowers are borne in upward-facing clusters, and are followed by pea-sized, green-turning-red berries, which provides the common name pea eggplant.

I find this plant quite striking and tropical in appearance, and would use it as a living backdrop in the rear of the herb bed or border to set off the appearance of more graceful looking herbs. The pea eggplant would also make a good herbaceous container subject or hedge plant, and it certainly is an interesting addition to the potager or vegetable garden. It does need a rich, water-retentive but well-drained soil and plenty of Sun to succeed, but it requires similar care to its better-known culinary cousins—the tomato, the pepper, and the eggplant. Like these vegetables, the turkey berry is frost-sensitive (hardy to USDA Zones 10 and 11), and it will succumb to autumnal chills. It makes a fine conservatory or greenhouse plant and is a definite horticultural conversation piece.

The young shoots and leaves of the pea eggplant are eaten raw or cooked. In the West Indies, especially Jamaica, the half-grown firm berries are boiled and eaten with salted fish, yams, *akees*, or in soups and stews. They have a distinctive bitter flavor. In tropical Asia, they are consumed raw, cooked with rice, or used in stews, curries, and chili sauces such as Thailand's famed *näm prik*. An extract of this plant is occasionally used as rennet in *domiati*, the most popular white, brined cheese in Egypt. *Solanum torvum* has ethnoveterinary importance as well, because the fruit provides needed nourishment for free-range poultry, the source of its other common name, the turkey berry. The turkey itself, *Meleagris gallopavo*, is a New World domesticated animal species that was first reported by British explorer Sir Edward Brown during his explorations of Venezuela in 1499.

In addition to being edible, *Solanum torvum* has several homeopathic medicinal applications, too. In Puerto Rican folk medicine, *berenjena cimarrona* is employed to assist suppurating sores and ulcers of the legs. The fresh leaves are put through a juicer or blender with a little water. A clean towel is soaked in the resulting strained and heated liquid and applied to ulcerations as a poultice. To aid uterine inflammations, a large quantity of leaves should be boiled up in a great volume of water. The patient is instructed to soak in the resulting liquid while it is still warm.

Four-o'clock (Mirabilis jalapa) *(Family:* Nyctaginaceae)

Four-o'clock, also known as *maravilla* in Spanish, is a much loved, old-fashioned flower garden plant that may grow as tall as four feet under ideal conditions. This bushy, undemanding plant fits well in a mixed and herbaceous border, and its scented, late-afternoon or evening-blooming, tubular flowers may be white to yellow, or purple to cerise-red, as well as any bicolor combination of these colors. Flowers may occasionally appear in different colors on the same plant. The genus name *Mirabilis* means "remarkable" or "wonderful" in Latin, referring to the aforementioned characteristics, and the species name, *jalapa*, is the Latinized form of Xalapa, a town in Mexico. The plant prefers full Sun, relatively rich soil, and adequate moisture. It is much appreciated by hummingbirds, butterflies, and nocturnal moths, and it is a perfect addition to the "evening-blooming flower garden" that is designed specifically for busy people who are not home during the day.

Although the four-o'clock is a native of Peru, and therefore considered tropical (USDA Zones 10 and 11), when planted in a warm, sheltered position—against a south-facing, brick wall, for example—in well-drained soil, it is hardy as far north as USDA Zone 6. Further north, its long, deeply penetrating roots may be dug up in the fall, and stored over the winter in the same fashion as the unrelated dahlias or cannas.

Mirabilis jalapa has a couple of unique culinary attributes. A crimson dye, obtained from steeping the flowers in water, is used for coloring Japanese and Chinese cakes and jellies made from seaweeds. The seeds are occasionally employed to adulterate black pepper *(Piper nigrum)*, and in South America, the leaves are sporadically eaten as a salad item.

Throughout Latin America four-o'clocks are considered to have remarkable curative powers. By virtue of its numerous components, the plant possess amazing antifungal, antiviral, and antibacterial properties. In fact, cysteine-rich peptides have been isolated from the seeds, and these have been documented in eradicating such important agricultural and horticultural fungal pathogens as *Alternaria brassicola, Botrytis cineraria*, and *Fusarium oxysporum*, just to name a few. Furthermore, this botanical is employed by the endemic populace of Amazonia as a diuretic, carminative, cathartic, hydragogue (a substance that promotes the discharge of water from the intestines), purgative, tonic, and vermifuge. It is applied as a poultice for rashes, sores, boils, and other dermatological maladies.

Beggar's Tick or Shepherd's Needle (Bidens pilosa) *(Family:* Asteraceae)

Beggar's tick is the common English name for two hundred or so species of New World wayside plants related to the familiar garden chrysanthemum and aster. It is known as *romerillo, aceitilla*, or *amor seco* in Spanish. A familiar North American cousin, *Bidens frondosa*, the tall beggar's tick, is a common garden weed in moist, well-watered plantings. Most of the species have little ornamental value and are not usually planted for their good looks. However, many species are cultivated by herbalists for their extensive medicinal merits, by apiarists for their value as honey plants, and by crafters for their usefulness as dye plants.

Bidens pilosa is native to moist, tropical areas of South America and the Caribbean. The genus name *Bidens* is composed of the Latin *bis*, meaning "twice," and *dens*, a "tooth"—hence the name means "two-toothed." This is an allusion to the pair of sharply hooked, fang-like structures at the top of the seeds, which grip on to the fur of passing animals or the legs of transitory humans. This assists in seed dispersal. The species name *pilosa* means "covered with long soft hairs," because the bases of the flowers are covered with them.

This multibranched herb grows to about two feet in height. The leaves are pinnately compound, bearing three to five lance-shaped leaflets with finely toothed margins. The white or yellow flowers are small, but obviously chrysanthemum-like. Beggar's tick is simplicity itself to cultivate. An area that is evenly moist suits them perfectly; they are not fussy about soil fertility. They will flourish in full Sun or part shade. They can be cultivated outdoors year round in USDA Zones 9 through 11. They are rampant colonizers, and great care should be taken to avoid having them spread throughout the garden to the point of ousting other herbs. They are easily propagated from seed saved from the previous year.

All plant parts of the beggar's tick have medicinal merits. This plant possesses antibacterial, antidysentric (dysentery-fighting), anti-inflammatory, antimicrobial, antimalarial, astringent, diuretic, emmenogogic, emollient, hepatoprotective (liver-protecting), and hypotensive (tension-relieving) properties.

Bidens pilosa has a long history of use by the indigenous peoples of the Amazon. Nearly all parts of the plant were used—roots, leaves, stems, and flowers. In the Peruvian Amazon, beggar's tick was utilized for angina, diabetes, dysentery, dysmenorrhea (severe cramps or pain during menstruation), edema, hepatitis, jaundice, laryngitis, and worms. The Cuna tribe partakes of a mixture of the crushed, fresh foliage with water to treat headaches. The Exuma people grind the Sun-dried leaves with olive oil to make poultices for sores and lacerations.

In Puerto Rico and Cuba, the plant is used to treat ailments of the eye, liver, lungs, stomach, joints, and teeth. Brazilians utilize beggar's tick as an astringent, diuretic, and emollient. It is used to treat blenorrhagia (or an abnormal discharge of mucus), diabetes, fever, liver ailments, sore throats, urinary infections, and vaginal infections.

Brittle Maidenhair Fern (Adiantum tenerum *and* A. capillus-veneris) *(Family:* Pteridaceae *Subfamily:* Polypodiaceae*)*

In botany, there is a category of primitive plants called cryp-togams, from the Greek *kryptos*, meaning "hidden," and *gamos*, meaning "marriage"—or, in other words, "hidden marriage," an allusion to their unobservable method of reproduction. This type of flora does not bear flowers or seeds, but instead bear structures called spores. This class includes some very familiar plants: ferns, mosses, hornworts, horsetails, club mosses, selaginellas, lichens, algae, mushrooms, and fungi.

About 200 tropical and temperate species comprise the genus *Adiantum*, the maidenhair fern, also known as *culantrillo de pozo* or *helecho culantrillo* in Spanish. This plant is one of the most familiar to hikers, as well as to gardeners. They are found throughout the moist woodlands of the world. The maidenhair fern is indigenous to the southern United States, to Central and South America, the Caribbean, and the West Indies. It is also found in Africa, India, Sri Lanka, Europe, China, Japan, Polynesia, and Australia.

The fronds of these ferns are elegantly bipinnate with each leaflet truncate ("broad-tipped") or cuneate ("wedge-shaped") in form. The petioles are shiny black or tinged deep purple in color. There are a couple of lovely cultivars worth seeking out. These varieties tend to a little bit more delicate than the straight species, so plant them outdoors in areas protected from pound-ing rains or shredding winds that will devastate their delicate fronds, or else simply keep them as indoor plants. *Adiantum capil-lus-veneris "Fimbriatum"* has finer, more contorted foliage than the norm, and *"Imbricatum"* has gracefully weeping fronds.

Adiantum tenerum "Scutum Roseum" possesses fronds that are colored pink when young.

Maidenhair ferns need a rich, compost-laden but well-drained soil. A shady spot in the herb garden, perhaps under trees or tall shrubs, is quite effective. Additionally, consider an ornamental container filled with ferns and placed in a nook out of the Sun or in a corner of a terrace or patio. They may be cultivated outdoors year round in USDA Zones 9 to 11. Farther north, they make superb greenhouse or conservatory specimens, but as house plants, they are very demanding—though their ethereal beauty may well warrant the effort. Maidenhair ferns, indoors, prefer temperatures on the cool side—in the 60s and 70s (Fahrenheit) during the day with a ten-degree drop at night. This is often more than a trifle difficult to achieve in our infernally heated apartments and homes. The ferns are extremely sensitive to both under- and overwatering.

The medicinal uses of this graceful fern have been known since the time of Dioscorides and Pliny. Indeed, the maidenhair fern is a veritable pharmacy unto itself. It has been incorporated into the medicinal inventories of practically every culture that has come into contact with it. Generally speaking, it is antibacterial, antifungal, antimicrobial, and antiviral. It has demulcent, antidotal, astringent, anti-asthmatic, depurative, diuretic, emmenogogic, emollient, expectorant, febrifugic, and sudorific qualities. The *Materia Medica Mexicana* recommends a sweetened infusion of the maidenhair fern as a tonic for chest ailments) and for stomach and liver blockages. In Brazil, this fern is employed to treat asthma, coughs, bronchitis, and all matter of respiratory ailments. It is used as an expectorant as well.

Avocado or Alligator Pear (Persea americana)
(Family: Lauraceae)

Whether or not you relish guacamole or avocado halves stuffed with crabmeat, practically everyone I encounter has at least tried to sprout an avocado seed. Its huge size seems to invite us to attempt plant propagation. The avocado, known as *aguacate* in Spanish, is the only member of the *Lauraceae* cultivated for its large, edible fruit. Its economically important botanical cousins, cinnamon, camphor, sweet bay, sassafras, and spice bush, are grown for their aromatic bark, roots, or foliage. The genus name *Persea* refers to a now obscure Egyptian tree once described by the first-century botanist Theophrastus, and the species epithet, *americana*, tells us this plant is from the Americas. Its common name, avocado, is derived from the Spanish word *aguacate*, which in turn is a corruption of the original Nahuatl Indian word *ahua-catl*, meaning "testicle," suggesting the shape of the fruit.

Technically speaking, the avocado has three distinct groups based on their region of origin, though the three are on the whole rather similar physically speaking. The main differences in these species have to with the size, shape, and skin texture of the fruit. There is *Persea americana* var. *americana*, the West Indian avocado, which produces enormous, smooth, round, glossy-green fruit that are low in oil and can weigh as much as two pounds. This is the giant green avocado found in groceries and markets. In addition, there is *P. a.* var. *drymifolia*, the Mexican avocado, which bears small fruit weighing only six to ten ounces. Its paper-thin skin turns glossy green or black when ripe. These are hard to ship, and are usually found locally in the areas they are cultivated. Lastly, there is *P. a. var. guatemalensis*, the Guatemalan avocado, which bears medium-sized, oval, or pear-shaped fruit with pebbled skin that turns from green to blackish-green when ripe. This species is by far the most oft-encountered avocado in the markets of mainland United States.

Botanists believe that the avocado may have originated in southern Mexico, but they concur it was cultivated from the Rio Grande, in Mexico, southward to central Peru long before the arrival of the Europeans. Thereafter, it was carried not only to the West Indies—where it was first reported in Jamaica in 1696—but to nearly all parts of the tropical and subtropical world with suitable environmental conditions.

Currently, the avocado is grown commercially not only in the United States, throughout tropical America, and the larger islands of the Caribbean, but also in Polynesia, the Philippines, Australia, New Zealand, Madagascar, Mauritius, Madeira and the Canary Islands, Algeria, tropical Africa, South Africa, southern Spain, southern France, Sicily, Crete, Israel, and Egypt.

Generally speaking, the handsome avocado tree is erect in growth habit and may attain a final height of thirty to sixty feet. The trunk is short and fissured with dark bark. The ovate or elliptic foliage is six to eighteen inches long and usually glossy and heavily veined. The Mexican form usually blooms November to March, while the West Indian varieties are usually spring blooming. The Guatemalan types bloom in late spring and early summer. The miniscule greenish blossoms are borne in large clusters towards the ends of the branches. As aforementioned, there is a great deal of physical difference between the fruit of the three varieties. It is advised to plant two different cultivars of the same race of avocados to ensure cross-pollination, which in turn results in greater yields.

Persea americana is a fine landscape plant for the herb garden, though all of the fruit should be harvested while still unripe and allowed to ripen indoors—to avoid an extremely untidy area on the ground under the tree's canopy. The avocado requires full Sun to flourish, and a rich, humusy soil with added sharp sand for perfect drainage. They need average, but regular, amounts of water. The main concern for the home gardener, however, is plant hardiness. The West Indian varieties are the least hardy to cold, only recommended to USDA Zone 11. The Guatemalan is slightly hardier, to USDA Zone 10; and the Mexican types are the most cold resistant, to the lower portions of USDA Zone 9. In northern climes the avocado deserves a place in the home greenhouse or conservatory. If they reach ceiling height, they handle hard pruning very well.

Starting plants from seeds is a wonderful family project, and the resulting avocado plant can, in time, become a large floor specimen, although it will never blossom or set fruit inside. Indoor examples need a good, unobstructed east-, south-, or west-facing window and plenty of fresh, circulating air to succeed. The avocado needs a slightly acid soil (as do other house plants, including citrus, camellias, gardenias, and coffee), and therefore needs regular applications of acidifying fertilizer.

We all delight in the avocado's buttery flesh in salads, guacamole, sandwiches, and spreads. In addition, avocados appear in ice creams, sherbets, and milk shakes in Brazil (believe it or not), and are served with tortillas, seasoned with salt, cracked pepper, and a squeeze of lime or lemon juice. Because of the avocado's high tannin content, the flesh becomes bitter if cooked. In Bali, the fruit pulp is added to sugar and water to create a popular iced drink known as *es apokat*, or it is mixed with other fruits, chipped ice, and brilliant red sugar syrup in a dessert called *es campur*. It is made into wine in many portions of South America. In Java, avocado flesh is thoroughly mixed with strong black coffee, sweetened, and eaten as a dessert. The flesh is the source of avocado oil—a mild, pleasant-tasting oil high in vitamins A, B, C, and E—that is used in salad dressings for strong-flavored greens such as arugula, chicory, or watercress. A tea made from the leaves is often sweetened with sugar cane juice. Toasted leaves impart a pleasant flavor to stews, molés, and bean dishes. The soaked foliage is occasionally used in smoke flavorings in Mexican barbeques. The rarely occurring, tiny, seedless fruits are marketed as cocktail avocadoes. For apiarists in locales where the avocado can be cultivated, the flowers are a resource for the production of a dark-colored, heavy-bodied honey.

Persea americana possesses a couple of other ethnobotanical uses as well—the most important of which is the production of an indelible, red-brown, or blackish pigment that is extracted from the seeds and used as dyes for fabrics woven by the indigenous Indios of Central and South America. The dyes were also made into inks during the Spanish exploration, and original letters written on parchment with avocado ink are still preserved in the archives of the Museum of Natural History in Popayán, Columbia.

The *Materia Medica Mexicana* recommends the seeds of the avocado as an anthelmintic, and considers it very effective (used externally) for pleurisy (an inflammation of the membranes surrounding the lungs). The oil pressed from the seeds, and the seeds themselves, roasted, is believed by the male population to be an excellent aphrodisiac. The flesh is so considered as well.

Within the arsenal of recipes used in Puerto Rican folk medicine exists a complex formula for a bath to treat fever, body pains, and other physical and mental complaints. To do so, bring five gallons of water to a boil, and add three good handfuls of fresh avocado leaves, Caribbean vervain *(la verbena* or *Stachytarpheta jamaicensis)*, castor bean *(la higuereta* or *Ricinus communis)*, ginger root *(el jengibre* or *Zingiber officinale)*, jointwood *(el higuillo oloroso* or *Piper marginatum)*, ground cherry *(el sacabuche* or *Physalis* spp.), and sawgrass *(la rompecota* or *Scleria* spp.). Boil the botanicals, covered, for a half hour. Cool, strain, and pour over the patient (standing in the shower), beginning with the head and working downward to the feet. Do not towel dry, but let the mixture evaporate in order to reap the benefit of the herbs.

In Brazil, an infusion of the foliage of the avocado is an important medicine. It is used as a diuretic to treat urinary retention and general swelling.

Sources of Eclectic Herb Plants and Seeds

Remember that it is perfectly legal to purvey seeds and plants from commercial overseas mail-order catalogs, because the material have undergone USDA inspection.

Tropical Fruit Trees
7341 121st Terrace North
Largo, FL 33773
813-539-7527

Stokes Tropicals
P.O. Box 9868
New Iberia, LA 70562-9868
800-624-9706

J. L. Hudson, Seedsman (ethnobotanical seeds)
Star Route 2, Box 337
La Honda, CA 94020
Catalog $1

The Banana Tree, Inc.
715 Northampton St.
Easton, PA 18042
610-253-9589
Catalog $3

Well-Sweep Herb Farm
317 Mt. Bethel Road
Port Murray, NJ 07865
908-852-5390
Catalog $2

Taylor's Herb Gardens
1535 Lone Oak Road
Vista, CA 92084
619-727-3485
Catalog $3

Peruvian Journey (ethnobotanical seeds)
75 West Main Street
Webster, NY 14580
561-344-7693
www.peruvian-journey.com

Jardin Naturel (ethnobotanical seeds)
Colimacons, 97436, Saint Leu
Ile de la Reunion, France
Int + 262247130
www.baobab.com

Gautam Global Seeds (ethnobotanical seeds)
34 Old Cannought Place
Dehra Dun-248001
India
0091-135-656222
www.seedman.com

An Herbal Sleeping Potion

❧ by Edain McCoy ❧

An eye of newt, a wart of frog,
A spider's web, and hair of dog;
Blend with bat's blood, curdle slow,
Deep in sleep, my pretty, you go.

The words "sleeping potion" tend to conjure up images of Macbeth's three warty Witches casting their foul ingredients into a large bubbling cauldron, or else the Wicked Witch of the West putting poor Dorothy into a comatose state as she runs through a lush field of scarlet poppies.

But to make a simple sleeping potion—better known in modern witchery as an herbal tea—you will need only a tea ball, some boiling water, and some dried herbs. This is something to make and drink just before going to bed.

For one large cup of a magic sleeping tea, you will need to gather the following:

      ¼   tsp. dried valerian (a strong sedative), or

      ½   tsp. dried catnip (a mild sedative)

Plus:

      1   tsp. dried peppermint or spearmint

      1   tsp. honey or rice syrup

If you opt for using the valerian, please note that it has a pungent aroma that some people find unpleasant. If you don't like the smell, try adding some more of the mint to cut the odor. Valerian is also reputed to be a great psychic enhancer that opens our eyes and minds to truths we may not want to see or know.

Catnip is a much gentler sedative, to be used when you need only a little nudge into dreamland, not a shove.

Be aware that any felines in your house will be attracted by the smells of both the valerian and the catnip. If they won't leave your tea alone, wrap up some of these herbs in an old sock. Tie off the top, and give it a toss. Your cats will follow.

Pour your boiling water into a large mug, then add the honey or rice syrup. Stir until the honey or syrup dissolves. Then place the tea ball containing the other ingredients into the mug. Allow it to steep while you think about having a peaceful night's sleep.

Remove the tea ball when the potion reaches the strength you prefer. Then relax as you sip your tea.

Herbs for a Lively Liver

by Leeda Alleyn Pacotti

Somewhere deep in your body lies the king of organs, your liver. Although you may have thought your brain, the way station for consciousness, or your heart, the mighty pump of the circulatory system, has more immediate importance, your healthy liver rules your fate if you want a long, fulfilling life.

How the King Rules

Many people may imagine the body just takes care of itself. We eat some food, we do things during the day—maybe we even exercise. We sleep a little or a lot. But beyond these cursory basics, we don't know or understand how the body finds energy to do what it does.

Let me be the first to say, if you have not heard this already, the liver is enormously important to the healthy functioning of our bodies. Larger than any other organ or gland in the body, a healthy liver weighs—depending on whether you are a woman or a man—about two to three-and-a-half pounds. It is attached by powerful ligaments to the upper abdominal cavity. A triangular semisolid mass, it occupies the upper right part of the abdomen, extending its narrow end past the diaphragm, our breathing muscle, to meet the spleen. Meanwhile, in front of and below the liver lies the purse-shaped stomach, our main digestive organ.

Midway behind and extending slightly below the liver is its companion bile storage reservoir, the gall bladder. From here, detergent bile acids—which make fat soluble in the small intestine—drip into the duodenum through a narrow duct after liquified food is moved out of the stomach. In the small intestine, these fatty acids move into protein envelopes for circulation within the lymphatic system, an integral part of the overall circulatory system.

Bile acids are very powerful, and the body is frugal with them. At the end of the small intestine, these acids are reabsorbed and deposited into the portal vein, which carries them back to the liver. Among all its blood-cleansing functions, the liver separates these bile acids, and reintroduces them into the gall bladder.

The liver itself needs a constant rich source of oxygenated blood to keep up its continual functioning. Through the hepatic artery, the heart pumps about one-fourth of all its fresh blood to the liver. This quantity, which is pumped constantly, amounts to about forty-two ounces (or one-and-a-third quarts) each day. At the same time, the portal vein returns bile acids from the intestinal tract at a rate of about twelve ounces, or about one-third quart per day. At any given minute of the day, the healthy engorged liver holds a constantly renewing one-and-two-thirds quarts of circulatory fluid.

The Body's Filter

Why is the liver so filled with blood? Simply put, the liver is the circulatory system's primary filter of pollutants. Just as you protect your car's operations with air and fuel filters to remove impurities, so your liver removes foreign chemicals and particulates from circulating blood. Without this filtration, the entire circulatory system would quickly become corrupted and filled with pollutants, and this would lead to potentially irreversible health consequences. Instead of carrying nourishment, blood would intoxicate cells with impurities, and the body would quickly become poisoned.

What Makes Your Liver Sick

As a filter, the liver's main duties are to detoxify and remove wastes from your body. When venous blood from the small intestine comes to the liver, toxic bile salts are recycled to the gall bladder. Other toxicities, however, must be processed for removal through the kidneys or colon.

To accomplish this, your liver needs huge amounts of vitamins and minerals to function. Fortunately, reservoir cells within your liver's mass can retain these nutrients for long periods—up to four years for vitamin A, and about four months for vitamins B_{12} and D. As a continual first line of defense against toxicity, the liver is easily overburdened from lack of nutrients or from their depletion, especially when you overeat food. Those exhausted reservoir cells reverse their duty and absorb toxins as a protection for the rest of the body, rather than allow toxicity to continue circulating.

Usually, when the liver loses its function toxicity is the culprit. This condition causes hepatitis or inflammation of the liver. As much as "toxic" is bandied about in everyday discussions, it is an insidiously pervasive problem where the liver is concerned. In some ways, virtually everything we eat, breathe, or touch passes into the liver. And since so much of the modern world is tainted with pollutants or foreign chemicals, the liver suffers. Whether the toxins eaten, breathed, or touched are removed is the other story.

Surprisingly, our bodies absorb toxins constantly throughout the day. Besides unnatural preservatives, chemical additives, and hormonal steroids found in foods, enemies of the liver are respired from polluted air, assimilated through the skin, and excessively generated within the body.

Overeating, especially of rich, fatty foods, depletes your liver, causing it to become congested and to filter blood inefficiently. A diet of fatty foods also introduces extra cholesterol, the foremost cause of liver congestion. On the other hand, serum cholesterol, which is naturally produced by the liver, aids cellular structure, especially in the brain and nervous system. But, when serum cholesterol is augmented with dietary cholesterol, the liver goes on overload and cannot eliminate all of it from the blood. Any excess cholesterol is then sent to the gall bladder, where it can combine with your bile salts to cause gallstones. Excessive cholesterol continues to circulate in the bloodstream, attaching itself to the walls of arteries and veins, and contributing to cardiovascular disease, high blood pressure, arteriosclerosis, and even atherosclerosis.

Respired pollutants, such as hydrocarbons, methane, nicotine, or sprayed chemicals, find their way straight to the liver after mixing with oxygen in the lungs. Because blood to the heart is deoxygenated, it must be refreshed. The heart pumps blood to the lung walls, where carbon dioxide is then released from blood molecules, and oxygen is attached. Molecules from pollutants, combined with this oxygen, move straight to the liver for removal and elimination—provided your liver is not already overburdened.

Seemingly innocuous personal care products, cosmetics, laundry detergents, and household cleaners are simply concentrations of chemicals. These items always carry warnings against ingestion or contact with the eyes. A few suggest that you avoid contact with the skin completely. However, we seem to give no thought to skin absorption as we shampoo, pat on, or rub in. The skin, although a major eliminative organ, has no choice but to soak up these offenders, bringing them in contact with capillaries, which transfer them into the bloodstream. Back at your liver, the choice is either to remove them or store them; that is, if the liver's function or capacity still exists.

Hormonal changes in the body, whether due to natural physical changes such as menopause, or artificial inducement from medicines or caffeine, take a powerful toll on your health. Medicines can stimulate an imbalance of hormonal production, stressing your liver with excessive detoxification. Therapeutic estrogen, if not processed by the liver, may result in a circulatory excess of the hormone. This increases risks of endometriosis, PMS, and cancer of the mammary and reproductive organs. If testosterone circulates in excess amounts, you can expect wide mood swings, aggression, and unhealthy heightened sexual energy. When estrogen or testosterone remain excessive, the body retaliates with disruption and dysfunction of the reproductive cycles. Your liver must also process all adrenal hormones. Stimulated adrenal production from coffee drinking or prolonged exposure to stress results in a complex range of emotional imbalances.

Symptoms of Liver Dysfunction

When your liver is ill or functioning poorly, some very obvious symptoms will show.

You will have an unexplained and persistent weight gain.

Your skin itches frequently and accumulates liver spots or large bruises.

Over the abdominal area of your liver, moderate fingertip pressure produces soreness.

You feel full and have no appetite.

You feel lethargic with weak muscles.

You feel excessive or prolonged anger or depression.

You get frequent headaches that are unrelated to tension or eyestrain.

You experience skin changes, such as a yellowish tint, unusual acne, or psoriasis.

If you allow stresses on the liver to go unchecked, the organ becomes susceptible to viral infections. This can lead to contagious hepatitis, which science has identified has five separate forms. Hepatitis A, caught from raw shellfish, fecal contamination of food or water, or person-to-person contact, carries the symptom of jaundice; this form is contagious two to three weeks before, and one week after the jaundice is observed. Hepatitis B, or serum hepatitis, comes from transference of infected blood through contaminated needles or blood transfusions. Of those ill with hepatitis B, 75 percent recover completely. Hepatitis C is spread through sexual contact, shared drug needles, or transmission during childbirth; this viral form, which is four times more prevalent than AIDS, is degenerative and often necessitates liver transplant. Hepatitis D is relatively uncommon but very serious. It occurs in some people who already have hepatitis B, and can be transmitted through sexual contact and childbirth. Finally, hepatitis E, rarely found in the United States, is spread by fecal contamination. It is very dangerous to pregnant women. This variant form does not cause chronic hepatitis in others.

Helping Your Liver Get Well

Fortunately, recent scientific discovery observes the liver is regenerative, even when the majority is removed from the body. Of course, some part of the original organ must be uncontaminated and reinforced against toxicities or other burdens during recuperative regeneration. Although symptoms of liver ailment do progress in severity, if you pay attention to your body, you won't have to resort immediately to extreme medicines or surgery.

Here are some tips for things you can do to help your liver naturally rejuvenate and regain its lively condition.

Diet: Unless your liver is very sick, you should eat between thirty and sixty grams of high-quality protein, either vegetable or animal, per day. If you choose animal protein, try to stay with fish—particularly salmon. Otherwise, buy meat at a health food store to assure you will not burden your liver with veterinary antibiotics or steroid hormones. Some people think eating animal liver is a good way to feed your liver. However, beef and pork liver are very difficult to digest and among the worst foods for adding cholesterol to your system. Unless poultry are range-fed, their livers may be jaundiced and worthless.

Eat foods with high sulfur content, such as garlic, onions, and broccoli, to help your body in its effort to break down fats. These foods have enormous beauty side benefits as well—increasing the elasticity and radiance of your skin.

About 60 percent of your diet should be comprised of vegetables, whole nuts, seeds, and semisweet fruits such as apples and pears. Keep all portions small, and eat frequently in small meals or snacks. In salads, use the bitter greens of endive and collard, which will stimulate the flow of bile.

Eliminate fat from your meals. Because fat in food continues liver congestion, you should avoid it. If you must use oil on your salads, keep it to one teaspoon of cold-pressed virgin olive oil per serving.

Refined sugars are out. Honey is naturally twice as sweet as sugar, so try it in your tea or oatmeal. The herb stevia, depending on how it is extracted, can be thirty to 220 times sweeter than sugar. If you have a sweet attack, go for a crisp, juicy apple.

Take supplements, especially the antioxidant vitamins C and E. Rather than taking vitamin A, consider its precursor beta-carotene, which is easier for the liver to store. Because your liver condition may change rapidly, consult your health professional regarding appropriate dosages and dosage alterations.

Exercise: Along with a low-fat, low-cholesterol diet, exercise does wonders for your liver by increasing oxygen, reducing body fat, and raising the level of high-density lipoproteins (HDLs) that carry cholesterol in the bloodstream back to the liver for removal. The best news is that you don't have to go on a strenuous regimen. All you need to allot is enough time to do eight miles of devoted walking or running per week. Take note—that's 1.15 miles per day. Because the average person walks about four miles per hour, you only have to walk a twenty-minute daily circuit. If you can run, don't shorten the time, just increase the distance. The easiest way to gauge your distance is to drive a pleasant route in your neighborhood. For added fun, take your dog or someone else's. As your body fat reduces, consider lengthening your daily exercise to thirty minutes or else add another physical activity you enjoy.

Exercise before breakfast, if you like feeling bright in the morning. Otherwise, take your moderate walk about one hour after any meal, to promote digestion. To develop your exercise plan, try to keep the same time each day.

Before you dismiss simple exercise, remember it is the only natural way to produce and increase HDLs that remove cholesterol from the walls of arteries and veins.

Cholesterol-lowering prescriptions take much longer to work, and they have some fairly serious side effects. However, these drugs are known to work better if you eat a low-fat, low-cholesterol diet and exercise regularly. Obviously, exercising regularly is the key.

Lifestyle: Eat your largest meal early in the day. Spreading out your daily food requirement throughout the day will prevent stress on your liver and other digestive organs to produce enzymes. *Note:* This should not be a daily all-you-can-eat deal. You simply need to practice moderation and balance. When your body produces insufficient enzymes for digestion, food can pass completely through the intestinal system without breaking down. Besides producing pain, undigested food in the colon causes alternating constipation and diarrhea, and it is the leading cause of severe colonic disorders.

Dump stressful situations, especially any that expose you to toxicities. Many people experience stress through employment and complain it is unavoidable. However, you can be practical. Are your employment take-home earnings, after you pay your living expenses, large enough to pay the extra medical charges for the illnesses generated by continual stress? If the answer is "no," consider why you are keeping a job that makes you sick and doesn't contribute to keeping you well.

Keep your total serum cholesterol level below 200. Regular monitoring can help you understand how well your diet and exercise are helping, but you don't have to go to the extreme expense of a doctor's visit and blood test every time. Check the home health equipment section of a better drugstore for an over-the-counter testing kit, which will give you a reading within fifteen minutes. If you follow the directions carefully, your test result will be 97 percent accurate.

Herbal purification: Herbs, especially those which act on the liver, can have very specific effects. Consult an herbalist if you do not know the current condition of your liver, and he or she will help you find an appropriate herb treatment. A herbalist can also tell you about using herbs while you are taking over-the-counter or prescription medicines or homeopathic remedies. The following herbs, however, have general tonic properties for the liver and can be taken separately or all together. As a tea, they can be enjoyed throughout the day and with meals. Expect to notice a difference of sensation around the liver area within two or three days.

Dandelion root is an excellent remedy for inflammation or hepatitis. An effective blood cleanser, dandelion root is also diuretic, meaning it helps keep the kidneys functioning if the liver releases toxins.

Fennel seed helps reduce general abdominal pain by stimulating the peristaltic action of the stomach and intestines. A comforting digestive, fennel seed also conducts the healing actions of dandelion root and milk thistle.

Milk thistle, one of the best liver tonics available, contains silymarin, a flavonoid that aids the healing and rebuilding of your liver. If jaundice is present, milk thistle helps purify blood. Although all thistles have a pronounced effect on the liver, milk thistle is unquestionably the premier remedy.

Organ cleansing: A serious detoxification process, organ cleansing should never be undertaken without the advice and guidance of your health care professional. Cleansing is a complicated and interactive organic process. If done only partially, other organs may be damaged. For instance, cleansing the liver puts extra burden on the kidneys, which can result in damage requiring dialysis.

An innocent series of enemas meant to detoxify the liver will open the gall bladder's bile duct. However, if, along with the bile the gall bladder releases stones created from fats, cholesterol, and bile salts, these stones can block the bile duct completely and cause intense pain.

A hot castor oil pack is a noninvasive method for relieving liver pain and gently drawing out toxicity. It is placed over the liver area of the upper abdomen. Castor oil has a deep drawing power that can penetrate four inches into the body. Applied with heat, a hot pack promotes sweating to excrete toxins and infection. This does not have to be done frequently. If you develop a rash after a castor oil treatment, do not repeat its use. You can also soak a white or an unbleached piece of cotton or wool in cold-pressed castor oil. Wring out the cloth before application, so that it is not dripping. Apply the wet cloth over the liver area and cover it with a piece of plastic and a towel. The plastic is important to keep the other items from contacting the wet cloth. Next, place a heating pad or hot water bottle over the towel, and cover with another towel or light blanket. The heat needs to be as warm as you can stand it. Leave the hot pack in place for sixty to ninety minutes, refilling the hot water bottle if it cools too quickly. Afterward, wash off any oil on your skin with a solution of water and baking soda.

You can massage your liver to promote healing. Just lie on your back and very gently massage the abdominal area over your liver with the flat side of your fingertips. Use a circular motion in a clockwise direction. If you feel any pain, continued soreness, or unusual tenderness, stop your liver massages and see your health care professional for an assessment. This treatment is not intended as a cleansing, but simply to stimulate the organ's functioning.

For Further Study

Castleman, Michael. *Blended Medicine: The Best Choices in Healing: The Breakthrough System that Combines Natural, Alternative & Mainstream medicine for more than 100 ailments.* Emmaus, Pa.: Rodale Press, 2000.

Feinstein, Alice, (ed.). *Training the Body to Cure Itself: How to Use Exercise to Heal.* By the editors of Prevention Magazine Health Books. Emmaus, Pa.: Rodale Press, 1992.

Krohn, Jacqueline, and Frances Taylor. *Natural Detoxification.* Pt. Roberts, Wash.: Hartley and Marks Publishers, 2000.

Lunar Herbs and Your Health

≫ by Jonathan Keyes ≪

A few days before I wrote this article, the Moon was waxing to full in the night sky. I went out walking in my garden and noticed that the plants seemed to be vibrating with an almost electric pulse. Herbs seem to really grow in power near this time of the month, and some herbs seem to have an even greater affinity to our Earth's satellite.

Long ago, each of the visible planets and the Sun and Moon were associated with certain characteristics and traits. Venus was associated with love and beauty; Mars with war and physical strength. The Moon was associated with traits of sensitivity, receptivity, the emotions, nurturing, and mothering. The planets were not only associated with human characteristics, but also with different types of herbs and

plants. The famous European alchemist Paracelsus summed up this philosophy when he wrote:

> *Every metal and every plant possesses certain qualities that may attract corresponding planetary influences, and if we know the influences of the stars, the conjunctions of the planets and the qualities of the herbs, we shall know what remedies to give to attract such influence as may act beneficially on the patient.*

Paracelsus also believed that human beings, the natural world, and the planets and stars above were connected as one interwoven tapestry. He also believed that each planet was associated with certain herbal medicines, and that by studying astrology one could gain a better understanding of which herbs worked best for individuals. Lunar herbs, therefore, are herbs that are most associated with the Moon and its qualities. These herbs have unique characteristics and are helpful for treating certain types of conditions and healing certain types of people.

Astrology and the Classification of Herbs

Astrology is the relationship of constellations and planetary movements to functions on Earth. Astrology not only helps us to understand and categorize human behavior and development, it also helps us to understand the relationship of the planets to the natural world, its plants and medicines, and how these interact with human health. Early astrologers categorized herbs into different planetary classifications. Traditionally, astrologers linked the herbs with five main planets and the Sun and the Moon. These planets were the closest to the Sun—Mercury, Venus, Mars, Jupiter, and Saturn. Each of these planets carried a symbolic mythology and an energetic focus that would help early physicians to categorize herbs.

To classify herbs, traditional European astrologer physicians would look not only to the effect of a plant, but also the appearance and location of the plant as well. These factors were known as the "Doctrine of Signatures," the theory that the physical characteristics of a plant helped one to understand its function and uses. For example, the herb lungwort was seen as being good for the lungs because of small darkish splotches on its leaves that looked like lung patches to early botanists. Lungwort indeed has a profound effect on the pulmonary tissues and is used today for the same reasons early herbalists used it.

There were differences of opinions on what herbs were associated with what planets. Meaning, there are no hard-and-fast rules. Each planet is associated with different organ systems, and herbs were often associated with planets based on their primary healing function. If an herb, such as eyebright, happened to heal the eyes, it was then classified with the Sun. If an herb, such as dandelion, happened to heal the liver, it was associated with the planet Jupiter, and so on.

Lunar Herbs

Herbs of the Moon have one or more of the following characteristics. They tend to hold water and are succulent and juicy in nature. They tend to help alleviate mood disorders because of their gentle, nourishing qualities. The leaves can have a round shape (such as nasturtium) or be wide and spreading. The plants can prefer to grow in damp places, such as in marshes or near lakes and streams. Their flowers or leaves are white, silver (such as willow), or pale yellow.

Willow, in fact, is a classic example of a lunar herb, because it tends to grow near rivers and streams and has long, droopy leaves that are silvery white in color. Willow has the ability to reduce inflammation and is therefore helpful for reducing hot or fiery type conditions. Overall, it has soothing, cooling, and watery powers. Another example of a lunar herb is wild lettuce, which grows in whorls that are round, holding moisture in its leaves. Wild lettuce also has soothing and cooling properties but works best for healing anxiety, as opposed to pain and inflammation.

The Effects of Lunar Herbs

Herbs of the Moon tend to be cooling, moistening, and nourishing to the body. Lunar herbs often help heal areas of the body that the Moon is associated with—the stomach, the breasts, the bladder, and the womb. Like the Sun, the Moon is also associated with the eyes. The famous astrologer William Lilly says that the Moon is associated with the right eye in females, and the left eye in males (it is vice versa for the Sun). I have yet to see this direct correspondence, but it is interesting to take note of this suggestion. Traditional herbals sometimes associated the Moon with the lungs, but I like to leave that connection to Mercury. To take the case of wild lettuce a little further, this is an herb that is helpful for bringing on lactation in mothers, as well as for strengthening digestion. Both the breasts and the stomach are associated with the Moon—showing wild lettuce to be a natural choice as a lunar herb.

Culpeper and Lunar Herbs

One of the most important herbalists who classified herbs astrologically was a seventeenth-century English physician by the name of Nicholas Culpeper. Culpeper's most famous book is called *Culpeper's Herbal*. It includes hundreds of descriptions of herbs, their effects, and their planetary correspondences. His book continues to be highly regarded by herbalists, and his writings on the subject often formed the basis for many modern herbals. Because of his importance as an astrological herbalist, I will quote some of his writings about lunar herbs.

For this article I will discuss five herbs associated with the Moon: chickweed, cleavers, lettuce, willow, and the California poppy. Though in his herbal Culpeper did not mention the then unknown California poppy, he did discuss the effects of several other poppies—including the opium poppy. I believe the California poppy carries a similar function to the opium poppy, but it is less potent and narcotic (and therefore better to discuss).

Five Herbs of the Moon

All of these herbs I mention can be used as medicine in tea form in infusions and decoctions. In fact, this is the method I prefer. All the herbs can be taken in tincture or capsule form. Chickweed can also be eaten as a lovely addition to salad. I recommend planting these herbs and trees in your garden to bring more lunar energy into your life.

Chickweed (Stellaria Media)

This small herb grows abundantly in all parts of the world and can usually be found growing in a patch of your garden (unless you are an expert weeder). It has six- to twelve-inch stems with ovate leaves growing oppositely. Chickweed expresses small white flowers blooming at the end of the stem.

Culpeper says of this herb that it "doth wonderfully temperate the heat of the liver, and is effectual for all imposthumes, and swellings whatsoever." He also wrote that it "helpeth cramps, convulsions and palsy." He felt it was good for "redness in the eyes," bloody stool, and pain arising from heat.

Among its modern uses, chickweed is often employed externally in poultices and lotions to help heal cuts and wounds. It is useful for decreasing itching due to rashes, eczema, and psoriasis. Internally, chickweed helps nourish and repair the stomach from any ulcers. Susun Weed recommends this little herb for "thyroid irregularities, reproductive cysts, swollen glands, ovarian cancers, and testicular troubles such as cancers, swelling, burning, or itching."

Chickweed is good for—externally: rashes, inflammation, cuts, wounds, eczema, psoriasis, red eyes; internally: ulcers, hepatitis, and inflamed liver.

Parts used: aerial parts. This herb can be munched as a fresh salad ingredient, juiced with other veggies, or made into teas and tinctures. For tea, infuse one ounce to one pint of water. Take one cup a day morning and evening.

Cleavers (Gallium aparine)

This annual herb grows wild in many places throughout North America. It has a square stem that can grow up to six feet in height. The leaves branch out in whorls around the stem and emit whitish flowers in cymes alongside the leaves. Cleavers is most noted for the sticky underside to its leaves that makes it attach to clothes and skin.

Culpeper wrote that this herb reduces heaviness for those who are overweight, and it "helpeth the yellow jaundice" and "stayeth the bleeding" of any wound. He also wrote that cleavers helps reduce and "hard swellings," "old ulcers," and "swellings in the throat."

Today, this herb is used to strengthen the lymphatic system and clean and purify the blood. It has a diuretic effect that makes it very helpful in healing urinary disorders. It is also used to heal liver inflammation and damage, and through its effect on the blood it can help to heal skin disorders. Externally, a poultice or salve of this herb helps to reduce swelling, burns, and wounds. Cleavers is also good for blood cleansing, urinary stones, infections, hepatitis, swollen glands, eczema, psoriasis, wounds, burns, and rashes.

Parts used: aerial parts. For tea, infuse one ounce to one pint of water. Drink two cups a day, one in the morning and one in the evening.

Wild Lettuce (Lactuca virosa)

Wild lettuce is a relative of the lettuce we grow in our gardens. This plant develops a long stalk and alternate flowers. Lettuce contains a bitter latex that is sedative and relaxing.

Culpeper wrote that wild lettuce cures headache, strengthens digestion, increases mother's milk, reduces heat and inflammation in the body, strengthens the heart and liver, relaxes spasms and convulsions, quiets the system, and reduces irritation.

Among its modern uses, wild lettuce is noted primarily for its sedative effects. Lettuce acts as a nervine to reduce anxiety and strengthen the nerves. It helps to reduce spasmodic problems such as coughing and menstrual cramps. It also has a general analgesic effect and helps to reduce pains associated with rheumatism and arthritis. Wild lettuce is good for anxiety, panic, mania, insomnia, cramps, whooping cough, and pains and aches in the body such as those caused by rheumatism and arthritis.

Parts used: the dried leaves. Use as an infusion with one ounce to one pint of water. Drink a cup twice a day. Do not overmedicate with this herb, as it can be overly sedating in very large doses.

California Poppy (Eschscholzia Californica)

This herb comes up as an annual and grows with numerous stemmed stalks and a brilliant gold and orange flower with four petals. Though its name shows its affinity for the California region, it likes to grow west of the cascades up into Canada.

Culpeper wrote mainly of the common opium poppy, but his words about that herb apply generally to this one as well. California poppy is gentler and much less dangerous to use than opium poppies. Culpeper wrote that "the syrup is a gentle narcotic, easing pain and causing sleep." Culpeper also felt this was a good herb for a "continual cough," and for "hoarseness of the throat." Culpeper wrote that poppy is beneficial to a women's reproductive system and good for healing headaches and other aches and pains.

Today, the opium poppy is the precursor to opiate drugs that originally were used in Asia. Their use has spread to a worldwide epidemic of drug users addicted to heroin, morphine, and narcotic pills. The California poppy, on the other hand, contains a negligible amount of addicting alkaloids. It is gentle and safe to use. As Culpeper wrote, California poppies can be used for their sedating, tranquilizing, and antispasmodic effects. They are also useful for easing aches and pains throughout the body. The California poppy is good for treating premenstrual syndrome, anxiety, insomnia, sore throat, cough, rheumatism, gout, and muscle pain.

Parts used: the aerial parts. California poppy can be used in tea form by infusing one ounce of herb to one ounce of water. Drink one cup in morning, one at night, or as needed throughout the day.

Willow (Salix alba)

The willow tree is found in North Africa, Europe, and North America. It has long, lanceolate leaves that are silvery underneath and appear alternately along tree branches. It often grows in moist places such as near marshes or along stream banks.

Culpeper recommended willow to help "staunch the bleeding of wounds" and "to stay vomiting." He also felt it was "very good for dimness of sight, or films that grow over the eyes." Culpeper said willow "clears the face and skin from spots and discolorings" and "takes away scurf and dandruff."

In 1828, salicin was extracted from white willow and later became the key component to aspirin. Willow has the effect of reducing pain and inflammation in the body—including cramps, muscle pains, and headaches. Willow bark can also be used in the same way aspirin is used to reduce clotting of the blood that leads to heart attacks. In my opinion, willow seems to have an elevating effect on the nervous system, simultaneously energizing and relaxing the entire body. This effect differs markedly from the effect of aspirin, thus revealing once again why plant remedies are generally superior to remedies based on their isolated chemical components.

Willow is generally good for treating headaches, cramps, arthritis, rheumatism, muscle and back pain, general debility, and fevers.

Parts used: the inner bark. Decoct one ounce of the inner bark in one pint of water for sixty minutes, then drink. *Note:* It is very bitter.

Herbal Treatments in Symptomatic and Temperamental Terms

In general, lunar herbs can be used in a number of ways. One common use, for instance, is to give an herb for symptomatic relief of a condition. An example of this is offering a cup of willow tea to someone complaining of a headache. Or, offering an infusion of chickweed for someone who suffers from the effects of an ulcer.

This method often works quite well, but there are times when deeper considerations need to be made. That is, it is often important to take note of the overall temperament of the person who is ill or striken, in order to assess what kinds of herbs they would do best to take.

For example, someone who runs hot and is often flushed and occasionally angry would likely do best to take lunar herbs on a regular basis. As lunar herbs are cooling, relaxing, and moistening, the hot and flushed person will be more balanced with such herbs. Meanwhile, someone who has a more lethargic and quiet nature with a heavier body type and cool skin would do better to take more heating, moving herbs.

The idea of assessing temperament to determine treatment plans is an age-old idea that continues to be used in ayurvedic and traditional Islamic *(unani-tibb)* medicine. Giving medicine according to temperament also formed the basis of traditional European medicine, as was outlined by the early herbalists Hippocrates and Galen.

Traditional European Medicine

In traditional European medicine, each person carried a dominant temperamental type that corresponded to the four elements. So, in this system, the choleric type corresponds to the fire element, and is generally thought to be passionate, exuberant, willful, playful, dynamic, and prone to anger. He or she also often runs hot. The sanguine type corresponds to the air element and tends to be merry, excitable, and intelligent, with a tendency towards nervousness and slight heat conditions.

The phlegmatic type, meanwhile, corresponds to the water element and tends to be sensitive, impressionable, artistic, and emotional. He or she also tends to run a little cool and can develop immune system problems. The melancholic type corresponds to the earth element and tends to be grounded, practical, productive, and steadfast. He or she also tends to run cool and can get into periods of feeling stuck and depressive.

If you learned to apply the temperamental method of assessing illness, and then developed a treatment plan based on your type, lunar herbs would tend to work best for the choleric and sanguine types. Lunar herbs are generally cooling, moistening, and relaxing. These qualities are more helpful for the hot-blooded choleric type and the nervous sanguine type.

Decumbiture and Lunar Illnesses

One other method used traditionally to diagnose health conditions was to consider a person's astrological chart at the time of illness. This method is known as *decumbiture* and is said to give clues as to the nature of the illness, as well as to the treatment principles needed for affecting a cure.

In this method, certain planets are seen as the cause of the disease. Each planet, including the Sun and the Moon, are associated with different illness patterns. For example, Mars is associated with hot, acute, and fast-acting illnesses such as high fevers. Saturn is associated with long-standing, chronic, and wasting diseases.

If the illness was associated with being cold and excessively damp, the Moon was usually the offending planet. With Moon-based illnesses, the sick person may tend towards lethargy and fatigue and often carry an excess of phlegm. Illnesses associated with the Moon include digestive problems, water metabolism problems, catarrh, menstrual difficulties, rheumatic and arthritic pains, eye infections or disability, poor immune system, intestinal diseases, and bladder and kidney stones.

Antipathic and Sympathetic Treatment of Illness

Once you determine the planet that is most associated with the illness in question, Traditional European medicine often prescribes one of two ways of healing the disease. In an antipathic cure, herbs were offered that would balance and offset the nature of the illness. For example, if the illness was lunar in nature, solar herbs were prescribed to balance the condition. (Solar herbs include such plants as St. John's wort, marigold, and angelica.) Of course picking the proper herb depended on the exact properties of the herbs.

The other method of curing an illness is to use the sympathetic cure. This method of treatment is most favored by homeopaths who believe that "like cures like." In this method, an herb of the same nature of the illness is used to affect the cure. For example, someone who has lunar health problems such as stomach tension and cramping would do well to take a lunar herb such as willow to reduce the pain. Again, the exact abilities of each herb would be examined to see what is most appropriate for a health condition.

Connecting with Lunar Herbs

Long ago, early astrologers and physicians classified herbs according to particular physical traits and according to their health benefits. These herbs were associated with the five planets, the Sun, and the Moon. Lunar herbs carry particular characteristics that make them unique and link them to each other. These herbs have been especially useful in treating a number of health conditions such as stomach problems, inability to lactate, and mood disorders.

The next time you go into your garden or to a nearby weed patch, examine how any herbs you find carry lunar qualities. Then experiment with them as medicines for healing common complaints. You may find through experimentation that you are particularly attracted to lunar herbs for healing.

Herbs
for
Beauty

Making Your Own Herbal Shampoo

⪢ by Edain McCoy ⪡

T he question I often get asked,
when I recommend an herbal
beauty tip, is how exactly does
the thing work.

People seem to want to know what
is the particular magic that makes it
possible that a plant, taken from a field
or from the garden, can be as effective,
and sometimes more effective, than a
product packaged in a fancy bottle.

The simple answer I give, at the
risk of sounding glib, is why shouldn't
it work? After all, humans for centuries
had no access to Johnson & Johnson
Company, or any other megaconglom-
erate purveyor of beauty as chemistry.
The thing is, when we were more in
tune with our Earth, and knew better
all of the plants that grew on it,
humans got along just fine. In many
instances, we were much better off.

Not only are herbal beauty treatments cheaper than the fancy packaged one, they are magical. Indeed, plant-based beauty is more in tune with the beautiful power of life itself. Everything in the universe can be found encompassed in the herbal beauty treatments of our forebears. I am amazed that more people do not perceive this connection.

So what do I mean to say exactly? Just this, in other, more mystical words. The power of herbs is much more attuned to the power of the life force, the stuff of creation. And as we can generally see that life itself is a remarkably beautiful thing, it makes sense that such plant remedies will tap into the beauty of life itself. Below are several simple remedies to get you started thinking about how you can beautiful yourself with this herbal life-force. If you find these remedies as refreshing and as simply beautifying as I think you will, then you can check back to future editions of this almanac for more such remedies.

Shampoo for Oily Hair

To start with, go to a drug store or deep discount store and find an off-brand shampoo base that is unscented. Make sure it does not contain the detergent borax, as this is too harsh to use on your hair. You will need eight ounces of shampoo base to make this recipe.

If your hair is not seriously oily, you can use pure liquid Castile soap. This is made in Spain from olive oil, and is a wonderful cleanser and softener. If you have a tendency toward greasiness however, soap may be too greasy for you hair.

You will also need a ten- to twelve-ounce container to mix your shampoo in, and you will want it to have a snug lid.

Into your simple base shampoo, add the following:

    ½ tsp. tea tree oil

    ½ tsp. baking soda

    ½ cup rosemary tea

    3 drops witch hazel

Mix the ingredients well, and refrigerate your shampoo between uses—unless you used the Castile soap, which does not need refrigerating. Castile-based products keep best in the warm dampness of your bathroom, as the refrigerator will harden this soap, and you'll have to melt your shampoo each time you want to use it.

Use your herbal soap for oily hair as you would any other shampoo. Take note of how quickly your hair responds to the magical and refreshing herbal ingredients.

Shampoo for Dry Hair

If you have dry hair, you can use luxurious liquid Castile soap. If you cannot find the soap in liquid form, it can be found in bars. You can grate the bars into flakes and melt them over a double-boiler to make an oil. Just make sure you're using a pan and wooden spoon that you don't mind throwing away. The soap will be almost impossible to remove once it dries.

Into the liquid castile base place:

2   tsps. apple cider vinegar
2   tsps. banana flakes (look in the babyfood section of your grocery store for this)
6   drops almond oil

Mix the ingredients well, and keep the shampoo in the bathroom between uses (as described above).

Moisturizing Hair Mask

To smooth, soften, and moisturize your hair, mix the following ingredients together in a medium-sized bowl:

¼   cup banana flakes (or ¼ cup puréed bananas)
½   cup oat meal
2   tsps. dried hyssop
¼   tsp. vitamin E oil

3 Tbls. apple cider vinegar

1 well-beaten egg

Mix the ingredients well, and work the mixture into your hair. Cover your hair with a plastic shower cap or towel, and leave on the "mask" for at least thirty minutes. You may want to use a blow dryer for a few minutes to help work the ingredient fully into your hair.

Wash out the mixture from your hair with cool water, and style as usual.

Gaia's Gift to the Gardener

by Stephanie Rose Bird

According to Patricia Telesco, in her comprehensive and encylopedic book, *365 Goddess: A Daily Guide to the Magic and Inspiration of the Goddess* (Harper San Francisco, 1998), Gaia is the goddess who stretched herself out at the beginning of time.

Gaia is the Earth. She is fertile, verdant, and lush, but she is also harsh and stormy. She is the giver of life—a symbol of abundance, graciousness, and providence. Gaia is the goddess whose hair we stroke as we tend our herbs and flowers. Hers is the delightful scent of the Easter lily and of new-mown grass.

Despite her loveliness, Gaia is not all romance. It is she who brings quick blood when we carelessly brush against her precious rose. It is she who makes the stones and brambles that we must on occasion remove from our gardens.

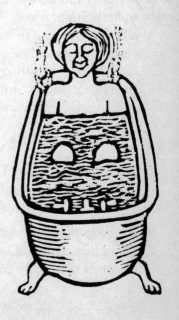

Still, Gaia resides everywhere—in the mountains, deserts, lakes, and seas. As patron goddess of gardeners, she offers us an opportunity for respite, healing, and renewal if we embrace her after tilling her depths.

The Polarity of Gardening

Gardening is an activity that embodies great polarity. It brings us peace, sweat, joy, nurturing, and sustenance. Ultimately, gardening is great for the soul, but it is not always so great for the body. Our hands become calloused, scratched, and cut. Our backs and joints ache after a few hours of gardening—especially as we grow older. And we are also subjected to assaults by mosquitoes and other insects.

Thankfully, if we work creatively in concert with Gaia, and make use of her natural ingredients—her greatest gift—we can enjoy her soothing embrace after a long session of gardening. The following recipes are designed to relax and heal the mind and body of the gardener.

The Gaia projects offered below include a soothing herbal healing balm for the hands, bath salts for tired or sore muscles, an herb-oil spray useful for repelling biting insects, and a dream pillow containing flowers, moss, and herbs that inspire a deep, peaceful sleep and prophetic dreams.

Before beginning the recipes, pour yourself a cup of chamomile tea, and drink in the rich lore and medicinal qualities of the herbs, flowers, and natural substances that we will use.

About the Supplies

Bay *(Laurus nobilis)*: Used in dream pillows by those seeking prophetic dreams; bay leaves also ensure protection and help build strength.

Beeswax pastilles: A natural substance used as a thickener in healing balms, salves, and creams. The pastilles, or small tablets, are convenient to use in measuring.

Burdock root *(Arctium lappa)*: Used to promote the healing of skin irritation and itchiness. It is sometimes recommended in the treatment of poison ivy or poison oak.

Calendula *(Calendula officinalis)*: Calendula flowers are a beautiful warm orange-yellow, similar to the color of the Sun. In Mexico, it is planted near the entryway of the home or business to bring prosperity. During the Day of the Dead, calendula flowers fill paths as an invitation to ancestral spirits. Medically, calendula is used in healing balms or salves for treating wounds, cuts, bruises, sprains, and pulled or sore muscles.

Chamomile essential oil (from Egypt) and dried flowers *(Anthemis nobilis)*: Used as an aromatic for inhalation and topical application. Chamomile promotes quick healing, and is calming to the nervous system and soothing to skin. Chamomile has long been respected as a sleep inducer. It also attracts positive influences.

Chickweed *(Stellaria media)*: Used topically in balms and salves to treat bruises, irritations, and other skin problems.

Citronella *(Cymbopogon nardus)*: This herb is burned as an essential oil in candle form to repel flying insects, especially mosquitoes. Citronella must be used sparingly when applied to the skin as a topical oil remedy, because it can be irritating. As an abortive, it should not be used on pregnant women or female animal companions and familiars.

Cocoa butter: This fixed oil is used to add body and solidity to healing balm formulas. Cocoa butter is known for its ability to encourage healing. It is purported to help tender, bruised, itchy, or cut skin return to normal appearance with minimal scarring.

Dead Sea salts: This natural substance from the Dead Sea in Israel is used as a bath salt to encourage relaxation of muscles and to reduce tension, body aches, and headache. Salt is associated with spiritual cleansing and nurturance.

Epsom salts: Salts are rejuvenating to the overworked body, mind, and spirit. Epsom salts are recommended for relaxing strained or bruised muscles. The combination of salts in my recipes works to help us reach a relaxed state.

Elder flowers *(Sambucus nigra):* As an infusion, elder flowers promote perspiration, and is helpful for rheumatic complaints. An elder ointment or salve is helpful for sunburn or other burns.

Hops *(Humulus lupulus):* This herb is recommended for nervousness, sleeplessness, tension, and stress. It is popular as a sleep aid in dream pillows.

Lanolin, anhydrous: This is a natural source material derived from sheep. The anhydrous form of lanolin is particularly used in oil-based balms and salves, as it does not separate. In addition to adding density and solidity to a healing balm or salve formula, lanolin also provides a barrier layer to help skin rest while it is healing.

Lavender *(L. officinalis):* As an essential oil, lavender is an insect repellent. It is also relaxing when inhaled, and it pampers tired, abraded, or sunburned skin. Lavender has a calm, purple influence on the weary, and is especially useful for women. It is upright in appearance and in effect on the spirit.

Lemon verbena *(Lippia citriodora):* In a dream pillow, lemon verbena is used both for its citrusy scent and for its property to strengthen other magical herbs. Lemon verbena has cleansing and purifying properties.

Marshmallow root *(Mallow spp):* This is an emollient that is softening when used on wounds and sores, as well as on irritations and inflammations.

Mullein *(Verbascum thapus):* This herb has many magical uses. Mullein is worn on the body in a pouch or pockets to keep wild animals at bay while hiking in untamed areas. In a dream pillow, it is used to ensure a peaceful sleep by guarding against the appearance of any stray nightmares.

Orris root *(Iris florentina):* Derived from the rootstock of the Florentine iris, orris root powder has a slightly floral and musky scent. It is used as a scent preservative. In the world of magic, orris root powder is thought to have protective properties and to help in matters of love.

Pennyroyal *(Mentha pulegium):* This herb is abhorred by flying and biting creatures. Like citronella, it should also be used sparingly, as it can be very irritating to some individuals. It also has abortive tendencies, so if you are pregnant replace citronella and pennyroyal with rose geranium and eucalpytus.

Rose Petals *(Rosa* **spp.):** This renowned healing herb is known to calm personal stress. Its heavenly fragrance makes rose a symbol of beauty, eloquence, and romantic inclination. Rose petals lend a superior soothing quality to our senses.

The Recipes

Gaia's Delightful Bedtime Soak

2   cups Epsom salt

2   cups coarse Dead Sea salt

2   cups fine sea salt

1   tsp. chamomile and lavender essential oils

1   large glass jar with a metal screw top

Put the salts in a large stainless-steel or ceramic bowl. Sprinkle and stir in the essential oils. Pour the salt mixture into the glass jar, and shake well. Let it rest for three or four days. Use one to two cups of the salt mixture per bath depending on how strong you like your treatment. Soak for at least twenty minutes, or longer if possible.

Herbal Insect Repellent Spray Mist

¼ tsp. French lavender essential oil

5 drops Virginia cedarwood essential oil

5 drops pennyroyal essential oil (Note: substitute rose geranium essential oil if pregnant)

3 drops citronella essential oil (Substitute eucalpytus or pine essential oil if pregnant)

7 oz. light carrier oil (such as safflower, sunflower, or sweet almond oil)

1 8-oz. spray pump bottle and funnel

Drop the essential oils into the carrier oil in a nonreactive bowl. Swirl the bowl gently. Adjust the oils if desired. Pour all of the oils through a funnel into the spray pump bottle, seal, and use before going outside. Repeat application every two to four hours.

Irritated Skin Treatment

1 tsp. of each of the following dried herbs: elder flower, calendula, chickweed, sage, chamomile

4 cups very hot distilled water

1 Tbl. of dried herbs: burdock root, marshmallow

½ cup apple cider vinegar

Infuse the elder flower, calendula, chickweed, sage, and chamomile by pouring 2 cups of hot, but not boiling, distilled water over them in a bowl or pot. Cover and let steep for 30 minutes. Bring the rest of the distilled water to a boil. Add the burdock root and marshmallow to the water. Cover, and lower heat to medium low and let simmer for 30 minutes. Strain the infusion and the decoction using a thin sieve. Pour through a funnel into a sterilized bottle with a screw top. Pour a bath and add 2 cups of the mixture along with a half cup of apple cider vinegar. If desired, toss a handful of rose and/or calendula petals into the water. Relax and soak. Refrigerate the remaining brew. There should be enough for two baths. Use the mixture within thirty days.

Gaia's Healing Balm

1 Tbl. beeswax pastilles

2 Tbls. anhydrous lanolin

2 Tbls. cocoa butter

½ cup sweet almond oil, olive oil, peach kernel oil, sunflower oil, or safflower oil

1 Tbl. wheat germ oil

¼ cup evening primrose oil

⅛ tsp. chamomile essential oil

¼ tsp. French lavender essential oil

Place the beeswax, lanolin, cocoa butter, and half cup of oil of your choice into a heavy-bottomed sauce pan on low heat. Allow the ingredients to melt completely, then remove from heat. Stir in wheat germ and evening primrose oils. Whisk in the essential oils. Quickly pour the mixture into jar with a wide opening, and screw it shut. Allow it to thicken for at least one hour before disturbing. Use it on sore muscles and when you need a dose of healing. Keep the balm in cool, dry place. It should have a shelf-life of 6 months.

Dream Pillow

1 handful of the following dried herbs: lemon verbena leaves, rose petals, chamomile flowers, French lavender buds, bay leaves, mullien, Spanish moss, and hops

⅛ tsp. chamomile essential oil

⅛ tsp. attar of roses (or quality rose fragrance oil)

¼ tsp. French lavender essential oil

2 tsps. orris root powder

Crumble the first six dried herbs into a bowl until small and relatively fine. Tear the Spanish moss into one-inch pieces, and then add to other ingredients. Stir in the hops. (Note: allergy sufferers should wear a dust mask for this project, as hops is a strong allergin.) Sprinkle the essential oils over the bruised herbs and stir well. Sprinkle orris root powder over the mixture, and blend. Allow the mixture to mature by placing it in a dark jar away from direct light. Shake daily for 4 weeks. While waiting, make a small dream pillowcase using gingham, linen, hemp, or some other fabric scrap. Use 2 nine-inch squares of fabric and some cotton thread. Stuff the herb mixture into the pillow when it is ready, and seal up the pillow. This particular dream pillow is designed for protection, strength, restful deep sleep, and prophetic dreams.

A Note to the Interested

Gaia's Gifts to the Gardener is offered as a hands-on workshop, that makes use of various herb-crafting recipes, by Stephanie Bird, at the Chicago Botanic Gardens in Glencoe, Illinois. Call the Gardens for upcoming dates and times.

Chicago Botanic Gardens
1000 Lake Cook Road
Glencoe, IL 60022
(847) 835-5440
TDD (847) 835-0790
http://www.chicago-botanic.org/

Botanical Arts and Herbal Suppliers

Liberty Natural Products
8120 SE Stark Street
Portland, OR 97215
(503) 256-1227
fax: (503) 256-1182
e-mail: sales@libertynatural.com
http://libertynatural.com/index.html

This is my favorite direct source of inexpensive essential oils; the only downside is that there is a $50 minimum on orders, and you need to set up a wholesale account in order to order.

Mountain Rose Herbs
85472 Dilley Lane
Eugene, OR 97405
(800) 879-3337
fax: (510) 217-4012
e-mail: customerservice@mountainroseherbs.com

Bulk herbs, essential oils, books, and herbal products at retail prices.

Penzeys Spices
1138 West Lake Street
Oak Park, IL 60301
(708) 848-7772
http://www.penzeys.com

This is an excellent source of exotic, fresh, high quality spices for potpourri and other uses. It does mail orders and has a catalog.

Sunfeather Natural Soap Co.
1551 State Highway 72
Potsdam, NY 13676
(315)265-3648
http://www.sunsoap.com/

This is a good source for supplies that are unusual and hard to find. It also has rare recipe books.

For Further Study

Bremness, Lesley. *The Complete Book of Herbs*. New York: Viking Studio Books, 1988.

Cunningham, Scott. *Encyclopedia of Magical Herbs*. St. Paul: Llewellyn Publications, 1999.

Davidow, Joie. *Infusions of Healing: A Treasury of Mexican-American Herbal Remedies*. New York: Simon & Schuster, 1999.

Edwards, Victoria H. *The Aromatherapy Companion*. Pownal, Vt.: Storey Books, 1999.

Freeman, Sally. *Everywoman's Guide to Natural Home Remedies*. New York: Doubleday Direct, 1996.

Lust, John. *The Herb Book*. New York: Bantam Books, 1974.

Roth-Harper, Jaqulene. *Beautiful Face, Beautiful Body*. New York: Berkley Books, 2000.

Rose Beauty Recipes

❧ by Chandra Moira Beal ❧

Y ou've heard about roses probably thousands of times in your
lifetime. Consider, for instance,
these well-known expressions of admira-
tion for the lovely rose:

*That which we call a rose by any
other name would smell as sweet . . .*

A rose is a rose is a rose . . .

My love like a red, red rose . . .

The days of wine and roses . . .

Literature is full of references to this
universal symbol of beauty. Roses are
flowers of antiquity. They have delighted
the senses for centuries. Red roses
especially are associated with beauty
and love. Once used more for their
medicinal, culinary, and fragrant qualities, and in many folk remedies, roses
are now valued for their inherent
beauty as well.

The beauty of the rose can be yours, too. That is, as modern people, we can still make our own rose beauty recipes using just a few simple and easy-to-find ingredients.

Beauty Treatments with Roses

Fresh Rose Petals

You may use any type of rose for these recipes, but the more fragrant roses—the heirloom varieties, generally speaking—will make better perfumes.

Whenever recipes call for fresh petals, seek out organically grown flowers if possible. In general, you can gather roses in the wild, grow your own, or buy yourself a bouquet at the grocery store. Fresh petals should be plucked from the flower before the flower falls from the bush, and before the morning dew has vanished. Use fresh petals immediately. Rose oil can be substituted, but it is highly concentrated and should be used sparingly. Rose oil can be found at health food or aromatherapy shops.

Dried Rose Petals

Some of these recipes require dried or powdered rose petals. You can buy dried rose petals, but you will not be certain of their quality. The best way to know if your petals are organic and healthy is to dry them yourself.

The way the flowers are gathered and dried makes a difference. Gather your fresh petals when the dew has dried, but before the Sun is at its peak for the day. The slowest method of drying is simply spreading the petals out on a table in a single layer. A better method is to spread them on a large wire screen. Old window screens work great for this purpose. You could also take a sheet of netting and fasten it to a wooden frame.

Don't expose the flowers to direct sunlight, and make sure the air circulates all around the petals so they dry evenly. Use a mesh screen that is fairly fine, as the petals will shrink as they dry and could fall through. When absolutely dry, the petals can be ground to a powder in a coffee grinder or food processor and stored in bottles or other airtight containers. Don't expose the dried petals to the environment or they will absorb moisture and lose their properties.

In Elizabethan times, women dried rose petals in sand, another perfectly acceptable way to dry flowers. This method helps the petals retain their shape and color. Take an old shoe box and spread a layer of sand on the bottom, then a layer of petals. Alternate petals and sand in layers. Leave the box uncovered so the moisture can escape. Store the boxes for about a week, then carefully remove the petals.

Drying roses allows one to enjoy them all year long.

Rose Perfume Recipes

Rosewater

One of the simplest rose recipes is rosewater. It is easy and inexpensive to make, requiring only fresh roses and water. Most washstands in Victorian times included a jug of rosewater for washing hands. Rosewater forms the base of many other recipes, so make up a big batch before proceeding.

Rosewater #1: Gather about two pounds of rose petals before they fall from the flower. Put the petals in an enamel saucepan, and cover with cool distilled water. Heat slowly until just under a boil. Then leave until cold, and strain off the water.

Rosewater #2: Gather 2 pounds of rose petals. Grind them into a paste with mortar and pestle. Let the mash sit in the mortar for five or six hours, steeping in its own juices. Put this mash into a canvas bag, and press out the juice into a jar. Add spring water and more fresh petals to fill the jar. Let this steep for 24 hours, then pour the contents into a saucepan and heat over a small flame until bubbles appear in the pan. Remove the liquid from heat, and let it cool. Strain and bottle.

Rose Steam

After you finish the rosewater cooking stage, remove the pot from the stove and use the rosewater steam as a mini-facial. Take a large towel and make a tent over your head, lean over the steaming pot, and inhale the rosy steam.

Rose Vinegar

Rose vinegar can help ward off headaches and is cooling and refreshing when applied to the skin. This recipe was popular with women of the French court.

Take a jar of good quality white wine vinegar, and fill to the brim with rose petals. Let it steep for twenty-four hours in the Sun, then strain off the vinegar. Dip a handkerchief in the vinegar, and lay it on your forehead. Or else apply it with a cotton ball as a toner after cleaning your face. Roses are naturally astringent and remove oil and dirt.

Old Fashioned Rose Perfume

Take a half-pound of rose buds, and cut the petals clear of the white part. Mash them with a mortar and pestle. Add 2 tablespoons of rosewater, and mix in a glass jar. Seal and leave overnight. Add ⅛ teaspoon of musk to the rosewater, and mix. Strain out to use.

Exotic Rose Perfume

Take a gallon of spring water. Add 3 handfuls of rose petals, a handful of lavender flowers, a handful of sweet marjoram, the rinds of 6 oranges, 12 cloves, and 1 ounce of orris powder. Steep the mixture for 24 hours in the Sun, then strain off into a quart jar. Add a few drops of musk. Add slices of juniper tied in muslin to the mix. Steep for another 24 hours. Strain out all the liquid, and add a few tablespoons to your laundry when the washing basin is full of water.

Sweet Rose Perfume

Add 2 handfuls of rose petals and ¼ pound of sugar to a quart of spring water. Let it steep for 30 minutes. Strain out the liquid to use.

Herbal Rose Perfume

Add a handful of rose petals to a quart of vodka, along with a handful of marjoram and 1½ ounces each of cloves, nutmeg, cinnamon, mace, and cardamom. Add a handful of lavender and rosemary. Shake the mixture well, and let it stand in the Sun for ten days. Strain and bottle. Dab on the temples and nostrils to fortify the brain and memory.

Rose Skin Recipes

Roses aren't limited to perfume recipes. They give numerous benefits to the skin and have many applications.

Rosewater and Lemon Toner

3 Tbls. rosewater

2 Tbls. fresh lemon juice

2 Tbls. distilled water

2 tsps. rubbing alcohol

2 drops rosemary essential oil

Mix all the ingredients together and place in a bottle. Apply with a cotton pad after cleansing the face. This toner must be stored in the refrigerator and used within two weeks. Shake well before using.

Rosewater Astringent

2 tsps. rosewater

1 tsp. witch hazel extract

1 tsp. apple cider vinegar or rose vinegar

1   drop orange essential oil

1   drop juniper essential oil

Mix the ingredients together, and store in a bottle. Apply with a cotton pad after cleansing.

Rose Eye Makeup Remover

Look for rose hydrosol at your local drugstore. Make sure it does not contain any alcohol as this can be irritating to the eyes. Soak a cotton pad in the hydrosol, and wipe away your eye makeup. Rinse with warm water.

Romantic Rose Bath Salts

½   cup sea salt

½   cup baking soda

1   tsp. sunflower oil

2–3   drops rose oil

½   tsp. vitamin E oil

Mix ingredients together in a ceramic bowl, or shake together in a glass jar. Store in an air-tight container. Add one or two tablespoons to your bath under the running water. For even more romance, float fresh rose petals on your bathwater.

Wake Up and Smell the Roses Toner

½   cup rosewater

1   cup white wine

2   bay leaves

6   clove buds

3   black peppercorns

This invigorating toner will get you started on the right foot in the morning. Rosewater's slightly acidic nature will help restore the skin's acid mantle. Place all of the ingredients in a saucepan, and bring to a boil. Remove the pan from the heat, and allow to cool completely. Pour the liquid into a container, and let it sit for at least two weeks. Strain and store in a clean air-tight container. Fill a misting bottle with the liquid, or just splash on after your bath.

Rosehip Facial Mask

20   fresh or dried rosehips
½   cup distilled water

Rosehips are the fruit of the rose. If gathering your own, pick them in the late fall before the first frost. The edible rosehips are packed with vitamin C and vitamin A, both nourishing to the skin. Dried rosehips are also available at most natural food and herb shops.

Remove any stalks from the rosehips, and wash the rosehips in cold water. Cut each open, and remove the seeds and fibers in the center. Place the rosehips in a saucepan, and cover with water. Bring the water to a boil, and simmer for fifteen minutes. Let it cool, and then pour it into a blender to purée. Smooth the mixture all over your face, and leave it on for about fifteen minutes. Rinse off and pat dry.

Rose Moisturizer

2   Tbls. grated beeswax
½   cup distilled water
½   cup apricot oil
½   cup rosewater
4   drops rose essential oil

Rose oil fights wrinkles and broken capillaries, making it a great choice for the face and hands. Melt the beeswax and the water over a very low flame, then pour into a blender and mix. With the blender running, gradually pour in the apricot oil, rosewater, and rose oil. The lotion will thicken as it cools.

Rose and Honey Mask

Rose is great for puffy or dry skin. Use this facial weekly.

2 Tbls. honey

2 tsps. almond oil

5 drops rose essential oil

Mix all of the ingredients together, and apply to face and neck in gentle circles. Leave it on for 15 minutes, then rinse with warm water.

Rosewater and Aloe Rejuvenating Lotion

Rose is anti-inflammatory, antiseptic, and toning. The aloe in this lotion adds moisture and will leave your skin feeling fresh and new.

½ cup olive oil

2 Tbls. aloe vera gel

3 Tbls. grated beeswax

3 Tbls. lanolin

4 Tbls. rosewater

Blend the olive oil and aloe in a small bowl. In a saucepan, melt the beeswax and lanolin over low heat, stirring constantly. Remove the pan from heat, and pour in the aloe and olive oil mixture. Keep stirring. Add the rosewater, and pour all into a blender. Blend until smooth. Pour into a clean container, and store in the fridge. It will thicken as it cools.

Beauty from the Inside Out

⪼ by Feather Jones ⪻

E ven though it's a rather old cliché, that beauty is more than skin deep is more than true. How we feel about ourselves and how we approach life contributes more to our well-being than how closely we resemble a magazine model. And after all, no one really truly looks like those magazine models; not even the models themselves.

As an example of the skin deep principle, just look at how emotional stress can wreak havoc on the skin. The skin has many functions, one of which is being responsible for excreting one-quarter of the body's waste products and water. As such, it will manifest the result of a stressful event. Stress causes adrenaline release, which puts one in the fight-or-flight response. This over-stimulation of the sympathetic nervous

system pulls blood and nutrients away from the skin to supply the muscles with the energy needed to run from a saber-toothed tiger, or whatever is the source of stress. This in turn causes excess uric acid in the blood. This may be enough to imbalance the pH of the skin.

Skin Health Starts Inside the Body

To protect itself, the skin has a natural layer of moisture and oil that forms an acid mantle. This mantle is antimicrobial, protects from infections, is pH balanced and a natural barrier to toxins in the environment. A high or low pH irritates the skin. The pH of skin varies through out the day and is primarily influenced by sweat. Skin is usually between 4 and 6.7 on the pH scale (which runs from 0 to 14; 7 being neutral, below 7 acidic, and above 7 basic). As food, stress, drugs, and alcohol can all affect the composition of your sweat, you can see how important it is to pay attention to our skin's pH.

As you may already be aware, healthy skin starts with a healthy body. The skin is a liver indicator and a barometer of basic good health. When the liver's metabolism is sluggish, the skin and hair will be dry; when the liver is in a hypermetabolic state, the skin and hair will be oily.

A healthy diet may well be the centerpiece to radiant skin. Eating organic whole foods and drinking lots of pure water is half the battle. This includes lots of vegetables, whole grains, nuts, seeds, and fresh fruit. Here are some basic tips that can help you keep your skin as healthy as possible.

The essential fatty acids obtained from fish and fish oils as well as flax, borage, and hemp seed improve skin quality and are especially good for atopic eczema where there is itching.

Royal jelly as a supplement contains hydroxyl fatty acids and protects the skin from dehydration. It is also anti-inflammatory; contains collagen, lecithin, vitamins A, C, D, E, and B (especially pantothenic acid); and decreases total cholesterol and triglycerides in the blood.

Wheat germ oil, an excellent source of vitamin E, has an estrogenic effect on skin—softening, increasing elasticity and blood supply to the dermal layers.

Things to Avoid

On the other hand, there are plenty of pratfalls to avoid if you want to keep your skin young and smooth.

Fried foods, chips, and cookies contain transfatty acids, which are all damaging to the skin.

Excess refined sugar and simple carbohydrates are quickly reduced to blood fats and clog the arteries as well as the lymphatic system (which is responsible for keeping the cells and interstitial fluid healthy).

High dairy intake also congests the liver and prevents the blood from being properly filtered.

Skin care products are everywhere, but beware of the ingredients. Many commercial products have BHT and BHA. Both are synthetic antioxidants often used to retard the rancidity of oils in foods and cosmetics. They are toxic and cause allergic reactions.

Methyl and propylparabens are petroleum byproducts that clog the pores. Petroleum products smother the skin and cause it to heat up—thus enlarging the pores, preventing natural oils from escaping, but allowing dirt and bacteria in.

Parabens are widely used as an inhibitor of microbial growth even though known to be toxic and highly allergic.

Aluminum can build up in the body through the use of cosmetics, food, and cookware that contain this metal. Aluminum toxicity is associated with Alzheimer's disease and should be avoided.

Making Your Own Skin Products

Even some good skin products sold in health food stores may contain at least some preservatives. Homemade body care products have ingredients you can trust. What you can make is superior to anything you can buy. These remedies will contain no colors, additives, harsh chemicals, preservatives, or alcohol, and they are naturally pH balanced.

One of the skin's jobs is to produce keratin and vitamin D, which is activated by ultraviolet sunlight and metabolizes calcium and phosphates through out the body. Using products with pore-clogging ingredients hinders this ability.

Oily Skin Types

Sebaceous glands pump lubrication to the skin. Overactive glands need calming without overdrying in order to keep your face soft. The daily use of facial soap is drying and can cause an oily rebound on the skin. When you strip all the oil off the skin with harsh soaps, it sends a signal to the oil glands to produce more oil. A simple rinse of a mildly astringent herbal toner will remove the oil yet not overly dry the skin.

If you have oily skin, it is important to use only water-based makeup—not oil-based. The following is a list of easy-to-make products that will remove excess oil while leaving some behind.

A clay mask increases blood flow, tightens the skin, and draws out excess oils and debris. Adding essential oils to your mask soothes inflammation and fights bacteria that inflame clogged pores. For weekly use, try this recipe. To 1 tablespoon clay or oatmeal, add 1 teaspoon water or lemon juice. Also add a dab of nutritional yeast to stimulate circulation. Add a small amount of honey to this as well for its acid-balanced, antibacterial, and antiseptic qualities. The bee pollen, enzymes, and propolis found in honey also stimulate new tissue growth. This mask draws oils to the surface and boosts circulation to stimulate blood flow and whisk away dead skin cells. It texturizes and smooths, removes grime, treats acne, and nourishes dermal layers.

An oatmeal mask leaves natural oils in place to protect and moisturize your skin. Just grind oatmeal, and add a little water to make a paste. Add a little cinnamon, and leave the mast on until it starts to feel tight. Afterward, rinse it away with water.

An oatmeal scrub cleans without robbing protective oils. Grind to a paste 2 teaspoons oats with 1 tablespoon water, and gently scrub your face. This leaves the skin clean without stripping natural oils. It can be made with green tea or rosemary powder, or you can add ½ teaspoon lavender for its antibacterial action and 1 teaspoon honey as a moisturizer.

Marshmallow moisturizer: Add 1 cup warm lavender tea to 1 tablespoon marshmallow powder. Let it sit for 10 minutes, and it will gel slightly. Apply liberally to your face.

Astringent toners can be used daily if one takes care. A good recipe is to take 1 teaspoon sage (for its drying properties) and 1 teaspoon peppermint leaf (for its cooling properties). Combine them with 4 ounces witch hazel liniment or yarrow tea to create an aromatic toner that restores the protective acid mantle. There is no need to strain this, just keep refrigerated up to two months.

Lemon juice diluted in water is a simple and effective toning rinse.

Tincture of benzoin is calming and astringing and can be added to calendula, yarrow, or chamomile tea at 15 drops to 1 cup tea. Add 6 drops lavender essential oil if you wish.

Sage in general is antihydrotic and can be drunk as a tea or tincture to help deal with excessive sweating associated with oily skin types. To help your sweat have a sweet scent, try rubbing on orange peel before your deodorant, and drink a cup of ginger tea once a day.

Bath Tea for Oily Skin

1   oz. lemon grass (for relaxing and invigorating qualities)

1   oz. cornmeal (for its drawing qualities)

1   oz. witch hazel (for astringent qualities)

1   oz. rose petal (for soothing and cooling qualities)

Steep all of these ingredients in hot water, and strain. Add this tea to your bath, and use the strained herbs in a muslin bag to scrub your skin.

Dry Skin Types

Desert-dry skin needs extra moisturizing. Help is available for the associated itchiness—the little dry lines around the mouth and eyes, the irritation that causes redness on the cheeks and forehead, and so on.

In general, oils are not the best approach for treating dry skin, as applications of oil make the skin "lazy." That is, the skin will stop producing its own oils. It's much better instead to hydrate your skin with emollients.

To start, make sure you drink plenty of water each day—preferably one-half gallon or so. If drinking that much water doesn't appeal to you, try adding a little lemon juice or a couple sprigs of mint to flavor your water mildly.

Here are some helpful remedies you can apply to battle the scourge of dry skin.

A basic skin cream might consist of 4 ounces olive oil, 3 tablespoons melted beeswax, 2 ounces herbal water (orange, rose, or lavender), 5 (broken) capsules of vitamin E, and 5 drops of your favorite essential oil (rose, lemon, or cedar). Stir the oils together, and add essential oils just before pouring the cream into a jar. Creams are more oily in general than lotions, and they are best used in nighttime applications for deep softening and moisturizing.

Oatmeal scrub contains ½ cup ground oatmeal, ⅓ cup ground raw sunflower seeds, 4 tablespoons almond meal, ½ teaspoon mint, and a dash of ground cinnamon or tumeric powder. Scrub gently this mixture onto your face. It will leave skin silky smooth. You can also try an oatmeal bath by putting the mixture into a muslin bag and washing with it. You can store this in the refrigerator.

Mullein oil is good as a body oil for aged skin that has lost its elasticity.

Chickweed and oatstraw tea are good applied to dry and itchy skin. These can be added to a bath as a strained tea.

The essential oil of lavender is good for dry, irritated skin. It is best used with ½ cup aloe vera as a toner.

An avocado mask is an amazing moisturizing treatment. It feels like a spring rain in the desert.

A loofah sponge invigorates dry skin and helps your skin keep its resiliency by increasing the blood supply. Use either before or in the shower.

Dry Skin Lotion

Lotions for day use are hydrating, stimulating, aromatic, antibacterial, and soothing. Here is a basic lotion recipe.

> 1 oz. cocoa butter
>
> 3 ozs. almond or jojoba oil
>
> 2 ozs. herb water
>
> 5 drops rose, orange, or lavender essential oil

Recipes for All Skin Types

An herbal steam: Applied weekly, an herbal steam stimulates circulation for any skin types. To start, gently wash face and leave moist. Bring to a boil 3 tablespoons of your favorite herb in 1 quart water. Cover with a lid and simmer for 5 minutes, and let it cool for 5 minutes. Tie your hair back and cover your head with a towel, making a tent with your towel. Sit for 10 minutes about eight inches from the pot, and close your eyes. Rinse afterward with warm and then cool water. Use an astringent splash to "close" the pores. Steams might include some of the following herbs—for normal to dry skin: chamomile, licorice root, or cloves. For normal to oily skin: lemon peel, calendula, rosemary, lemongrass, rose, witch hazel, or lavender. For acne: lavender or licorice; for a stimulating steam: nettles, rosemary, fennel, peach leaves, or lemon. For a cooling steam: mint. And for a sweet steam: roses.

A honey pat is a great way to rejuvenate the skin. Honey is a non-oily moisturizer. It cleans the skin and naturally disinfects. Apply a small amount to the face, and massage in gently with circular movements. When it becomes tacky, pat the honey with your fingertips. You will feel a tingle as circulation increases to the area. Rinse with warm water, and feel the glow. In time you will notice your skin is softer.

Masks in general are intended to remove dirt and oil without stripping the natural oil base. They deep-clean your pores, soften dry skin, peel away dead skin cells, boost circulation, and force you to relax for at least the ten to thirty minutes it takes for them to dry.

Fruit masks in particular refine and clean out pores, tighten droopy skin, and stimulate a nice healthy glow. Mango, papaya, apple, and pear add smoothness and exfoliating qualities—removing dead skin cells. Lemon, orange, and grapefruit act as a tonic, moisturizing and rejuvenating the facial muscles. Apricot, peach, nectarine, and melon refine and texturize the skin. Blueberry protects skin capillaries. Strawberry and raspberry reduce oiliness and make skin soft as velvet.

To perk up tired skin that's pasty or sallow looking, try a mask first, then a gentle cleanse or scrub, followed by a toner. This will be the key to soften and exfoliate skin that has lost its luster.

Washing with Grains

½ cup finely ground oats

½ cup cornmeal

1 cup white clay

¼ cup ground almonds

⅛ cup powdered lavender

⅛ cup powdered roses

5 drops lavender, peppermint, orange, or lemon essential oil

Mix these ingredients, then moisten with honey and a little water to reach the consistency of a paste. Use this daily instead of soap.

Recipes for Treating Acne

Acne forms due to several conditions. Hyperactive glands, in teenagers for example, cause excess lanolin formation. Try liver-cooling herbs such as burdock and dandelion (in teas or tinctures) to treat persistent teenage acne.

Another acne-causing condition may be clogged pores. This can occur due to lack of good circulation. That is, the liver is overburdened and not cleaning the blood well. It can't break down stray hormones and waste products effectively. The lymph system may be congested as well. Liver stimulants such as oregon grape root and yellow dock root may help. If acne flares up right around menstruation, it is probably hormonal-based and may respond to chastetree berry. Teenage acne is influenced by hormones that stimulate oil glands. Puberty and adolescence are peak levels of such activity.

As a good general rule, resist the urge to squeeze pimples. It can lead to scarring and prolongs the healing process. Try a pimple juice on blemishes:

  ½ oz. golden seal powder (organically grown only)

  ½ oz. echinacea root powder

  ½ oz. black walnut hull powder

  ½ oz. myrrh gum powder

  1 pint vodka

Let the herbs sit in the vodka for a week. Strain, and throw the herbs away. Store your liquid extract in a squeeze-top plastic container, and use daily as needed.

Calendula is excellent for acne that scars easily, as it improves tissue strength and causes wounds to contract faster.

St. John's wort oil keeps the skin from overproducing oil, even though this seems unlikely to heal acne because it is an oil. However, the herb is calming to oversensitive oil glands and promotes wound healing. It is astringing, anti-inflammatory, and antiviral. The best application is to wash your face first and put a hot washcloth over it to open the pores. Then massage the oil into the trouble areas and return the hot washcloth to the face, keeping it warm for a few minutes. Have a final rinse to remove all extra oil with yarrow toner or lemon water. Do this weekly.

Lavender essential oil is useful for hyperactive oil glands and can be used for dabbing on blemishes.

Grain masks are good for acne. (See recipes above.)

A honey mask is acid-balancing, rids face of blemishes and blackheads, and is a natural hydrater that leaves skin taut and firm with a warm feeling and pleasant smell.

Herbal steams open the pores. Essential oils from the herbs soothe the skin, ease tension, and calm the nerves. Try lavender or thyme.

Light moisturizers are necessary for treating acne. Skin that is moisturized is not likely to overproduce oil.

Sunlight is also valuable as ultraviolet light sterilizes the skin. Be mindful that excess salt causes acne, and fast foods contain extremely excessive amounts of salt.

Vitamin A, in the form of beta carotene, is essential to good skin quality.

Zinc is a bacterial suppressor.

The B complex vitamins reduce facial oiliness and black-head formation. Stress uses up our B vitamins.

Vitamin C aids in resisting the spread of acne and vitamin E helps prevent scarring.

Herbs for the Skin

The following list of herbs are good for topical applications to the skin, unless otherwise noted.

Aloe *(Aloe vera)* is considered the plant of immortality in ancient Egypt. It is a skin rejuvenator for acne, fungal infections, and skin ulcers. Its polysaccharides promote fast healing of skin tissue through anti-inflammatory, immune-stimulating, and antimicrobial action. Fresh aloe vera gel contains twenty of the twenty-two amino acids required by the human body, as well as zinc and vit-amins E and C. The best application method is to get the fresh aloe plant and cut off a piece of the stem. Apply the exposed inner section directly to treatment areas, and cover with a Band-Aid or first-aid tape.

Burdock root *(Arctium* spp.) clears liver heat and pulls impurities from the blood. It has keratolytic action as a skin softener, and it is used for all types of acne when taken internally as a tincture, tea, or food that can be added to soups or stir-fry. It is nutritive and anti-inflammatory when used as an herb steam. This plant has benefits in treating a sluggish lymphatic system.

Calendula *(Calendula officinalis)* flushes poisons from the body, is antiseptic and anti-inflammatory, and tones and soothes the skin. Calendula is effective in treating wounds where there is a possibility of infection by inhibiting pus formation, and it is nonirritating to burns and sores. It relieves pain and swelling and has the ability to curtail bleeding. As an antimicrobial, it boosts the immune system.

Chamomile *(Matricaria* spp.) has a relaxing action on facial muscles and is beneficial when applied to dry skin and wounds. Be mindful of potential allergic reactions. Chamomile is anti-inflammatory.

Chastree berry *(Vitex agnus-castus)* helps normalize the pituitary gland and regulates hormone production for menses-related acne and herpes when taken internally.

Echinacea *(Echinacea* spp.) is an immune stimulant, and it is anti-inflammatory and antimicrobial. It can be used internally as well as topically.

Jojoba oil *(Simmondsia chinensis)* softens skin and hair. It is not really an oil, but a liquid wax ester. Our skin's sebum secretions are comprised of about 30 percent liquid wax ester of the sort similar to jojoba. Jojoba oil is nonallergenic and penetrates the skin rapidly. Jojoba treats the itchiness of psoriasis and is a good carrier of essential oils, improving absorption into the skin. It will condition dry hair and moisturize the skin, being beneficial to sunburn and wind burns. It removes makeup and eliminates diaper rash.

Licorice *(Glycyrrhiza* **spp.)** soothes irritated tissue.

Marshmallow root *(Althea officinalis)* is an emollient herb that moisturizes dry skin and irritated tissues.

Nettle *(Urtica* **spp.)** improves circulation and overall liver and kidney health. As a nutritive for the body, it makes a tea that is nice to drink daily.

Oregon grape root *(Mahonia* **spp.)** will detoxify the blood by its stimulating action on the liver. It promotes digestive enzymes and bile flow, and so helps break down food allergins before they make it to the blood stream and cause allergic reactions. It can be taken internally as a tea or tincture.

Plantain *(Plantago* **spp.)** draws out infections, is soothing, and clears heat from irritated tissues due to its emollient action.

St. John's wort *(Hypericum perforatum)* is an excellent wound healer with the ability to calm nerves associated with hyperactive oil glands. It also astringes swollen tissues and speeds up the healing process.

Witch hazel *(Hamamelis virginiana)* is astringent and healing to damaged blood vessels.

Yarrow *(Achillea* **spp.)** opens the pores when used internally and facilitates waste removal through the sweat when applied to the skin as a toner. Yarrow tightens enlarged pores and draws out infections.

Yellow dock *(Rumex crispus)* helps the liver detoxify the blood. It is especially useful in treating acne caused by constipation. It improves psoriasis, rashes, and staph infections.

As a final note, exercise is essential to a healthy lymphatic system and makes your skin glow with warmth. Sleep is also an often neglected ingredient in healthy skin. A good night's rest of eight uninterrupted hours is important for the body to repair itself from a day's worth of stress.

Remember what we think affects how we look. Anger reddens the face, fear whitens it, and joy makes us radiant. Be happy.

For Further Study

Gladstar, Rosemary. *Herbal Healing for Women: Simple Home Remedies for Women of All Ages*. New York: Simon & Schuster, 1993.

Griffin, Judy. *Mother Nature's Herbal*. St. Paul, Minn.: Llewellyn Publications, 1997.

Harrar, Sarí, and Sara Altshul O'Donnell. *The Woman's Book of Healing Herbs: Healing Teas, Tonics, Supplements, and Formulas*. Emmaus, Pa.: Rodale Press, 1999.

Keville, Kathy, and Mindy Gree. *Aromatherapy: A Complete Guide to the Healing Art*. Freedom, Calif.: Crossing Press, 1995.

Rose, Jeanne. *The Herbal Body Book*. New York: Grosset & Dunlap, 1976.

Winter, Ruth. *A Consumer's Dictionary of Cosmetic Ingredients*. New York: Three Rivers Press, 1999.

Herb
Crafts

Making Herbal Bookmarks

⚜ by Elizabeth Barrette ⚜

Y ou love herbs and you love books—so why not combine the two? Whether done in a traditional or a more contemporary style, herbal bookmarks are a delightful and practical art form. They're rather easy to make. You can work with just the materials you happen to have on hand, or for more elaborate projects you can track down goodies at a craft store or other supplier.

There's no such thing as too many books, or too many bookmarks.

The Three Parts of an Herbal Bookmark

An herbal bookmark has three basic parts: the base, the herb(s), and embellishment. The base forms the main body of the bookmark, and it is usually comprised of some kind of paper—

although it can be plastic or some other material as well. Choose something thin enough to fit between the pages of your books, and sturdy enough to withstand some use.

The herbs give the bookmark its charm, both visually and magically. Different herbs do different things, so pick the right herbs for the job.

Embellishment includes everything from protective covers to tassels to glitter. These touches make a bookmark more durable, convenient, or pretty. Not every bookmark necessarily has all three parts, though. You can pick and choose what combination appeals to you.

The Language of Herbs and Flowers

You may already be aware of the custom of using plants to send messages. This "flower language" dates back at least 150 years. During the Victorian period, this tradition reached a height of popularity, as lovers used it to exchange secrets. Although flowers are more commonly associated with this custom, many lists include herbs as well, and there are a few lists devoted entirely to herbs.

Is it a real language? Well, yes and no. It's one of the most complex and versatile forms of invented communication ever to achieve some kind of popular use. Each plant represents a word, phrase, idea, or emotion. The flower language has no grammar, so it's not quite a real language—but it does have an impressive vocabulary. You can mix and match symbolic plants to create precise, unique expressions.

Today, flower fans still use this esoteric but fun code when designing arrangements for family and friends, or when planning special Victoriana parties. Pressing plants into bookmarks allows you to make the message permanent, and to get your meaning across as well. For the sake of clarity, you might want to list names and interpretations on the back of each bookmark—especially if your friends are not familiar with this custom. Here are some herbal associations to get you started.

Agrimony: Gratitude

Angelica: Inspiration

Dandelion: Fidelity, happiness, indestructibility

Basil: Love and good wishes

Bay: Reward for merit, glory, will power, "no change till death"

Chamomile: Initiative, energy in adversity, patience

Clover, red: Industriousness, "be mine"

Clover, white: "I promise"

Coriander: Hidden worth

Costmary: Sweetness, sanctity

Dittany of Crete: Birth

Eglantine: Poetry, "I wound to heal"

Fennel: Strength, praiseworthiness

Foxglove: A wish

Garlic: Courage, strength

Hawthorn: Hope

Hyssop: Cleanliness, sacrifice

Lavender: Silence, "sweets to the sweet"

Marjoram: Blushes, happiness

Mint: Virtue, warm feelings

Mistletoe: Affection, surmounting difficulties

Mugwort: Good luck, happiness

Nasturtium: Optimism, patriotism

Parsley: Useful knowledge, festivity, entertainment

Poppy: Consolation, compassion

Rose, red: Congratulations, "I love you"

Rose, white: Purity, secrecy, youth, "I am worthy of you"

Rose, yellow: Joy, friendship, "welcome back," "remember me"

Rose leaf: "You may hope"

Rosemary: Remembrance, "your presence revives me"

Sage: Esteem, wisdom, domestic virtue

Sorrel: Parental affection

Thyme: Energy, affection

Verbena: "You have my confidence"

Vervain: Enchantment

Willow: Freedom

Witch hazel: Spellcraft, "a spell is on me"

Yarrow: Cure for heartache

Magical Correspondences

Plants also carry the energy of many other influences: gender polarity, the elements, planetary rulers, and so forth. Spells often call for the use of herbs which embody certain mystical properties. Many deities have special plants associated with them, too.

All these correspondences can help you create herbal bookmarks with clear magical signatures. Consider beginning with these herbal associations.

Feminine: dittany of Crete, foxglove, mugwort, oat, poppy, rose, sorrel, thyme, vervain, willow, yarrow

Masculine: agrimony, bay, chamomile, fennel, garlic, hawthorn, lavender, marjoram, mint, parsley, rosemary, sage, witch hazel

Air: agrimony, borage, clover, elecampane, fenugreek, hops, lavender, mint, parsley, sage

Earth: bistort, cypress, fern, horehound, mugwort, oat, primrose, sorrel, vervain, vetivert

Fire: angelica, basil, bay, fennel, garlic, hawthorn, hyssop, mandrake, rosemary, St. John's wort, witch hazel

Water: chamomile, dittany of Crete, foxglove, lady's mantle, poppy, thyme, valerian, willow, yarrow

Jupiter: agrimony, borage, meadowsweet, sage, witch grass

Mars: basil, garlic, hawthorn, pennyroyal, woodruff

Mercury: bergamot, clover, elecampane, fennel, lavender, mint, parsley

Moon: balm, eucalyptus, poppy, willow, wintergreen

Saturn: bistort, comfrey, fumitory, mullein, quince

Sun: angelica, bay, chamomile, mistletoe, rosemary, rue, witch hazel

Venus: catnip, dittany of Crete, mugwort, oat, rose, sorrel, vervain, willow

Courage: borage, garlic, mullein, pine, thyme, yarrow

Fertility: bistort, hawthorn, hollyhock, mistletoe, poppy

Happiness: catnip, hawthorn, lavender, mugwort, St. John's wort

Healing: angelica, bay, fennel, garlic, mugwort, thyme, vervain, willow

Love: basil, catnip, elecampane, lady's mantle, poppy, thyme, yarrow

Luck: fern, poppy, rose, strawberry, vetivert

Mental powers: caraway, eyebright, horehound, rosemary, rue

Money: basil, chamomile, fern, marjoram, oat, poppy, vetivert

Peace: dulse, lavender, meadowsweet, pennyroyal, vervain

Protection: agrimony, bay, clover, hyssop, mint, sage, witch hazel

Purification: bay, chamomile, fennel, lavender, parsley, thyme, valerian

Success: balm, clover, ginger, High John the Conqueror

Witchcraft: enchanter's nightshade, oat, vervain, witch hazel, witch grass

Elegant and Eloquent Herbal Combinations

An herbal bookmark is like a bouquet pressed and frozen in time. Sometimes you might choose the spare elegance of a single flower, other times the exuberance of many herbs together. When combining different plants, consider both their appearance and their meanings. You want herbs that look good together, complementing or contrasting each other's color and shape. You also want to send a clear message—that is, when you tuck a bookmark inside a book that you give as a present.

Try these combinations for special occasions, or experiment with your own.

Book of Shadows: Angelica for inspiration, eglantine for poetry, eyebright for mental powers, parsley for useful knowledge, and witch hazel for spellcraft. Add lacy parsley leaves and spidery witch hazel blossoms to create a delicate beauty; find eyebright blooming in white or purple.

Four Aspects Charm: Parsley to know, bay to will, pine to dare, and lavender to keep silent. The greens offset the lavender flowers in this homage to traditional witchcraft.

Get Well Soon: Chamomile for energy in adversity, mint for warm feelings, nasturtium for optimism, and willow for healing. Bright nasturtium flowers give color to this bookmark; make pretty patterns with the willow leaves.

Elemental Charm: Borage to represent air, horehound (earth), St. John's wort (fire), and lady's mantle (water). The round, scalloped leaves of horehound and lady's mantle balance the flowers of borage and St. John's wort.

Initiation: Bay to reward merit, enchanter's nightshade to evoke witchcraft, mistletoe for affection, red rose for luck, and parsley for useful knowledge. The dark green leaves of bay, mistletoe, and parsley form a quiet background for the celebratory fireworks of the rose petals.

Sympathy: Chamomile for energy in adversity, poppy for consolation, vervain for healing, and yarrow as a cure for heartache. Choose leaves for a subtle card, or flowers for a brighter one. Yarrow comes in many colors, while chamomile and poppy both work as leaves or flowers.

Wiccaning/Baby Shower: Dittany of Crete for birth, lavender for happiness and peace, sage for domestic virtue and protection), and sorrel for parental affection. The round leaves of dittany of Crete and the pointed leaves of sorrel make a subtle base for the pretty lavender flowers; you can use sage as leaf or flower.

Pressing and Drying Herbs

When drying herbs to use in bookmarks, keep your format in mind. For simple or appliqué bookmarks, you need to use pressed, dried herbs. For making herbal papers, hanging, screen-drying, or oven-drying will work. It's best to avoid silica flower-drying powders because of the difficulty in later getting all the powder off the plants.

Start by picking your fresh herbs in midmorning—when they are fresh and dry. Choose intact leaves and flowers; avoid any with spots, insect holes, or other flaws. Sometimes you get better results with new shoots, as opposed to mature ones. Also bear in mind that thick, fleshy parts are harder to dry than thin ones. For paper, you can also use the stems.

To press plant parts, first lay them out on sheets of paper. Blotting paper is best, but tissue, newspaper, or paper towels also work well. You may need to separate large leaves into smaller pieces, and you may need to pluck and dry only the petals from bulky flowers. Once you have laid out appropriate plant parts, cover them with another sheet of paper. Press the paper and herbs between weights for one to four weeks, until the plant matter is perfectly dry and flat. Any heavy weight, such as books or bricks, should work. If you do a lot of pressing, you might want to buy a craft press, which uses a clamp to exert pressure on two flat surfaces.

Other methods of drying tend to yield more three-dimensional herbs. You can hang bunches of herbs to dry in a cool, dark place. You can spread them out on screens. You can even put them on a cookie sheet and dry them in an electric oven—on the lowest heat with the door open. Try these when you need large amounts of herbs for making paper, or when you plan to crush the dried plants for colorful flakes.

Simple Bookmarks

Have you ever been reading outside, suddenly needed a bookmark, and just grabbed a nice big leaf to use? I have. Single leaves are probably the oldest form of bookmark. One herb in particular, costmary, has proven so popular in this regard that its nickname is "Bible leaf." Its large oval leaves dry exceptionally well, and it gives off a pleasant and invigorating scent—just the thing for dozing parishioners or college students.

Some other herbs stand out as good candidates for the whole leaf bookmark. Besides costmary, consider: elecampane, foxglove, hops, lady's mantle, mullein, sorrel, and vervain. These all have relatively solid, sturdy leaves that will survive occasional use. Other herbs have more delicate leaves with interesting patterns: clover, fennel, fern, hawthorn, meadowsweet, mugwort, parsley, poppy, rose, St. John's wort, thyme, woodruff, yarrow. These look great enclosed in clear plastic film to protect and show off their intricate shapes.

You can also make bookmarks based on a single flower, or a flower accompanied by a few of its leaves. This is a little more challenging than working with leaves, because blossoms tend to be more fragile. However, flowers also offer more color. For this purpose think about using: foxglove, hollyhock, lavender, nasturtium, poppy, rose, yarrow. Protect with clear film.

Appliqué Bookmarks

Most herbal bookmarks fall into this category. It involves arranging your pressed dried herbs on a sturdy background. This technique offers great flexibility and durability.

Start with the background. You need something stiff enough to provide a little support for the plants, and opaque enough to display them nicely. Thin cardboard or poster board works well and comes in a modest range of colors; this is a good choice if you don't plan to cover your bookmarks with plastic film.

For covered bookmarks, you have a wider range of choices. Heavy paper or light cardstock works beautifully. You can also consider art paper or fancy printer paper, which comes in many colors and fancy designs. If you want to go all out, consider scrapbook paper—it's more expensive, but specially designed for archival purposes and available in every imaginable hue and design. Another spectacular choice is a herbal or other handmade paper. These are both sturdy and beautiful. You can make your own (see "Handmade Paper Bookmarks" below), or buy some in an art, craft, or stationery store.

In general, as you work on this think about contrasts. Keep in mind the color and character of the herbs you plan to use. Choose a light background for dark plants, a dark one for light plants. Large solid leaves or flowers sometimes look good against a patterned paper. Smaller, more detailed plants look better against a plain or subtle background.

Next, decide the size and shape of your bookmarks. They should be long and wide enough to fit your herbs comfortably, but there is no set proportion. Bored with rectangles? Try something different. Relatively simple shapes work best, but you can do a lot with this. Experiment with ovals, long triangles, and broad curves. You can also begin with a rectangle and then trim around your herbal arrangement, leaving a quarter-inch margin of paper around the edges. This gives the bookmark a bit more definition without making it too baroque.

Also, you can dress up the edges of any bookmark by cutting it with craft scissors. Remember your mother's pinking shears that left a zig-zag edge? Today you can find craft scissors that cut dozens of different patterns: zig-zag, scalloped, wavy, deckled, Victorian, and more. Use these on uncovered bookmarks, on background paper before covering the bookmark with clear film, or on covered bookmarks after applying the film. Each creates a different effect.

After you trace or cut out your bookmark base from the background paper, arrange your herbs in an attractive pattern. Because dried plants are very fragile, handle them as little as possible; and use a light touch always. Lay out your choices on a white cloth beside your base, and you'll have an easier time moving the bits around to see how they look in different configurations. This technique works a lot like an appliqué quilt, where you sew fabric shapes onto a background.

When developing your design, place large leaves or flowers first. They define the arrangement and usually look best when centered. You can also offset them toward the top or bottom, or a bit to one side, and balance them with something else at the opposite point. Small leaves and flowers can be used alone or in combination. Try making shapes or borders with these.

Another fun technique is herbal confetti. For this you will want to use a plain background, usually white. Choose dried leaves or flowers in one or more colors. Then crumble them into pieces, as fine as you want. Sprinkle them over the base. The effect mimics herbal paper, with a lot less work and mess. To help make the pieces stick to the base, you can brush the paper with a thin coat of glue, or you can simply press clear film on top of everything.

It is usually best to glue down the herbal arrangement before applying a protective layer. If you feel confident of your pattern, you can start from the bottom. First attach the largest leaves and flowers to the base, then add smaller ones on top. If you tend to change your mind in midprocess, you can start from the top. Finish your whole arrangement, then glue the uppermost herbs to the ones right under them—and so on until you reach the bottom layer. Use a high-quality, acid-free craft glue, and do not overapply it.

Handmade Paper Bookmarks

Shop at the right store and you may find a few herbal papers for sale. Lavender paper, with its rich scent and subtle coloration and texture, is very popular. It makes a lovely background for intricate arrangements. Petal paper has tiny bits of colored petals embedded in it, and potpourri paper has larger bits of petal and leaf clustered thickly together. These work well alone, or as a base for large, simple leaves or blossoms. Flower paper has small pressed flowers added during the final stage of paper-making. It works best when used by itself; you probably don't want to cover up the pretty flowers.

For a more challenging project, consider making your own herbal paper. In addition to the above, you can make papers such as the smooth and refined dandelion paper (pastel in color, with leaves and petals creating flecks of gray, green, and yellow), hop vine paper (fine-textured, with silver-gray speckles), fern paper (lightly textured, with pieces of leaf for an earthy touch), garlic paper (made with the dried skin from garlic bulbs, a smooth and subtle paper), or fiber paper (made with the stems of sunflower, chamomile, fennel, or mullein for a rich, lined texture). You can also experiment with the blends from the "Elegant and Eloquent Herbal Combinations" above.

The basic paper-making process involves mashing plant matter to form a pulp, then dipping a screen into the pulp and letting the coat of wet paper slowly dry into sheets. You can start by making your own pulp from raw herbs, or save steps by recycling other paper such as newsprint or computer paper. Making paper is a messy and rather complicated process, but it offers you complete control over the materials and can yield exquisite results. For more complete instructions, see the resource list at the end of this article.

Herbal papers offer a variety of advantages in bookmark construction. Most are attractive and sturdy enough to use alone without further decoration or protection. This allows their natural beauty, fragrance, and magical energy to come out with no interference. If you want to dress them up just a little, cut the edges with craft scissors and attach a tassel. Smooth papers with subtle patterns also make ideal backgrounds for writing quotations. If you're handy with a pen, you can even write quotations that wind around the blossoms pressed into your flower paper.

Finishing Touches

There are many touches you can add to dress up your herbal bookmarks. Some of these touches are best applied early in the process, others later, and some you can use at varying stages. Craft scissors can work at any phase of the construction. Punches, which cut out decorative shapes, do nicely in the middle phase when you are arranging herbs. But you can also use them as accents after creating a design on an appliqué bookmark, or by themselves to make an herbal paper bookmark more interesting. Corner edgers are a special kind of cutting tool designed to make neat patterns on paper corners—a more subtle touch than cutting out the whole bookmark with craft scissors.

You don't have to restrict yourself to herbs alone in decorating your bookmarks. Glitter makes a beautiful addition to any of the three types. Craft confetti—shaped like leaves, stars, or other symbols—can also work well if you lay down a thin coat of glue and then sprinkle the confetti over it. Also consider stickers, which come in all colors and subjects—but get the acid-free kind intended for scrapbooking. Fairies, Moons and Suns, leaves, garden baskets, cauldrons, and other images mix well with herbs.

Stickers work especially well alongside simple leaves or flowers, or as an embellishment on herbal paper bookmarks.

Bookmarks often have a message printed on them. If you're using background paper light enough to go through your computer printer, then you can print out the text first and cut out your bookmarks around them. For heavier background materials, you can hand-write your message. Choose archival quality pens for best results. Metallic inks are widely available today and look spectacular. You can even make herbal inks—see Lesley Bremness's *The Complete Book of Herbs* for instructions. Because herbs appear in a great deal of classic literature, there are many famous and evocative quotes you can use. Choose one about the plants themselves, or the qualities represented by their symbolism.

Most herbal bookmarks benefit from protection. The easiest and most secure method is to cover them with clear plastic film. If you have access to a laminating machine, this also works nicely. Alternatively, bookmarks made from a single leaf or flower may be sealed by placing them between two sheets of waxed paper and pressing with an iron on low heat. If there's not enough wax on the paper to get a good seal, shave crayons or colored candle wax over the bottom sheet and the plant before adding the top sheet. Art stores also sell a variety of spray-on or brush-on fixatives. These work best for herbal papers when you want some protection that will not obscure the paper's natural appeal.

Toppers make a bookmark easier to find and grasp. Tassels are the most common form of topper, but some bookmarks have a ribbon instead. You can find tassels and ribbons in any craft or fabric store. Look in the scrapbooking or embroidery aisle, and you may find some especially intended for bookmarks. Small upholstery or ornament tassels work just as well, and any narrow ribbon will do.

To attach a topper, first punch a hole at the top of the bookmark. For tassels, thread the tassel's loop through the hole, then spread the loop and pass the body of the tassel through it. Pull tight and you're done. For ribbons, pass one end of the ribbon through the hole, pull until the ends are even, and then tie a knot near the bookmark to keep the ribbon from sliding out.

One current fashion is putting beads on bookmark toppers. To do this, choose an attractive bead with a large enough hole for the ribbon or thread of your tassel to pass through. Beads shaped like leaves, roses, or other flowers look great for this. For tassels, thread the tassel's loop through the bead, then slide the bead all the way down to the head of the tassel. Proceed as above for attaching the tassel to the bookmark; use your fingers to keep the bead pressed against the tassel head so it doesn't get in your way while you work. For ribbons, first attach the ribbon to the bookmark as described above. Then thread one or more beads onto each end of the ribbon. Knot the ribbon's ends to keep the beads from slipping off.

Happy Bookmarking

Herbal bookmarks are both beautiful and practical. They offer a nice way to enhance the energy of your magical and spiritual books. As magical tools, they are perfectly discreet.

If you are looking for child-suitable activities, making bookmarks is a fun way to spend an afternoon together. These pretty crafts also make excellent gifts.

However you make them, whatever you do with them, herbal bookmarks preserve a bit of nature's bounty for future enjoyment. Use your imagination—the possibilities are as infinite as the diversity of herbs themselves.

For Further Study

Bremness, Lesley. *The Complete Book of Herbs: A Practical Guide to Growing and Using Herbs.* New York: Viking Studio Books, 1988.

Includes brief notes on flower language (pp. 154–5), plus detailed instructions for making herbal papers and inks (pp. 200–02).

Cunningham, Scott. *Cunningham's Encyclopedia of Magical Herbs by Scott Cunningham*. St. Paul, Minn.: Llewellyn Publications, 1991.

An excellent guide to magical correspondences and properties of herbs.

Holt, Geraldene. *Geraldene Holt's Complete Book of Herbs*. New York: Henry Holt and Company, Inc., 1991.

See chapter on "Herbs for Decoration" for brief guide to flower language.

Kowalchik, Claire, and William H. Hylton. *Rodale's Illustrated Encyclopedia of Herbs*. Emmaus, Pa.: Rodale Press, 1987.

A comprehensive guide to herbs with chapters on crafts, history, and other topics. See pages 132–133 for herb and flower language information.

Websites

Carlin's Florist & Gifts website: http://www.carlinflorist.com/-flowerlanguage.htm. Includes an extensive guide to the meanings of flowers and some herbs.

Flower Symbolism website (by Weddingbokay): http://www.weddingbokay.com/symbol.html. This is a medium-sized guide to flowers, with plenty of herbs included. It lists each plant by name.

Handmade Paper website (by Karen Mendelow): http://www.exploratorium.edu/exploring/paper/handmade.html. This site lists detailed instructions on making paper, including tools and herbal enhancements.

The Language of Flowers website (by Katherine Bryant): http://www.cybercom.net/~klb/flwrmeanings.html. Use this resource to find flowers with a desired meaning (as the list is arranged in order by meaning); also includes some herbs.

The Mystical World Wide Web website: http://www.mystical-www.co.uk/plants.htm. Includes a brief guide to meanings of herbs by name; the website has other resources and information on flowers in general.

Scrapbooking-Online website: http://www.scrapbooking-online.com. A shopping site that carries a wide array of papers, punches, stickers, craft scissors, corner edgers, and other supplies.

Tear It Up Papermaking Supplies website (by Anne Heinrichs): http://www.papermaking.net/stpbystp.htm. This site includes comprehensive instructions for making paper, with attention paid to using herbs and flowers. The site also offers tools and supplies for sale.

The Ancient American Art of Incense

⚜ by Stephanie Rose Bird ⚜

As the seasons change, now is the perfect time to find meaningful ways to connect our bodies, minds, and spirits with the Earth. This article provides recipes that encourage an understanding of Native American plant lore in relation to seasonal celebrations, ritual, and invocation.

Smudging

One of the most familiar Native incense-burning practices is smudging. A smudge stick is a dried medicine bundle that is lit and waved like a magical fragrance-wand to clear spaces and bring healing energy to humans and animals. Sage (*Salvia officinalis*) is the most highly touted and popular smudging substance, but American sage (*Salvia divinorum*) is a slow growing plant indigenous to a very small

area of the southwestern United States. American sage, however, is rapidly becoming an endangered species as a result of its ever-increasing popularity as a smudging herb. Therefore I cannot endorse its use despite its traditional importance in Native American incense rituals.

My favorite alternatives to sage as smudging herbs are mugwort *(Artemisia vulgaris)*, lavender *(Lavandula officinalis)*, and juniper *(Juniperus communis)*. Each of the three herbs are traditional Native American healing herbs, much as American sage. Create the smudge stick below to use during your spring cleansing activities. Each herb has well-known medicinal and magical qualities.

Spring Clearing Smudging Ritual

Gather mugwort, juniper branches, and lavender in the morning, after the dew has evaporated. Cut each to between twelve and eighteen inches. Bundle the herbs, and tie up with hemp string or raffia. Bring the bundle inside, and hang it upside down away from direct sunlight. Dry for several days—not fully; the bundle should still be pliable—then lay the bundle on a natural fiber cloth. Untie the bundle, then roll and fold it until you have a neat six- to eight-inch long bunch. Bundle using natural hemp string or natural cotton string.

To use your smudge stick, simply light it. Carry the smoking wand in your dominant hand, and pass through your home, allowing the smoke to penetrate areas that need cleansing or where unfortunate occurrences have taken place. You may use a feather to spread the smoke. Traditionalists follow the four directions, as indicated by the medicine wheel, as they travel. Use the same approach when you wish to purify a sick or unhealthy person.

Afterward, you may choose to dampen your smudge stick with salt water or sea water and hang it up to dry. Or you may simply tamp the burning part of your smudge stick on a nonflammable surface (a stone or seashell, for example) to put out the smoldering fire.

This ritual is enhanced by the power of the Moon. In particular, you may choose to gather your herbs, or perform your actual cleansing ritual, during the waning Moon—as this will allow you to take in the power of the orb's spiritual cleansing and habit-purging energies.

Seminole New Year Incense and Summer Ritual

At the beginning of July, the Seminole people of Florida and southeastern United States celebrate their New Year by evoking Corn Mother. Corn Mother is a divine spirit and goddess who ensures continuity, growth, prosperity, health, and strength among her people. She is associated with children, birth, and an energy of growth and expansion. The following loose incense blend is an appropriate accompaniment to Seminole New Year celebrations, as it features herbs of bountiful harvest and good fortune.

Incense Recipe

- 2 Tbls. each: orange peel, calendula flowers, sunflower petals, and finely ground copal
- ⅛ tsp. each sweet orange oil, amber, and lavender essential oils
- ¼ tsp. of charged jade or green jasper chips

The Florida orange represents the bounty of a rich harvest and good medicine; calendula and sunflower petals are emblematic of the warming rays of the Sun. Copal is connected by the Aztec and Mayan people with maize. The two—maize and copal—are sacred herbs used in high rituals. Copal comes from several sources. It is the resin from *Bursera bininnata*, extracted by making incisions in the bark. This procedure produces tear-like resin droplets that the Mayan people call the "Tears of the Moon Goddess."

Copal is also extracted from some species of the *Pinus* genus of trees. And in certain areas of Mexico, Guatemala, and Belize *Elaphruim bipinnatieum* is used instead to produce copal. To make matters slightly more confusing, copal is also sometimes called *pom*, and it comes in varieties that may be either crystal clear or black in color.

However, you can tell that you have true copal by the heavy, sweet, lingering scent and dense smoke produced when you burn it. Copal is a revered offering to the gods, and as such is appropriately appealing to the senses. Corn, at the same time, is a gift to the goddess of abundance, Corn Mother.

To make the Seminole New Year incense, grind the herbs and resin together, and place them in a nonreactive bowl. Drop the essential oils in with care—one drop at a time. Mix in the stone chips, and let the mixture rest for a moment before storing it.

Store the incense in a tightly sealed container for two weeks. To use, spread blue, white, or yellow corn meal on the bottom of a censor or small cauldron. Place a piece of charcoal and several pieces of mesquite wood inside, and light. Once the wood is white-hot, sprinkle a pinch of the incense on top.

Use the incense to bless a couple, or to bless the area used in a wedding ritual. This incense is also useful for rituals such as house blessings, prayers for safe passage of a child, or any other new beginnings.

Combining the two deity herbs of copal and maize with calendula, sunflower, and orange will produce a sacred incense that is intensely fragrant and uplifting. Charging the copal by using it in conjunction with chips of jade or green jasper, a combination used traditionally by the ancient Maya to inspire prosperity and luck, will produce a superior healing incense useful for wedding or birth blessings, ancestor celebrations, or other significant rites of passage.

Autumn Kinnikinnik

Apart from the smudge stick, the peace pipe is another Native American ritualistic practice that many people have at least a cursory understanding of. Smoke is perceived to be a phenomena that makes spirits feel comfortable.

Most often, smoke is used to create an inviting atmosphere to attract positive helpful spirits. These spirits are invoked to facilitate smooth communications between visitors or even strangers, and to share their heavenly blessings with humans. The Algonquin people are renowned for creating complex smoking blends that are fragrant, healing, and, above all else, spiritually charged. The following blend is inspired by the Algonquin people's *kinnikinnik*, an ancient word for their healing smoking blends.

Kinnikinnik blends often contain the pure herbal tobacco or other smoking ingredients, but they are not always smoked. Sometimes they are added to medicine bundles to bring good health and to get rid of bad vibes, or they are burnt on their own to please the ancestors.

To create your own healing-giving kinnikinnik, gather the finest ingredients you can find.

Kinnikinnik Recipe

1 cup evergreen needles; use what is available, including: juniper, cedar, spruce, pine

Handful crushed juniper berries

Handful dried willow, oak, or birch branches, shredded dried leaves and bark

1 cup herbal blend: dried sage, rosemary, bearberry leaves *(uva ursi)*, lavender buds

½ cup pure smoking tobacco

¼ tsp. each of juniper, bergamot, and white pine needle essential oils

Break the evergreen needles into half inch or so pieces, and mix in the crushed juniper berries. Add the tree branches, broken into one-inch (or so) pieces, along with the leaves and the bark, followed by the herbal blend and the tobacco. Stir this mixture well and allow to rest while you take a breath. At last sprinkle on the essential oils, and blend the mixture with great care. Try not to spill any or upset the mixture in any way.

Once your mixture is fully blended, put it in a sterile glass or stainless-steel container with a tight-fitting lid, and store it out of direct sunlight in a cool place. Shake the mixture daily for four to six weeks while focusing on your intentions for the blend. This recipe makes twenty ounces of kinnikinnik, useful for rituals and simply for a dose of healing energy (try pulling it out just to smell it on occasion). It should keep for up to a year if it is kept sealed in a cool place.

Kinnikinnik Offering

Place a charcoal block inside a chimena (a type of gourd-shaped ceramic oven), or on top of your favorite flat rock or fossil. Light the charcoal, and allow it to heat thoroughly. Take out a pinch or two of the kinnikinnik, and put it on the charcoal. For this you can also choose to use your incense burner—whatever you feel comfortable with.

Now, close your eyes, and smell the aroma. Think back, and remember your ancestors with a special song, memory, or chant—whatever you tend to use before beginning any ceremonial healing work. This ritual is a special way to honor and remember your loved ones on their birthday or an anniversary. Simply call them to mind as your kinnikinnik burns, and its purifying scent fills your space.

You can also make a small medicine bundle of kinnikinnik to carry on your person or in your purse or handbag. This will attract good health and deter negative spirits. Simply wrap one-half cup of the matured kinnikinnik blend in muslin, and secure it with a ribbon. On occasion during the day, simply take out the bundle and get a nostril-full of its pleasantly pungent and indescribably purifying scent.

Winter Blessing Sweet Grass Braid

A new healing tool for spiritual cleansing is sweet grass *(Hierochloe odorata)*. Sweet grass is another fragrant herb that is beloved by various First Nation peoples such as the Lakota. The Lakota connect this vanilla-scented rush with the compassionate creation goddess Wohpe.

Wohpe is a stunningly beautiful, well-balanced, and very spiritual goddess associated with the seventh direction. She generally is thought to appear at the moment that a puff of smoke clears. Fittingly then, she is associated with sweet grass, a herb that creates a quietly seductive incense that helps us understand the mysterious seventh direction.

While many Western holiday observances are firmly anchored in the particular seasonal moment of each particular celebration, often Native American rituals project forward to the next season. The projection forward from the winter, for instance, creates a holiday that is an invitation for a fertile, vibrant spring with abundant rains to ensure a safe harvest. If you are interested in creating your own winter ritual that looks to the coming of a spring renewal, start by obtaining a braid of sweet grass at the height of the winter season—such as on the Winter Solstice, or at the New Year.

Stroke the grass gently, and whisper your wishes for the oncoming spring. Treat the sweet grass as though it is the actual braid of the beautiful Lakotan wisdom goddess Wohpe. As you light the braid in the darkness of winter, implore Wohpe to open the way for you and your family to have an enlightened and abundant spring.

Tamp out the flame and travel through your home spreading her delightful vanilla scent and whispered wisdom along the way.

Further Native Scents

So there you have it: sowing seeds, harvesting herbs, grinding flowers, burning resins over hot mesquite and charcoal, burying the remaining ash of your Native American–inspired incense blends in your garden—all of these activities will bring you ever further into the sacred hoop.

Indigenous people have understood for several millennia that the sacred hoop of continuity and the circular life cycles inspire a spiritually rich life. It is time that the rest of us catch on.

Magical Herbal Brooms

≈ by Raven Kaldera & Tannin Schwartzstein ≈

For centuries, traces of ancient Pagan religions could be found in ordinary household customs. And such customs helped give rise to the enduring tradition of kitchen witchery.

The broom, that most ubiquitous of old-fashioned household implements, became a common symbol of witchcraft over the last few centuries. Brooms have been used magically for all kinds of purposes, and they can be made by anyone with access to woods and an herb garden.

Reasons to Make a Broom

There are many different modern reasons why one would build a magical broom. One, of course, is for weddings—many Pagan weddings use the symbolism of jumping over a broom, so it has become common to create something unique and magical by hand for the ceremony. Another sort of broom can be a protective fetish that creates good fortune for the household. Still another can be an actual practical floor-sweeper, used for house purification rituals. You can also make a broom to honor your ancestors who worked the land, and possibly to honor those foremothers and forefathers who were wrongly accused of witchcraft and executed for it.

Ancestor brooms honor the peasants who eked out a living in the dirt so that we might survive. They are generally hung in the kitchen, or the heart of the home, and the brush can be made of traditional Witch's herbs such as mugwort, wormwood (both sacred to the Moon goddess), yarrow, vervain, mullein, or elder twigs. They are especially appropriate for a Samhain altar.

Broom Plants

The traditional plant for broom brushes is the broom plant, *Cytisus scoparius*. Broom plants are easy to grow in the back of the herb garden. They can grow as tall as five feet, so give them lots of space. The American equivalent is broomcorn, which looks like a tall maize plant with a seeded brush instead of ears. This can be grown pretty much like food corn, although do not grow broomcorn together with food corn, as they may end up cross-pollinating.

Either broom brush or broomcorn are traditional for protective brooms. For the brush of your broom, you can also use twigs of the trees that provided the stick-handle.

Making the Broom

The simplest brooms consist of two parts: a stick-handle and bundles of plant matter as a brush. The wood of the handle should be of a sort that corresponds to the purpose of the broom. For instance, wedding broomsticks should be made from fruit-wood, such as apple, pear, or cherry; from "love" woods, such as maple or hawthorn; from flowering woods, such as lilac or crape myrtle; or from birch, which symbolizes beginnings.

Protective broomsticks, meanwhile, are made from woods such as oak, ash, or hickory. Broomsticks for purification are best made of oak and pine. Brooms for honoring ancestors should have sticks of elder, aspen, cypress, or sycamore.

Broom-brushes can be made of grasses, twigs, or fresh or dried herbs—all depending on their eventual purpose. For brooms that are actually going to be used for sweeping, leafy stuff is a hindrance, and so all leaves should be stripped off. For magical brooms that will be hung over doorways or used ceremonially to brush negativity out of someone's aura, it is preferred that you make the brush of herbs. You can wrap the brush while the plants are still green or after they are dried.

To wrap the brush onto your broom-handle, make sure that the plant matter has long stems, and divide this material into an odd number of bundles. Using string, rough twine, or cord (which can be in a color appropriate to the occasion), tie the bundles evenly to one end of the stick, just enough to hold them in place. Then wind the string over one bundle and under the next, and so on around the broom. With an odd number of bundles, the lashes should alternate in a spiral several times around, until you reach the end of the stick, at which time you tie it off.

Wedding brooms are ceremonial, and don't need to be sturdy enough to sweep floors with, unless they are to be used in a purification spell for the couple's new home. Here, the brush is often made of wheat, or of sheaves of some other grain—in order to evoke fertility of body and spirit. Another nice option is to let the couple gather long grasses from some place that has special meaning to them, and use those for the brush.

Some good love herbs to add into wedding brooms include: lemon balm, lemon verbena, agastache, cilantro, summer or winter savory, heliotrope, lavender, or rosemary. Use large sprigs of these herbs, incorporating them carefully into the brush.

In practice, the wedding broom is usually held up by two volunteers so that the couple can jump over it. It can also be placed along the doorstep during the ceremony.

Afterward, the broom is usually hung on the wall, as a spell for marital harmony. It can also be used as a ceremonial purification broom before the wedding ceremony, bringing the energy of love and banishing any evil spirits. If there are children at the wedding, here is a good job for them—have them rush about with the magical broom making loud noises and shouting loudly, "Away, evil spirits! Away!" Make sure an adult is supervising them so they don't knock things off shelves or end up in areas that are off-limits to them.

Some protective herbs to add to a "door broom" are tarragon, vervain, agrimony, hyssop, and thistle. If you don't intend to handle it very much, the brush can be made of thorny plants such as raspberry brambles; this is especially good for hanging over doorways as a spell to keep intruders out.

Herbal brooms with the leaves still attached can be used to sweep a floor. They will strew fragrant bits around, rather like the medieval custom of strewing sweet herbs in the floor rushes for ambient perfume (see page 233 for more information about this custom).

A broom that is actually going to sweep the floor and make it clean has to be made differently than simple ritual broom. You can make a traditional-style floor broom, but it had better have strong twigs that will not continually break off and make more of a mess than it cleans up. If you use broom plant or broomcorn, strip out all the seeds first. The fuller the broom brush, the better it will work. Another sort of handmade broom is made with wood and cornhusks. First find your broomstick—which should be a straight, smooth pole rather than a bumpy sapling—and cut a twelve by four-inch piece of wood to a length of eighteen inches. Drill two-inch wide holes in two or three rows down the length of this board, and then make bundles of green cornhusks. Fold them in half around a loop of cord and pull each bundle through a hole; its folded top should just protrude.

Tie all the cords together on top, drill a hole through it at a slant, and glue in the handle. This will make a floor broom suitable for sweeping. You can also use bundles of green twigs or stems; willow works well and is associated with the Moon and with women's mysteries. With this broom, it's better to insert the plant material while green and let it dry in place. Thicker twigs are better than thinner ones that will become brittle. When a bundle wears out, it can be untied and replaced. This cornhusk broom sounds too fragile to use, but mine lasted for more than two years with no problems.

Ceremonial purification brooms are used by shaking them at the walls, floor, windows, doors, and so on. It is actually good if this sort of broom is noisy and rattles or rustles loudly. Encourage this by leaving the tails of your plant material for the brush extra long. Your purification should begin with a thorough space-cleansing—as it is likely this broom will be too fragile to do any real cleaning. It helps to visualize the space in your mind while you're cleaning it. Afterward, go around the room with the purification broom, swiping in the same direction that you cleaned. Aim the broom up and down corners, around the ceiling and the floor. Circle windows and doors. Pick a window or door to sweep the energy out. You can also sweep around someone's aura as a preritual cleansing.

You can grind dried herbs to a powder with mortar and pestle (or a coffee grinder if you're a bit lazy) for a purification dust. Sprinkle it around on the floor, and then sweep it out the door with your ceremonial broom. Some people use a filler to bind and stretch the mixture; sawdust is good, but don't use flour as it sticks to everything. This is a good use too for used herbal teabags; empty the contents onto a tray and leave them in the Sun to dry. It's also a good use for old bunches of herbs that you want to get rid of as you turn over your yearly supply. Herbs that are easily powdered include: flower petals, basil, tarragon, and parsley. Dried commercial kitchen herbs are acceptable for this purpose as well.

Of course, none of these brooms will stand up to getting wet. For that, you want a more conventional broom or mop. Herbal floor washes can be made from strong tea or essential oil dissolved in water. (For the latter type, measure a tablespoon of oil per gallon of water, and make sure that you shake it up well or it will separate.)

You may want to take some time to experiment first, because some essential oils are gooey and won't mix at all. Teas are cheaper and easier, especially if you have an herb garden. Some suggestions for this include using mint tea for money, chamomile tea for peace and quiet, rosewater for love, or cinnamon-nutmeg-clove tea for prosperity. Good protection washes can utilize vetiver oil, bay leaf tea, or tarragon tea.

If you're in a first-floor room with a noncarpeted floor and a door to the outside, you can finish your floor-washing the old-fashioned way. Sweep all the suds and dirt out the door. While you're doing it, imagine the psychic "dirt" in the house being swept outside. This ritual works the same way with a dry floor and a magical broom.

Medieval and Renaissance Strewing Herbs

≈ by Lynne Smythe ≈

Renaissance home owners used strewing herbs liberally throughout Europe in the late medieval to early Renaissance periods—between AD 1000 and 1650. Rushes or straw were often used to cover the floors of houses before carpets were commonly used as a floor covering. The herbs were used because the rushes ended up being a depository for spilled food, drink, and domestic animal droppings. In short, these floor coverings served as breeding grounds for all sorts of fleas, lice, other nasty vermin, and general filth and disease.

By strewing herbs around, then, on the top of, or in place of, the rushes or straw, home-dwellers could affect their own health. Herbs exhibited aromatic and insect-repelling properties that were crucial to the times.

What Are Rushes?

Rushes encompass a variety of plant species that are found in abundance in wet areas such as stream and river banks, swamps, and marshes. Sweet flag *(Acorus calamus)* is another very aromatic plant with iris-like leaves that grows abundantly in wetland conditions. It was often used as a strewing material on floors in houses and other buildings. Common rush *(Juncus conglomeratus)* and common bulrush *(Scripus lacustris)* were also commonly used for floor coverings.

As people went about their daily activities, they crushed the rushes underfoot, causing their aromatic fragrance to be released into the air. The rushes not only helped soften the tread, but they freshened the air and provided protection against cold.

During the later medieval through Renaissance periods, rushes were replaced in European churches once a year on what was called rush-bearing Sunday. On this day, the old layer of rushes would be cleaned out and a new layer added to help keep the feet of churchgoers warm and dry. Aromatic herbs such as meadowsweet would sometimes be strewn along with the rushes.

The History of Strewing Herbs

Because of improper personal hygiene and sanitation habits, pest and odor control in the past could be an intense problem. Public bath houses were in common usage during the early Middle Ages, but they went out of favor in the later part of the era. This was due to the belief that bathing promoted the spread of diseases such as the plague. Officials began to close down the public baths at the end of the fourteenth century, and the poor peasants who made up the majority of the population no longer had the luxury of public bath houses at their disposal.

As peasants often had to haul their own water from the nearest well, stream, or pond, and then had to heat the water before bathing, it is no surprise that in those days baths were not an everyday occurrence. The wealthy nobles and royalty would have servants to perform these chores for them in the privacy of their own homes, but overall a bath was not a very frequent event for the majority of the population.

Though nobility and royalty would more often have floors of stone, plaster, or wood, the floors of peasant houses were usually made of beaten earth. Carpets were an expensive luxury item only available to nobility and royalty, and even then they were more often hung on walls or draped on tables as a status symbol rather than used as a floor covering. English monarchs such as Queen Elizabeth I and King James II employed royal herb strewers who strewed about a variety of aromatic herbs during various royal processions. Unfortunately, not everyone at the time could afford such luxuries.

Along with the straw or rushes, a variety of aromatic and insect-repelling herbs were often thrown on the floor. These herbs were called strewing herbs, and as these herbs were crushed underfoot, their volatile essential oils were released. The aromatic essential oils present in the herbs would evaporate rapidly, and the herbs would rot or dry out in a very short time— so the strewing materials would have to be replaced periodically.

Strewing herbs served two main purposes. The aromatic herbs helped to disguise the build up of potent odors—from food, unwashed bodies, accumulated garbage, food scraps, animal droppings, and so on, and they also served as a form of vermin and pest control. Many of the herbs acted as flea, lice, mice, weevil, and moth repellents. Some of these strewing herbs even exhibited strong antiseptic and/or antibacterial properties.

Strewing herbs were most likely introduced into England via the Romans during the early medieval period. The Romans used a variety of herbs for their aromatic and insect repelling properties. They covered entire floors with sweet smelling rose petals and the flowers of the saffron crocus *(Crocus sativus)*. Strewing herbs would be used in all areas of the household, including the dinning hall, kitchen, and bedrooms. Strewing herbs would also be used for the same purposes in public buildings such as churches, infirmaries, and courthouses.

From time to time the rushes, straw, and strewing herbs would be swept clean from the floors. New material would be added to begin the cycle all over again. Old strewing materials cleaned from kitchen floors and other areas would commonly be used to start the next day's cooking fires.

Strewing Herbs and the Plague

A major outbreak of the bubonic plague (also known as the "black death") occurred in Europe between 1346 and 1351. Plague outbreaks recurred throughout the next several hundred years in Europe. It was spread to people via black rats that were the hosts to infection-causing fleas. The disease actually came from an invisible microbe that infected the fleas. When their black rat hosts began to die off, the fleas would bite humans and domestic animals instead, and spread the microbe.

The cause of the plague was unknown during the medieval and Renaissance periods. Unlike the modern-day brown rat, which prefers to live in the sewers away from close human contact, the black rat of the medieval and Renaissance periods was more visible. It often lived in close proximity to humans in order to access the abundant of food that could be found in kitchens, dining halls, stables, and other common areas. Houses that used strewing herbs, and especially insect-repelling herbs such as pennyroyal (*Hedeoma pulegioides*, also known as fleabane), may have had an advantage in resisting outbreaks of the plague.

Rue (*Ruta graveolens*) was another herb believed to help prevent the plague. It was strewn on the benches and floors of courtrooms. Judges carried branches of rue to help guard themselves against jail fever (also known as European typhus), which was transmitted by fleas and lice.

Southernwood (*Artemisia abrotanum*) was used by the medieval crusaders, as it too was thought to ward off the black death. Southernwood was also commonly used as protection against jail fever. The lemon-scented leaves of southernwood have since been proven to have insect-repelling properties.

Fleawort *(Plantago psyllium)* was thought to ward off fleas and was used as a strewing herb for this purpose. The seeds, which are black when dried, resembled fleas—and this may have been why the herb was thought to be an effective flea repellent. Modern herbalists have not shown this herb to exhibit any insect-repelling properties.

Tansy *(Tanacetum vulgare)* mixed with elder leaves *(Sambucus candensis)* was also thought to be a very effective flea repellent. In modern times, the black elder *(Sambucus nigra)* has been shown to have strong antibacterial, antiseptic, antiviral, and insecticidal properties.

Some Specific Medieval and Renaissance Strewing Herbs

Thomas Tusser, in his 1557 book *A Hundreth Good Points of Husbandrie*, lists twenty-one plants that could be used as strewing herbs. His original spelling has been maintained for historical interest:

1. Bassell
2. Bawlme
3. Camamel
4. Costemary
5. Cowsleps and paggles
6. Daisies of all sorts
7. Sweet fennell
8. Germander
9. Hop
10. Lavender

11. Lavender spike

12. Lavender cotton

13. Marjoram

14. Mawdelin

15. Peny ryall

16. Roses of all sorts

17. Red myntes

18. Sage

19. Tansey

20. Violets

21. Winter savery

Modern-Day Strewing Herbs

To expand on Tusser's list, here is a more modern list of some herbs that could be used for strewing purposes. The common name is followed by the Latin name in parenthesis. The major strewing herb properties of each plant are also listed.

Anise *(Pimpinella anisum)*: Aromatic

Anise hyssop *(Agastache foeniculum)*: Aromatic, moth-repellent

Basil *(Ocimun spp.)*: Insect-repellent

Bay *(Laurus nobilis)*: Antiseptic, insect-repellent

Catnip *(Nepeta cataria)*: Insect-repellent

Cedar *(Cedrus spp.)*: Antiseptic, aromatic, moth- and flea-repellent

Costmary *(Tanacetum balsamita)*: Aromatic, insect-repellent

Cowslip *(Primula veris)*: Aromatic

Eucalyptus *(Eucalyptus* spp.): Antibacterial, antiseptic, aromatic

Feverfew *(Tanacetum parthenium):* Aromatic, disinfectant, insect-repellent

Germander *(Teucrium chamaedrys):* Antiseptic

Hops *(Humulus lupulus):* Antibacterial, antiseptic

Hyssop *(Hyssopus officinalis):* Insect-repellent, aromatic, cleansing, antiseptic

Juniper *(Juniperus communis):* Antiseptic, aromatic

Lavender *(Lavandula* spp.): Aromatic, antibacterial, antiseptic, moth- and fly-repellent

Lavender cotton *(Santolina chamaecyparissus):* Aromatic

Lemon balm *(Melissa officinalis):* Aromatic, antibacterial, antiviral, insect-repellent

Marjoram *(Origanum majorana):* Aromatic, disinfecting

Meadowsweet *(Filipendula ulmaria):* Aromatic (meadowsweet was a favorite herb of Queen Elizabeth I)

Mint *(Mentha* spp.): Antibacterial, antiseptic, insect-repellent; note of interest: horsemint *(Mentha longifolia)* has a stronger scent than either peppermint *(Mentha piperita)* or spearmint *(Mentha spicata)*

Mugwort *(Artemisia vulgaris):* Aromatic, moth-repellent

Oregano *(Origanum vulgare):* Aromatic, ant- and rodent-repellent

Pennyroyal *(Mentha pulegium):* Insect-repellent

Roman chamomile *(Chamaemelum nobile):* Aromatic, insect-repellent

Rose *(Rosa* spp.): Antibacterial, antiviral, aromatic

Rosemary (*Rosmarinus officinalis*): Antibacterial, antiseptic, aromatic, moth- and insect-repellent

Rue (*Ruta graveolens*): Aromatic, insect-repellent

Sage (*Salvia officinalis*): Antiseptic, antiviral, aromatic, insect- and rodent-repellent

Southernwood (*Artemisia abrotanum*): Antiseptic, aromatic, moth- and ant-repellent

Sweet cicely (*Myrrhis odorata*): Antiseptic, aromatic

Sweet fennel (*Foeniculum vulgare*): Aromatic, insect-repellent

Sweet myrtle (*Myrtus communis*): Antiseptic, aromatic

Sweet violet (*Viola odorata*): Antiseptic, aromatic

Sweet woodruff (*Galium odoratum*): Aromatic, insect-repellent

Tansy (*Tanacetum vulgare*): Disinfectant, insect-repellent

Thyme (*Thymus vulgaris*): Antiseptic, aromatic, disinfectant, insect-repellent

Winter savory (*Satureja montana*): Antiseptic

Wormwood (*Artemisia absinthium*): Insect-repellent

Strewing Herbs Today

Here are some tips to help you make use of the ancient practice of herb-strewing in your present-day life.

1. When entertaining outdoors, strew fresh herbs around your decks and patios. Herbs with insect-repelling properties—such as tansy and pennyroyal—work especially well outdoors.

2. Hang dried bundles of herbs such as lavender, cedar, and southernwood in your closets and cupboards. The herb bundles will help repel moths and impart a pleasant fragrance to your clothing.

3. The practice of strewing rushes and straw onto bare floors was eventually phased out by the late seventeenth century as carpets and rugs became more affordable and readily available. Wool carpets were used on the floors during the winter months, and mats made out of straw were used during the summer. A layer of aromatic strewing herbs would often be used underneath the carpets and mats. You can emulate this practice by placing dried herbs in muslin bags under area rugs throughout your home. You could also place these bags of herbs under mattresses and cushions.

4. A romantic use of these herbs is to strew aromatic flowers such as roses and lavender on your bed linens. You could also use sweet woodruff (also known as lady's bedstraw) on top of your pillows and comforters. Dried lady's bedstraw has the scent of new-mown hay and was often used as a mattress filler during the Middle Ages. A less messy method would be to make sachet bags to contain the herbs, and then place the bags in your bed linens.

5. A historical herb-strewing that is still seen today are flower girls at weddings. We have all seen little girls tossing rosemary and roses in front of the oncoming bride.

6. Grow a garden that features strewing herbs to add a historical medieval or Renaissance flare to your yard.

Strewing Herb Garden Designs

Here are two designs that can be used by gardeners interested in growing their own strewing herbs. Raised planting beds were commonly used in both medieval and Renaissance garden designs. The beds can be edged with materials such as landscape timbers or bricks. The spaces between each type of plant can be delineated with bricks, polished river stones, marble chips, or lines of mulch, depending upon your preference.

Either garden design can be filled with plants purchased from your local nursery center or from a reputable garden catalog. The more ambitious gardener may want to start these herbs from seeds.

All the plants listed are perennials unless otherwise noted. The USDA plant hardiness is listed for each plant. To find out what zone you live in visit the USDA website at www.usna. usda.gov/Hardzone. (More information on USDA zones can be found in pages 10 and 11 of this edition of the *Herbal Almanac.*) If you are interested in growing a plant that is not hardy in your zone, you can still plant it in your garden. Treat these less hardy plants as an annual either by starting new plants from seed or planting new plants every year.

A Culinary Strewing Herb Garden

All the the plants featured in this garden can serve double duty—both as strewing herbs and as culinary herbs. This is a garden that should be planted in an area that receives full Sun.

The bay and myrtle in this garden can be clipped into topiaries if you so choose. Topiary shrubs were a common medieval garden design feature.

1. **Bay *(Laurus nobilis):*** Grow in a container that can be moved indoors during the winter. If you live in Zone 8 or higher, the bay may be left outdoors year round.

2. **Plant seat:** Use landscape timbers, bricks, or interlocking blocks to build a raised planting bed tall enough to sit on. Fill the center of the bed with potting soil (a combination of composted cow manure, peat moss, and perlite works well), then plant the bed with varieties of thyme—which are hearty enough for you to sit on. When you sit on the seat, the plants will release their essential oils onto your clothing. This is portable pest control that smells great. Plant zone hardiness varies according to the specific type of thyme used.

3. **Myrtle** *(Myrtus communis):* Grow in a container that can be brought indoors during the winter months. If you live in Zone 9 or higher, you may plant myrtle to form the dividing lines between each type of herb. Periodically prune the myrtle to keep it from growing out of control and taking over the other herbs.

4. **Place a sundial** on top of a pedestal in the center of the main planting bed. Sundials were a common feature of Renaissance gardens. The main planting should measure eight-feet square, or as close to this as fits your space.

5. **Plantings:** Include the following herbs in your garden— fennel *(Foeniculum vulgare;* hardy to Zone 6); rosemary *(Rosemarinus officinalis;* hardy to Zone 8); sweet cicely *(Osmorhiza longistylis;* hardy to Zone 3); lemon balm *(Melissa officinalis;* hardy to Zone 4); sage *(Salvia officinalis;* hardiness varies according to variety); winter savory *(Satureja montana;* hardy to Zone 6); oregano *(Origanum vulgare;* hardy to Zone 5); marjoram *(Marjorana hortensis;* hardy to Zone 9); spearmint *(Mentha spicata;* hardy to Zone 5).

A Bouquet Strewing Herb Garden

All the the plants featured in this garden can serve double duty as strewing herbs and in a variety of floral arrangements. This garden can be grown in either a full Sun or partial shade location.

This garden is intended for a sixteen square-foot plot, or as close to that size as you can fit. Place paths between the beds to allow ample room to walk around and visit with your plants.

1. **A fountain** is a nice focal point for the center of your garden. Such fountains were a common during the Renaissance.

2. **Sweet flag** *(Acorus calamus):* Likes moist growing conditions, so plant it around the base of a fountain. This plant is grown for its decorative and aromatic foliage; its flowers are not terribly interesting. Hardy to Zone 3.

3. **Meadowsweet *(Filipendula ulmaria)*:** This plant has clusters of small creamy-white flowers and is hardy to Zone 4.

4. **Dog rose *(Rosa canina)*:** Single white or pink flowers. Hardy to Zone 3.

5. **Rue *(Ruta graveolens)*:** Has ornamental blue-gray foliage that complements many floral arrangements and yellow-green flowers. Hardy to Zone 4.

6. **Lady's mantle *(Alchemilla mollis)*:** tiny yellow-green flowers. Hardy to Zone 5.

7. **Damask rose *(Rosa damascena)*:** Semi-double rose-red to pink flowers. Hardy to Zone 5.

8. **Lavender *(Lavandula officinalis)*:** Spikes of small blue flowers. Plant hardiness varies depending on the variety used from Zone 5 to Zone 8.

9. **Hyssop *(Hyssopus oficinalis)*:** Spikes of blue flowers. Hardy to Zone 4.

10. **Sweet violet *(Viola odorata)*:** Comes in various colors, including purple, violet, pink, and white. Plant hardiness varies depending on the variety.

11. **Cowslip *(Caltha palustris)*:** Yellow bell-like flowers. Hardy to Zone 5.

12. **Tansy *(Tanacetum vulgare)*:** Flat clusters of yellow button-like flowers. Its fern-like leaves can also be used in floral arrangements. Hardy to Zone 4.

13. **Feverfew *(Chrysanthemum parthenium)*:** Small yellow and white daisy-like flowers. Hardy to Zone 5.

14. **Clipped hedges** can be used to surround your garden. Such hedges were a common component of Elizabethan-style knot gardens and will lend an authentic historic flare to your landscape.

Mail-Order Sources of Herb Plants and Seeds

Horizon Herbs
P.O. Box 69
Williams, OR 97544-0069
Phone: (541) 846-6704
http://www.chatlink.com/~herbseed/

Richters Herbs
357 Highway 47
Goodwood, Ontario L0C 1A0
Canada
(905) 640-6677
http://www.richters.com

Sandy Mush Herb Nursery
316 Surrett Cove Road
Leicester, NC 28748-5517
Phone: (828) 683-2014

For Further Study

Bown, Deni. *New Encyclopedia of Herbs and Their Uses.* London and New York: DK Publishing, 2001.

Burke, Nancy. *The Modern Herbal Primer: A Simple Guide to the Magic and Medicine of 100 Healing Herbs.* (The Old Farmer's Almanac). New York: Time-Life Books, 2000.

Griffin, Judy. *Mother Nature's Herbal.* St. Paul: Llewellyn Publications, 1997.

Kowalchik, Claire, and William Hylton. *Rodale's Illustrated Encyclopedia of Herbs.* Emmaus, Pa: Rodale Press, 1987.

Oster, Maggie. *Ortho's All about Herbs*. Des Moines, Iowa: Meredith Books, 1999.

Whiteman, Robin. *Brother Cadfael's Herb Garden: An Illustrated Companion to Medieval Plants and Their Uses*. Boston: Little, Brown and Company, 1997.

Crafting Magical Herbal Perfumes

≫ by Peg Aloi ≪

Many modern Pagans enjoy using incenses, oils, and scented candles for ritual. They simply love preparing the space, and employing various herbs or oils during rites.

Aromatherapy, the science of using essential oils for healing, is also of interest to many Pagans. In general, Pagans enjoy deepening their connection to nature through magical crafts and other activities such as gardening, cooking, or soap-making. Because so many products are now available that are scented with pure essential oils, the holistic benefits of these pure plant essences can now become part of our everyday lives. We can also use herb essences to perfume and magically alter everything from shampoos to housecleaning products.

Essential Oil Perfumes

The use of essential oils in perfumery is a subtle art that goes beyond freshening a room or taking a fragrant bath. Making perfume oils that correspond to magical purposes can be, in fact, a very satisfying endeavor.

Any Pagan who walks the herbalist path knows there is much knowledge to learn from the many books published over the years. This ranges from the old "herbals" by masters like Culpeper and Gerard to the myriad "green witchcraft" sites on the Internet. Making natural perfumes is just one aspect of the green Witch's art, and one that comes out of a long historical precedent.

Herbal Perfumes in Egypt

In ancient Egypt, perfumes were employed in many religious rituals. Oils, unguents, and resins were also used in complex Egyptian funerary rites. The elaborate preparations made by these people before burying the dead reflected their deeply held belief that the soul lives beyond the corporeal existence. The magical herbal applications were meant to ease the burden of the soul in eternity.

There are many artifacts which tell us of the Egyptian fascination with perfumes. For instance, wall murals, as well as jars and bottles, have been found intact after thousands of years and still smelling of cedar, myrrh, or sandalwood.

These substances were prized not just for their pleasant aromas but for their antibacterial, preservative qualities. The herbal essences in these oils, unguents, and resins acted much like the modern embalming substances of today—though their scents are much more pleasing to the nose than the formaldehyde that is in use today.

Medieval European Perfumes

Medieval Europeans were also fascinated by perfumes and spices. During the era of the black death, it was believed that sweet-smelling herbs and oils could help clear the "pestilence" from the air. Therefore, special perfumes and toilet waters using lavender, rosemary, and other plants were employed to prevent the spread of disease.

As it turns out, these plant materials did in fact help slow the rates of infection somewhat because of their antimicrobial properties. Though the record is spotty, it is known for instance today that apothecaries who dealt in herbal compounds all day long were mysteriously immune to the plague.

Properties of Aromatherapy

One of the most fascinating aspects of the study of aromatherapy is that it combines divergent properties of beauty and science. That is, the essences give pleasure even as they improve health.

As anyone who has researched herbal folklore knows, there are also many magical properties associated with plants, and thus with the essences derived from them. Writers from Nostradamus to Aleister Crowley, from Sybil Leek to Scott Cunningham have written about the magical uses of perfumes and incenses.

The table of magical correspondences used by many modern Witches is based in Western esoteric tradition and the Qabala of Judaic tradition. Just as it is believed magic is more effective when certain astrological conditions are met, so it is believed that the use of certain colors, symbols, gemstones, and incenses or perfumes enhance one's magical efforts.

Today, Witches can enjoy a wide variety of essential oils that can be made into perfumes with magical properties. The tiny molecules that give essential oils their scent also affect our brain chemistry and our emotional and psychic states. Overall, choosing just the right combinations of essential oils for our magical work is a very important, and very pleasurable, enterprise.

An excellent book for anyone interested in magical perfumery is *The Magic and Ritual Use of Perfumes* by Richard Alan Miller

(Inner Traditions International, 1992). Scott Cunningham also wrote a well-loved and useful book on magic herbalism called *The Complete Book of Incenses, Oils & Brews* (Llewellyn, 1989).

Both of these books offer valuable insights and suggestions for experimenting with the fascinating art and science of aromotherapy. Still, though reading is the first step toward gaining herbal knowledge, there is never any substitute for hands-on experience. After all, one cannot smell the essences of herbs just by reading words on a page (even if the book is from a dusty used bookstore).

To Begin Making Perfume

To begin making your own herbal essence perfume, you need to purchase an assortment of quality essential oils and a base or "carrier" oil with which to dilute the concentrated essential oils. Sweet almond oil works fine as a carrier oil, as does very light (extra-virgin) olive oil, or any unscented oil that is also suitable for massage.

Mineral oil or other petroleum-based products should not be used, as these oils tend to clog pores in your skin. Ultimately, you want to be concerned with what you are putting on your body— as much of it ends up being absorbed in your body.

As a general rule, you should keep your perfume in a glass container, away from direct light or extreme heat or cold. The correct ratio is generally twenty drops total of essential oils to a quarter-ounce of carrier oil, but in this you can also use your own discretion. Some people as a rule prefer a lighter concentration of oils in their perfumes, and some prefer heavier concentrations.

Keep in mind, however, essential oils are expensive. So start with some moderately priced ones to see what works for you. In building perfumes, you will want several of each of the three perfume categories known as top notes, middle notes, and base notes. These categories refer to the strength, "weight," and staying power of a scent. Here are some general rules regarding the "note" of essential oils.

Woods or resins are base notes, as a general rule.

Grasses, leaves, and spices tend to be middle notes.

Light florals and fruit scents are top notes.

As the base note is what remains the longest on the skin, fragrance-wise, perfumers usually start from the bottom and work up.

Notes on Base Notes

Some inexpensive base notes to try are patchouli or cedar-wood.

Vetiver and frankincense cost a bit more, but both have wonderful scents.

Sandalwood or myrrh are quite expensive, but a little goes a long way.

Patchouli, vetiver, and frankincense are relaxing and sensual; the first two are woodsy and warm, while frankincense is somewhat lemony and cooler.

Frankincense slows the breathing, which makes it excellent for meditation.

Myrrh is rather bitter and mysterious, but also soothing and entrancing.

You will want to add to your array of essential oils as you become more experienced with blending perfumes.

Notes on Middle Notes

For middle notes, try lavender, cypress, juniper, rosemary, clary sage, petitgrain, palmarosa, or oakmoss. These are wonderfully "herby" scents and all impart a relaxing quality when inhaled.

Rosemary stimulates memory, clary sage brings prophetic dreams, and lavender clears the mind and calms the nerves.

Petitgrain and palmarosa are balancing and very green in character.

Notes on Top Notes

The top notes are what one smells first when one first opens a bottle of perfume. These fleeting fragrances—like rose, jasmine, or neroli (the bitter orange blossom)—are often precious and rare.

Be careful with top notes; a little goes a long way!

Top notes tend to be very expensive and impart a sensual, romantic quality. Other nice top notes are the citrus scents of bergamot, mandarin, sweet orange, grapefruit, and lime; these are all uplifting and help to focus thought.

Blending Your Perfumes

So you have your essential oils. Now you need to know how to blend all these together.

Your research and reading will help you familiarize yourself with the properties of each, as well as describe what scents blend well together. Many books will also list recipes. I offer some very basic recipes below, using my favorite combinations of the essential oils mentioned above.

In general, you should add the suggested amounts of essential oils to a quarter-ounce of your carrier oil. Feel free, however, to experiment with different amounts to find a blend that pleases you.

Remember too that a perfume will change after several hours, and again after a few days until it "sets" and takes on its more permanent finished scent.

If you are not immediately satisfied with the results of an experimental perfume blend, don't throw it away—as it may change into something a few days later that you magically find rather appealing.

I hope you enjoy making your perfumes the natural way. Don't be afraid to experiment with your own blends—just be sure to make small batches at first.

Meditation Perfume

3   drops patchouli

8   drops frankincense

4   drops lavender

5   drops sweet orange

Sensuality Aphrodisiac Perfume

4   drops vetiver

3   drops frankincense

5   drops sandalwood

2   drops clary sage

3   drops oakmoss

(Note: If it is available, try adding 5 drops Bulgarian rose and/or 3 drops neroli.)

Vision Perfume

5   drops frankincense

6   drops clary sage

4   drops lavender

3   drops lemon

Protection Perfume

4 drops cedarwood
4 drops rosemary
3 drops cypress
5 drops sweet orange
5 drops lavender

Herb
History,
Myth, and
Magic

The Magic of Garlic

≈ by S. Y. Zenith ≈

The healing, protective, and culinary virtues of garlic (*Allium sativum*), a member of the lily family, have been lauded for over 5,000 years. Ancient pharmacopoeias in Mesopotamia, Egypt, India, China, and Greece recorded the uses of garlic in therapeutic and restorative remedies and for treating numerous physical disorders.

For instance, the Greek historian Herodotus noted that builders of the Great Pyramid of Giza were given garlic to strengthen resistance to infections. In Homer's *Odyssey*, Ulysses ate garlic to prevent himself from being turned into a pig by Circe. Garlic was also found in the tomb of King Tutankhamen. When ancient Roman soldiers went into battle, they wore garlic for courage and strength.

Garlic has long been used magically as well. In ancient Greece and Rome, garlic was placed at crossroads as an offering to the goddess Hecate. Brides once carried cloves of garlic in their pockets for good luck. Those who slept with a garlic bulb or clove under their pillow were shielded from unseen malignant intrusions and nightmares. In Japan, pilgrims and visitors are not allowed to bring garlic or leeks into temples, as they are considered too powerful and would hinder the training of priests within sacred temple grounds.

The Magical Uses of Garlic

In general, garlic is a potent deterrent against the evil eye and is powerfully protective against demons, vampires, and other malefic supernatural forces. Garlands of garlic hung in the house or in the kitchen ward off evil entities and harmful spells or hexes. As these garlands are specifically used for protective purposes and absorb negative energies, you should never eat this garlic or use it for cooking. The garlands may be replaced every three or six months.

To negate the effects of a magical magnet or lodestone, rub it with garlic. In healing spells, garlic can be used for absorbing diseases by rubbing the freshly peeled cloves on to afflicted parts of the body. In banishing spells, ground or powdered garlic can be strewn on the floor and around the property to eliminate unwanted influences.

It is also possible to carve rune scripts associated with protection on peeled garlic cloves and bury them at the front entrance or in the backyard of the home. Apartment dwellers may bury them in decorative potted plants placed either indoors or on the balcony.

Constituents and Health Benefits of Garlic

Garlic is valuable as a mild natural antibiotic and considered to be an herb of inner cleansing by many herbalists and naturopaths. The antibiotic properties of garlic are known to kill bacteria, fungi, and other pathogens, and to dilate blood vessels and so improve blood circulation.

Among its other bountiful properties, garlic contains the vitamins A, B_1, B_2, and C, as well as niacin, traces of sulfur and iodine, steroids, and two important protective minerals—selenium and germanium.

Daily consumption of garlic may help to reduce blood cholesterol levels, lower high blood pressure, and assist in dissolving blood clots—hence preventing strokes and heart attacks and regulating blood sugar levels.

Garlic extract has been found to reduce free radicals and peroxide formation relating to degenerative diseases and premature aging. It is also able to detoxify a wide range of harmful and naturally occurring toxins, thus providing protection against the cancer-causing substances rampant in our world, such as air pollutants and cigarettes.

The effectiveness of garlic at enhancing the body's resistance to, and recovery from, illness and infection has been consistently well documented through the centuries. In modern times, the benefits of garlic have been studied in laboratories all over the world. German scientists are known to clinically administer garlic to patients suffering arteriosclerosis. The Russians favor the vapors of steamed garlic bulbs for inhalation in combating respiratory disorders.

Garlic Treatments

As garlic contains antibacterial, antifungal, antiviral and anti-inflammatory properties, it is useful for treating colds, coughs, influenza, bronchitis, and cystitis, as well as numerous other infections. It is also known to be of assistance to some asthmatics.

Known to eliminate pinworms from children, garlic is also useful for the prevention or treatment of recurring skin eruptions such as pimples, boils, abscesses, and carbuncles. Being antifungal, garlic is also of assistance to those prone to thrush.

Eaten raw, garlic also helps ease coughs, colds, nasal congestion, and mucus. Utilized as a permanent tonic for longevity, garlic assists the cell structure in preserving the natural tone of tissues. Garlic also enhances the memory, strengthens the immune system, and promotes general good health.

Side Effects

The pungent and lingering odor of garlic on the breath or in some cases through the pores of the skin is the most common side effect. In some social surroundings, the scent of garlic is considered objectionable.

Allicin, the most effective antibacterial component in garlic, is responsible for this odor. Do not despair, however. Cardamom is well-known for reducing the smell of garlic. Just chew cardamom seeds or blend some ground cardamom into a glass of juice or other beverage. Chewing some fresh basil or thyme leaves also helps clear the odor of garlic. Peppermint and coffee beans are also known to lessen or disguise "garlic breath," as it is expelled through the respiratory passages.

Allergies and Caution

Those who are allergic to garlic, and to related herbs such as chives, leeks, and onions, should avoid them completely. It is often said that the difference between a remedy and a dangerous substance is a matter of dosage. Some people may find that large doses of fresh garlic and garlic oil could irritate their digestive systems. Taken in large quantities, garlic may also induce migraines in some individuals.

Those with sensitive skin should wear gloves to prevent contact dermatitis when handling garlic. Individuals who are highly allergic to garlic are likely to develop a rash from eating it. Consuming more than five cloves of garlic a day may cause heartburn, flatulence, and gastrointestinal bleeding in susceptible individuals. It is important for pregnant women, and those taking anticoagulants, to consult their health care practitioner before consuming large quantities of garlic. Advice regarding physical health matters should always be sought from suitably qualified medical professionals.

Garlic and Gardens

To yield a good crop of garlic, country folk advised that garlic cloves should be planted on the year's shortest day, and the corms harvested on the longest day. The soil should be fertile, well drained, and weed-free. The garlic plant enjoys the full Sun or partial shade.

Garlic tends to form clumps as it grows, and so it can easily be propagated by dividing the root system or cloves. It is also suitable as a companion plant, as the sulfur in garlic deters some plant diseases.

Apart from its health benefits, there are also numerous uses for garlic in the garden. The planting of clumps of garlic near rose bushes will help keep them free of aphids. Grown under apple trees, garlic protects against scab. Planted near outdoor eating or sitting areas, the odor of garlic is also known to keep mosquitoes away.

Garlic Spray

To prevent ants, spiders, tomato worms, and caterpillars, make a simple but effective natural deterrent by steeping five crushed garlic cloves in a quart of water for several days before straining and storing in a plastic pump-spray bottle for use.

Garlic Infusion

Infusions are easy on the digestive system, and when diluted further they are ideal for both children and adults with sensitive stomachs. A gentle garlic infusion may be used in douches, compresses, and rinses. Applied as a fomentation, a garlic infusion improves circulation, draws abscesses, and relieves inflamed joints.

To make a garlic infusion, cut 6 cloves of fresh garlic, and add to 1 cup of cool water. For a weak infusion, steep the mixture for ten to fifteen minutes. A strong infusion with added potency requires steeping for 6 hours before use.

Garlic Tincture

As a tincture prepared in wine spirits, garlic protects against influenza and stomach ailments. A handy garlic tincture can be made using ½ pound of peeled garlic cloves soaked for 2 weeks in 1 quart of brandy at a temperature of 85°F in a bottle with an air-tight seal. Shake the bottle several times daily. After 2 weeks, strain the tincture and return it to the bottle for storage in the refrigerator.

Take five to twenty drops of this tincture each day after meals, or as instructed by your health practitioner.

Garlic in Traditional Asian Medicine

Garlic forms part of the staple diet in many eastern countries. In the ayervedic medical traditions of India, it is known as *rashona*, which meaning "lacking one taste." This refers to the fact that garlic possesses five of the six tastes in the ayervedic system—that is, its root is pungent, its leaf is bitter, its stem is astringent, its stem-top is saline, and its seed is sweet. Garlic only exhibits an absence of sourness.

In traditional Chinese medicine, garlic was first mentioned around AD 500, and was characterized as acrid, bitter, and warm. Some Asian households often soak garlic in vinegar or wine for two to three years in order to produce a health tonic. This aging process is believed to convert some of the compounds into beneficial and biologically active amino acids that provide extra therapeutic effects. After the two-year aging process, small portions of the liquid can be used with a fresh clove of mashed garlic in salad dressings or as a healthy flavoring agent in soups, stews, casseroles, and other dishes.

Some Garlic Recipes

Roasted Garlic

Place a bulb of garlic on an oven tray, and coat it with olive or peanut oil. Roast at 350°F for thirty minutes or until soft. Let cool, and squeeze the flesh from the shell for use as required.

Garlic Salt

Place alternate thin layers of salt and chopped garlic in a jar, and store it for several weeks. Those who prefer to remove the garlic can do it with a sieve. The salt will retain the flavor of garlic. Garlic lovers who crave more pungency can simply add more chopped garlic during the preparation process.

Garlic Oil

Oil flavored with garlic turns simple foods into gourmet delights, and also makes an attractive present. Apart from its use in salad dressings, bastings, stir-fries, and other dishes, a small phial of garlic oil can also be kept with other occult oils and used for rubbing on candles for protective spells.

An easy homemade recipe for garlic oil requires 10 sliced cloves of garlic and a quart of virgin olive oil. Place the garlic into a jar containing olive oil, and allow the contents to stand for 1 week before straining through muslin or coffee filter paper. Pour the oil into a labeled bottle, and seal.

You can also experiment with walnut, macadamia, and almond oils rather than using olive oil. Nonaromatic oils such as safflower or sunflower oils are also good alternatives.

Garlic Ointment

Ointments contain greasy ingredients such as fats or oils thickened with wax. Beeswax is a popular ingredient favored by herbalists as it brings additional healing properties to salves, liniments, and other similar preparations. The thick texture of ointments ensures that they stay longer on the skin, forming a soothing and protective layer while keeping body heat and water in. Ointments should not be applied to hot, inflamed, or weepy skin conditions. Garlic ointment can be applied to corns or used as a rub for treating rheumatic pain, muscular sprains, and strains.

Garlic ointment can be made at home by mixing 1½ cups of garlic-infused oil to 1 ounce of beeswax. To do this, put the oil and beeswax into a heat-proof jug, set it in a large pan, and place the pan on the stove. Add water to the pan until the level is slightly below that of the oil in the jug. Bring the water to a boil, then turn the heat down to a gentle simmer. Stir contents in the jug with a metal spoon until the beeswax melts and fuses with the oil.

Remove the jug from the pan and turn off the heat. Place the jug on a heat-proof surface so the mixture may cool. Before the ointment begins to set, pour it into clean jars. Do not cover or seal the jars until the ointment has completely cooled and set. Label the jars with date and ingredients. Some of us may reek of garlic while using this ointment, but the versatile remedial effects make it worthwhile.

Garlic Vinegar

Herb vinegar is made in general by placing fresh herbs into a bottle of vinegar and letting it stand for two or three weeks. Ensure that the bottle is properly sealed. The flavor will disperse more readily if the bottles are placed in a sunny spot.

Vinegar flavored with garlic is one of the easiest and quickest herbal vinegars to make. It can be added to salads dressings, marinades, sauces, and stews. Store yours in decorative bottles with a sprig of rosemary, thyme, mint, or basil. It can make a great gift idea for Christmas or other special occasion.

Note: It is essential to use good quality vinegar as a base, since cheap varieties of white or malt vinegars are likely to dominate the added flavorings. As vinegars are acidic, it is important to use jars or bottles with acid-proof lids.

In many health diets, vinegar is cooling and antiseptic. It is used as a cleanser and regulator. Drunk in the morning with warm water, garlic vinegar is known to keep the skin clear while toning the body system. This routine generally helps rheumatism and arthritis sufferers. It is useful for thrush as a douche, and for other skin itches and irritations as a topical treatment.

To make garlic vinegar, simply crush 4 cloves of garlic, and put them into a large jar with 1 quart of good quality white wine vinegar. Allow the mixture to stand for twenty-four hours before straining. Store your garlic vinegar in a cool and dark place in sealed bottles.

Garlic Butter

This recipe makes approximately one-half cup of garlic butter suitable for use as a spread for toasted sandwiches or simply for bread. Steamed vegetables may also be enhanced with a tablespoon of garlic butter. (You may also substitute margarine for the butter if you choose.)

You need the gather the following ingredients for this recipe: 4 ounces of softened butter (or margarine), 2 crushed garlic cloves, and salt and pepper to taste (always go easy at first with these; you can always add more). Combine all the ingredients well. Those who like it a little spicy may add ½ teaspoon of curry powder to the ingredients before blending. Store unused garlic butter in the refrigerator.

Old Garlic Brew to Beat the Flu

An old brew for beating influenza consists of 1 large teaspoon of sliced garlic, 1 teaspoon of chopped ginger, 1 tablespoon of raisins and ½ teaspoon of crushed aniseed. Simmer these ingredients with the juice of one or two lemons in 1 cup of water for ten minutes. An optional dash of brandy can be poured into the brew as an additional boost—this is especially effective during the cold and flu season.

Hot Garlic Sauce

This hot and spicy dipping or topping sauce is derived from a simple Indonesian recipe. Depending on your individual palate, you may adjust the recipe for a range from mildly spicy to hopping hot. To make ½ cup of Hot Garlic Sauce, gather the following ingredients:

4	cloves minced garlic
1	Tbl. minced onion
2	Tbls. vegetable oil
1	tsp. shrimp paste, or *blachan* (available from Asian grocers)
1 to 2	tsps. minced fresh green chili
1	tsp. salt
1	tsp. sugar

Heat up a saucepan, and sauté the garlic and onion in the vegetable oil for two or three minutes. Add the shrimp paste, chili, salt, and sugar, and stir constantly until the sauce is well blended. Let the sauce stand until room temperature before serving with your favorite dish. You may also choose to store it in a small jar in the refrigerator until it is needed.

Garlic Soup

This is a modern version of a Central European garlic soup popularly used for preventing colds.

1	head garlic
1½	quarts vegetable or chicken broth
4	oz. two-day old bread
	Salt and ground pepper, to taste

Peel the garlic cloves and poach them in 2 cups of simmering broth for ten minutes or until the cloves soften. Remove the cloves, and purée the mixture in a blender. Trim and discard the crust from the bread. Cut the bread into cubes and cover them with warm water in a bowl to soak for ten minutes. Squeeze out excess water, and crumble the bread. Add the puréed garlic to the remaining broth, then add the bread. Add salt and pepper according to personal taste. Simmer for ten minutes, then serve while hot. Garnish with a sprinkle of cut basil leaves and a dash of olive oil if you wish.

Garlic and Herb Bread Sticks

For something a little different from the usual garlic bread, some bread sticks will add flair to a meal. Eaten on their own or with soups, they make savory and healthy snacks. The ingredients are easily available:

    2   cups whole-meal flour

    2   tsps. dried herbs of your choice

        Cracked black pepper to taste

    1   egg

    ⅔   cups milk

    2   Tbls. melted butter

    ½   tsp. minced garlic

        Sesame seeds

Combine flour, herbs, and pepper in a bowl. Beat the egg with milk in another container, and mix with the dry ingredients to make a soft dough. Lightly knead the dough on a floured board until smooth. Roll it out in a rectangular shape and cut into twelve even-sized strips. Melt butter in a rectangular cake pan, and stir in the minced garlic. Without removing the garlic, arrange the dough strips in rows in the pan, then sprinkle with sesame seeds. Bake in a hot oven between ten and fifteen minutes. Serve with soup and salad.

Japanese Soy Sauce Garlic Pickles

This Japanese-style pickle is believed to be indispensable for developing stamina. Gather the following ingredients:

3 to 4   cloves garlic

2   cups soy sauce

½   cup sweet sake (Japanese rice wine)

1   tsp. ginger juice

Separate the garlic into individual cloves, and remove all layers of their skin. Sterilize a jar in boiling water, put the garlic cloves in the jar, and pour soy sauce over the contents. Seal the jar, and store it in a cool, dark compartment of the kitchen cupboard for about three or four weeks before slicing thinly for eating.

Garlic Curry

This Indian dish takes thirty minutes or so to prepare and serves approximately four people. It is a delight to garlic and curry lovers. I first learned the recipe some twenty years ago while I was living in Singapore. I found it to be a source of food and medicine that was suitable for eating in both warm and cold climates. For those who are deterred by the thought of the quantity of garlic used in this recipe, small quartered potatoes may be substituted in place of some of the garlic. This curry is usually served with rice, although the adventurous may try it with ordinary bread or a variety of Indian ones.

8   oz. garlic bulbs with large individual cloves

8   small red onions

3 to 8   fresh red chilies

2   Tbls. oil

1   tsp. fenugreek seeds

½   tsp. chili powder

½   tsp. turmeric

3½   cups coconut milk

Salt to taste

3½   cups water

½   cup tamarind purée

Peel the garlic cloves and onions, but leave them whole. Remove chili stalks and discard. For a cooler spice, remove the seed from the chilies (for more heat, keep the seeds). Heat the oil in a heavy saucepan, and fry the garlic, onions, and fresh chili over very low heat. Do not let them brown too much. Remove the garlic, onions, and chili from the saucepan with a slotted spoon to set aside, leaving the oil in the pan. Add fenugreek seeds to the flavored oil, and stir over low heat until they begin to darken. Stir in chili powder and turmeric to fry for a few seconds before adding coconut milk, salt, and 3½ cups water. Bring the saucepan to a simmer, stirring constantly.

Add the fried garlic, onions, and chilies to the saucepan, leaving the curry to simmer uncovered until the garlic cloves become tender. If the liquid in the saucepan evaporates too quickly, add more coconut milk and water. After the pan has been cooking for twenty minutes, stir the tamarind purée into the curry. Let the dish sit for at least five minutes before serving.

For Further Study

Belsinger, Susan, and Carolyn Dille. *The Garlic Book: A Garland of Simple, Savory, Robust Recipes.* Loveland, Colo.: Interweave Press, 1993.

Cunningham, Scott. *Cunningham's Encyclopedia of Magical Herbs.* St. Paul, Minn.: Llewellyn Publications, 1994.

Garland, Sarah. *The Complete Book of Herbs and Spices.* Pleasantville, N.Y.: Reader's Digest Association, 1993.

Guiley, Rosemary. *The Encyclopedia of Witches and Witchcraft.* New York: Facts On File, 1999.

Little, Brenda. *The Illustrated Herbal Encyclopedia*. Leicester: Abbeydale Press, 1999.

Lust, John. *The Herb Book*. New York and London: Bantam Books, 1974.

Roehl, Evelyn. *Whole Food Facts*. Rochester, Vt.: Healing Arts Press; distributed to the book trade in the U.S. by Harper & Row (New York), 1988.

Thomson, William A. R., M.D. (ed.). *Healing Plants: A Modern Herbal*. London: Macmillan Limited, 1978.

The Rose

❧ by Ellen Dugan ❧

Oh thou beautiful Rose! So fair
and sweet . . .

    – Julia C. R. Dorrhe

The captivating tale of the rose stretches far back into our history. The romantic, sentimental appeal of this flower is due to its charms, its usefulness, and the folklore that has built up around it. Roses supplied the ancient Egyptians, Greeks, and Romans with petals for fragrant oils, flavorings for wine and food, and decorations for their warriors. And the rosehip provided both a food source and medicine.

There is really no other flower that has inspired such a passion among poets, gardeners, royalty, and even average folk throughout the ages. The ancient Greek poetess Sappho called the rose the "Queen of flowers," a title that still more than fits our beloved rose to this present day.

Rose History

The first known paintings of roses were found in Crete at the palace of Knossos. These renditions of a five-petaled pink rose date back to 1800–1700 BC. Egyptian tombs had roses for decoration. The rose is also recorded in clay tablet depictions that show the flower's role in the Egyptian daily life. Cleopatra was thought to have greeted Marc Antony in a rose-laden room. Her mattress was stuffed with the fragrant petals. The two lovers wore garlands of the flowers, and rumor has it that the petals were knee-deep on the floor of her love nest.

The rose was wildly popular in ancient Greece and Rome. Old Roman politicians would hang roses from the ceiling to indicate when a meeting was secret. This practice gave rise to the term *sub rosa*, literally "under the rose," but now meaning "in secret." Roman farmers cultivated roses as field crops. (Probably an older version of the *gallica* species.) This was a profitable business and fairly common. In fact, the Roman poet Horace once complained that too many roses were being grown in Italy, and not enough corn.

The ancestor of all old European roses is the Apothecary rose *(Rosa gallica)*. It forms a dense shrub and produces deep red-pink blooms. It can grow up to five feet and has upright and arching canes. The canes are bristly and sport a few thorns. This rose tolerates poor soils and is intensely fragrant. It also produces rosehips in the fall.

Today, most rose aficionados agree that modern rose breeding began in 1867 with the development of the hybrid tea rose. Any rose that was produced before this time is classified as an old rose. While I adore hybrid teas, they can make some gardeners a little nervous. If that is the case for you, then consider raising the older roses. Old garden roses are tougher (some may be winter hardy to a Zone 3), and they are more disease-resistant and easy to care for. Old roses may only bloom once a year, but the fragrance of these flowers is strong and old-fashioned. They also add some historical character to the garden.

Rose Classifications

Here are some rose classifications and varieties for you to consider trying out in your garden.

Old Garden

This classification describes any rose introduced before 1867. Cold-hardy types such as the "Alba" variety grow upright anywhere from four to eight feet in height and are used as hedge or specimen plants. The blooms are semidouble and double flowers in pink or white. These were cultivated in the Middle Ages for medical use. Another Old Garden rose is the "Gallica." This rose typically blooms heavily once in the late spring or early summer months. Look too for the red "Apothecary's rose," which grows three to five feet tall, or the "Cardinal de Richelieu," which grows four feet tall and has double purple blooms. Both of these are *gallica* varieties.

Hybrid Tea

This classification of rose has pointed buds that open to high centered, deeply petaled, long-stemmed flowers. The hybrid tea rose may grow in excess of six feet in height. Hybrid teas bloom repeatedly during the summer, and they are hardy in USDA Zones 6 to 9. Some popular varieties include: "Double Delight," a fragrant cream and red blend; "Tropicana" and "Voodoo," both orange shades; "Peace," a traditional yellow and pink blend; "Honor," which has lovely white blooms; and "Oregold" and "King's Ransom," which both have yellow blooms.

Floribunda

This classification has cup-shaped blooms that are set in clusters. The floribunda usually grows to about three feet in height and has a compact rounded look as a bush. They bloom repeatedly and are hardy in Zones 5 to 8. Some popular varieties to check out are: "Europeana" and "Sunfire" (red), "Cherish" (pink), "Sun Sprite" (yellow), "French Lace" (ivory), "Iceberg" (white), and "Angle Face" (purple). This last rose has lavender petals with a ruby-colored blush around the edges and is very fragrant.

Grandiflora

This rose classification resulted from crosses between floribundas and hybrid teas. This group combines the free flowering characteristics of the floribundas, with the size and quality of the flowers of the hybrid tea. They grow about four feet in height and make a great garden bushes. They are typically vigorous, though their zone hardiness may vary. Some of the highest rated varieties are: "Ole" or "El Capitan" (red), "Love" (red and white), "Queen Elizabeth" (pink), "Gold Medal" (yellow), and "White Lightnin'" (white).

Miniature

This classification is comprised of dainty little rose plants that are replicas of their larger cousins. The leaves, flowers, and thorns are perfect miniatures. The plant size may range from six to twelve inches. There are many varieties and colors of the miniature rose to choose from—even green. Zone requirements vary according to variety.

Polyantha

This rose classification's flowers are smaller than the floribunda but are borne in large clusters. The plants are hardy and disease-resistant. My favorite variety of the polyantha is called "The Fairy." It produces soft pink clusters of miniature blooms. "The Fairy" stays under three feet in height but sprawls charmingly outward in a loose shrub (it can be almost six feet in width). It is a knockout in my gardens and is hardy to Zone 4. Other popular varieties include "China Doll" and "Mrs. R. M. Finch."

Rugosa

This rose classification's hardiness makes it ideal for windy and exposed sites—many are winter hardy to Zone 2. Some varieties can grow up to six feet tall. These roses are easy to care for. They bloom throughout the season and into the fall months, and they develop a good orange foliage color and bright red hips. The flowers may be single or double. One of the most popular of the rugosas is "Hansa." It has large reddish-purple flowers and is strong and spicy in scent. "Therese Bugnet" has clusters of ruffled and bright lilac-pink flowers and has a sweet heady fragrance. It also has a great display of rich red foliage in the fall, and the canes remain deep purple throughout the winter.

Climbing

This classification includes all varieties of rose that produce long, vigorous cane growth that can be trained to grow along fences, trellises, or pillars. Its hardiness, flower shape, and rebloom varies depending on variety. Some of the more popular climbing roses include "New Dawn" (pink or white), "Climbing Peace" (a yellow and pink blend), "Golden Showers" (yellow), "Blaze" (red), and "Queen Elizabeth" (pink).

Myth and Folklore

Very few flowers have so many ties and connections to folklore and mythology as the rose. In Scandinavian countries, the rose was believed to be protected by the fairies and the elves. Fairy lore tells us that fairies are attracted to strongly scented flowers such as the rose.

The rose became a symbol of love and beauty thanks to the goddess Aphrodite/Venus. According to legend, as this goddess rose from the sea the opalescent sea foam that clung to her was transformed into roses. Portraits often show her crowned with roses or carrying a rose-tipped scepter. It is thought that originally all roses were white, until Aphrodite accidentally scratched herself on the thorns of a rose and her blood turned the petals blood-red.

The rose was a symbol of alchemy and Hermetic lore. The number five is the sacred number of the rose, which in days past also represented Aphrodite. Before hybridization, the five-lobed, or five-petaled, rose was common. The petals of the rose formed a natural pentacle and this shape is sacred to goddesses everywhere. According to some plant folklore, a seven-petaled rose stood for the seven planets or the seven days of the week, while the eight-petaled rose represented regeneration. The rose is also a emblem for the Virgin Mary. She was called the "Mystic Rose," as was Aphrodite before her. Other goddesses with ties to the rose are: Cybele, Diana, Flora, Freya, Juno, Lakshmi, Our Lady of Guadalupe, Selene, and the Fairy Queen Titania.

Rose Symbolism and Colors

Florigraphy, also known as the "language of flowers," was widely popular during Victorian times. This floral language was based on the traditions of older mythology and plant folklore. It was an enchanting and "secret" way to communicate your feelings to your intended. This custom of sending a little "message" bouquet (sometimes called a tussie-mussie) developed into today's language of flowers.

Here is a classic example that you are already familiar with. Most of us know what the red rose symbolizes—love, lust, and romance. But did you know that the corresponding messages change with the many different colors of the rose? Take a look at this list of rose colors and their meanings.

White: Peace, love, new beginnings

Yellow: Joy and happiness

Orange: Vitality and energy

Pink: Innocent love and friendship

Purple: Power and passion

Ivory: Romance and steadfast love

Red: Love, beauty, romance

Red and white blend: Unity and creative force

Red and yellow blend: Gaiety and joviality

Burgundy: Simple yet beautiful

Blue: Impossibility and miracles

Deep pink: Gratitude and appreciation

Peach: Charm

Creating Enchanting Bouquets

The Tussie-Mussie

Flower folklore and the language of flowers enables us to choose our blooms with intent and purpose. The nosegay and tussie-mussie are simple arrangements that you can create yourself at home. All you need are garden flowers, foliage, garden scissors, some green floral tape, a bit of ribbon, and some creativity.

Start the arrangement with a larger central bloom, such as a rose, for your focal point. Then encircle the bloom with contrasting foliage, herbs, and flowers. Work out from the center in a circular pattern. Bind the stems together, wrapping with green florist's tape as you go—to keep the tussie-mussie tight. Build up the layers, and emphasize the outer rim with large leaved herbs, such as lady's mantle, ferns, variegated ivy, or lamb's ears. Finish off the bouquet by tying the ribbons around the stems into a decorative bow. The tussie-mussie bouquet should stay fresh in water for about a week.

A rose and complementary herbs and foliage from your own garden mean so much more to a friend than an arrangement bought from a florist. You can also use some of your own ingenuity and send them a floral-herbal message at the same time. For example, combine a peach colored rosebud, a bit of fern foliage, and a few sprigs of white yarrow. This carries the message of charm, fairy magic, and bewitchment. Yarrow is traditionally a wisewoman's herb used for all sorts of benevolent charms and spells. The fern is associated with the fairies and bestows protection and fairy magic. (Some more herbal flower-language associations appear on pages 205 and 206 of this edition). The peach rose, as listed above, stands for charm. In other words you are saying, "Your friendship is like a magical charm."

Well, now that I've gotten you to thinking, let's take this a step further. Let me stroll out into my gardens and see what I have blooming at the moment. Currently, it's July and the garden is in full swing. Here we go—let's make a small arrangement of red grandiflora roses, tall purple garden phlox, Queen Anne's lace, a few sprigs of lavender, and some trailing ivy. These flowers would symbolize: love and beauty (roses); "I'll return" (Queen Anne's lace); you and the receiver of the bouquet are "soul mates" (phlox); devotion (lavender), and promises of fidelity and trust (ivy).

What a wonderful tussie-mussie message. Traditionally the rose was the central flower in a tussie-mussie type of bouquet. So pick your favorite rose and herbs from the garden and get busy! Use your imagination, and see what you sort of magical floral messages you can create.

Rose Gardens and Herbs

To grow a rose garden is in itself a magical act of creation. Folklore tells us that growing both herbs and roses encourages benevolent nature spirits such as the fairies to come reside in your garden. If your roses happen to be strongly scented, then that is all the better for attracting fairies. (See Vivian Ashcraft's article "Gardening for Fairies" on page 53 for more details on attracting fairies to your garden.)

If you wish to grow a enchanted rose/herb garden, try adding some fragrant herbs and flowers to grow beneath your rose bushes. There is nothing sadder than roses growing all by themselves with no company. Sweet-scented lavender is traditionally grown at the feet of rose bushes. Another harmonious plant would be catnip, but you can also try growing tricolored sage. In my formal rose garden I also grow the herb rosemary. Rosemary enjoys the full Sun and seems to be happy growing along with the roses. All of these scented plants would turn a plain rose garden into a fabulous "fragrance garden."

In the language of flowers, these herbs and plants add the following energies to the rose garden. The lavender brings love, devotion, and purification. Catnip is for cat magic and to encourage a sense of playfulness. Sage encourages a sense of family solidarity and brings wisdom both to the garden and into your life. There are several varieties of thyme that would do well in a rose garden. Look for a variety that will stay low to the ground or is a "creeping" variety. Thyme connotes bravery, courage, and strength, and magically it is worked into enchantments for purification, love, healing, and to increase psychic abilities. Lastly, rosemary traditionally signifies remembrance. It also brings good luck, and inspires fidelity and devotion. If you place a sprig of fresh rosemary beneath your pillow, it is thought this will help you to get a good night's sleep free from nightmares.

As a final practical note to adding edibles into a rose garden, I would caution you that if you are growing herbs such as lavender, rosemary, thyme, and sage in the rose garden then please be very careful with chemicals. In other words, don't eat anything that may have been sprayed. Try sprinkling systemic rose food directly at the base of your roses and watering it well. This type of selective fertilizer feeds the roses and discourages insects. It also keeps your edibles safe.

Magic in the Rose Garden

The rose, a symbol of the great goddess, is a very popular flower to be employed in magical herbalism. Roses and rose petals often play a significant role in a Witch's herbal charms. Besides the obvious associations of love and beauty, rose petals are often added to charms to "speed things up." If you look back at the rose symbolism color chart, you can see how different types of roses can be worked into floral love charms. Look over the language of flowers information before you plan your magical workings.

When gathering flowers and herbs, remember to cut them gently and cleanly from the plant. Only take what you need, the smallest amount possible. If you are harvesting a herb for a charm or spell, then only take a bit of the herb—a sprig or two is usually just fine. Gather your plants gently, with a positive intention and with reverence, and the Goddess will smile down on you.

Since I am a "hands on" type of garden Witch, let me give you some ideas and a few quick and easy rose spells for you to perform for yourself and your loved ones.

The Healing Rose Spell

Gather together these supplies:

- 1 yellow rose (for joy and happiness)
- 1–2 sprigs of yarrow blooms or a leaf of the foliage (to promote health)
- 2–3 stems of lemon balm (refreshes and revitalizes)
- 1 bud vase full of fresh water
- 1 blue ribbon (for healing and peace)

Place the flowers and foliage in the bud vase. Fasten the ribbon into a bow, and add it to the arrangement. Repeat these words:

Yellow is the color of joy, freshness, and spring,
May these herbs cheer; health and energy they will bring.
This rose, a magical charm, a loving gift from me to you.
May the Goddess bring health, and protect you in all that you do.

Take the charmed flowers to the person who is feeling under the weather. Drop the arrangement off, and tell the person to keep it near them until the flowers begin to fade. After the flowers fade, the person can tie them and the herbs together with the ribbon and hang them up to dry. Or he or she can simply dispose of the faded flowers and save the vase for another time.

The "Passionate Partner" Rose Spell

This spell is intended to bring a little spark back to a relationship between partners. With this spell you magic yourself, not your intended. That is, you are preforming the spell on yourself to bring about a little more sexual allure. Gather these supplies:

- 1   red rose (for love and romance)
- 1   red and white blended rose (for unity)
- 1   purple rose (for power and passion)

     Various filler herbal flowers such as feverfew ("you light up my life") or white yarrow (all purpose)

     Fern foliage (for fascination)

- 1   red ribbon
- 1   bud vase full of fresh water

Arrange the roses, filler flowers, and ferns in the vase. Tie the ribbon into a bow, and add it to the arrangement. Say this charm:

With these few enchanted herbs and roses, one times three,
I call for love, desire, and sensuality.
Ferns add fascination; feverfew a love that shines,
Red and white for unity and to stand the test of time.
Purple brings passion and power; red brings love,
May the goddess hear my call and answer from above.

Close out this spell by saying: "For the good of all with harm to none and by the earth and sea, this spell is done."

The Rose, the Flower of the Heart

From the earliest days, the rose was considered a magical flower. It is not only a lovely flower to grow in your gardens, but among all the treasures of the garden the rose is the sweetest. This symbol of love and heartfelt emotions is universal. Enjoy these wonderful, sacred, magical flowers. Check out as many different varieties as you can.

Roses can add structure to the garden. They encourage pollinators such as the bee and butterfly. They can add a little romance to an arbor or trellis. You could even grow climbing roses along fences to gently encourage stray animals and the neighbors kids to stay out of your yard. The thorns discourage fence climbing, the vines add privacy, and the plant is pretty.

And once your roses are grown, try your hand at creating a few of your own rose spells. Remember, the strongest magic comes from the heart.

For Further Study

Dugan, Ellen. *Garden Witchery*. St. Paul, Minn.: Llewellyn Publications, 2003.

Laufer, Geraldine Adamich. *Tussie-Mussies: The Victorian Art of Expressing Yourself in the Language of Flowers*. New York: Workman Publishing, 1993.

Skolnick, Solomon M. *The Language of Flowers*. White Plains, NY.: Peter Pauper Press, 1995.

Walker, Barbara G. *The Woman's Dictionary of Symbols and Sacred Objects*. San Francisco: HarperSanFrancisco, 1988.

The Magic of Yarrow

≫ by Eileen Holland ≪

Y arrow *(Achillea millefolium)* is a weedy perennial herb of the Northern Hemisphere. Its dark green, feathery leaves are pungently aromatic. Other names for yarrow include yarroway, yerw, gearwe, field hop, devil's nettle, snake's grass, devil's plaything, bad man's plaything, arrow root, death flower, old man's pepper, and carpenter's weed. Because of its segmented leaves, yarrow has also been called milfoil, thousand leaf, thousand seal, and thousandweed.

Yarrow has been used in herbalism to help stop bleeding, so it has many names that refer to this property, including: bloodwort, staunchweed, sanguinary, nose bleed, saigne-nez, woundwort, soldier's woundwort, herba militaris, knyghten milfoil, and knight's milfoil. In the old

language of flowers, yarrow meant "healing," "war,"and "cure for heartache."

The botanical name of yarrow—*Achillea*—refers to the Greek hero Achilles, who is said to have discovered herbs with the ability to heal wounds. Legend has it that Achilles, who had been trained in herbalism by Chiron the Centaur, used these herbs at Troy to staunch the bleeding wounds of his men.

Magical Yarrow

Yarrow is a Witch's herb. It increases the power of spells, and amplifies the action of other medicinal herbs. It is associated with the planet Venus, the elements air and water, with female essence, and with yin energy. The entire plant can be used magically for love spells, divination, courage, clairvoyance, consecration, longevity, fertility, evocation, tranquility, good luck, protection, dream work, releasing, banishing, breaking spells, psychic power, defensive magic, self-confidence, animal magic, recovering from heartbreak, and reaching other planes of awareness. Yarrow treats the blues, but it is not a substitute for medical care.

Yarrow attracts love, friendship, courage, and fairies. It is a charm for creating or maintaining a happy marriage, and for fidelity in marriage. Sprigs of yarrow are charms for courage and protection. Wear a sprig of yarrow to avert negative energy. Nettles and yarrow, together, are a charm against fear. Writing everything you are afraid of on a piece of parchment paper, and placing this in a yellow mojo bag with some yarrow, is said to help you to overcome all of your fears—especially if you carry this charm with you.

Yarrow is an appropriate herb for the sabbats of Lammas and Mabon. Add yarrow to incense mixtures for divination, banishing, and love. Essential oil of yarrow is used for balance and in psychic work. Yarrow stems, which are very straight, were used in China as the original *I Ching* sticks. The Druids are said to have used yarrow stems for weather forecasting and divination.

There are some old occult beliefs about the magical properties of yarrow. Buried with a clover leaf, yarrow was believed to engender red and green serpents. Powdered and burned in an oil lamp, it was supposed to induce hallucinations of serpents. Placed under a man's head while he slept, yarrow was said to prevent him from ever dreaming of himself again.

In a dream pillow, yarrow is said to grant a dream of one's future spouse if one recites this traditional spell before sleeping:

> *Thou pretty herb of Venus' tree,*
> *Thy true name it is Yarrow;*
> *Now who my bosom friend must be,*
> *Pray tell thou me to-morrow.*

Some people are allergic to yarrow, and it isn't good for pregnant women, but infusions of yarrow have long been used for magic and healing. Yarrow tea is a bitter tonic. It is a traditional remedy for melancholy, and it strengthens psychic abilities. Yarrow tea with molasses and cayenne pepper is an old treatment for the common cold. The herbalist Gerard recommended yarrow broth, taken faithfully every day, for general good health.

Yarrow Facts

Yarrow has ribbed, upright stems and grows to three feet. The whole plant is covered with silky white hairs. It blooms with dense clusters of tiny daisy-like yellow, white, pink, or lilac flowers from June through the autumn. Yarrow can be propagated by division, or by seeds sown one foot apart in the spring. It likes moisture, and it can become invasive in gardens.

Harvest the entire plant while it is in bloom, and hang it to dry. Yarrow provides both cut flowers and dried flowers. Distilled water of yarrow is used in making cosmetics.

Other varieties of yarrow include: sweet yarrow (*Achillea ageratum*, also called sweet milfoil, sweet nancy, moonwalker, and maudlin); silver yarrow (*Achillea clavennae*, also called lady's smoke; it is sacred to Mary); and sneezewort (*Achillea ptarmica*, also called pearlwort). This last is an upright perennial European herb with hairy stems and long, pointed leaves. It grows to two feet and has long, thin, fleshy roots. Sneezewort blooms from June to August with loose clusters of white flowers. It grows wild near water and in damp places.

English mace *(Achillea declorans)* is also called mace yarrow, mace, and nutmeg thyme. This is an aromatic perennial herb that grows to twenty inches with narrow, bright green leaves. It has long, arching stems and blooms from July to September with creamy-white flowers that resemble daisies. Its leaves are used as a kitchen herb in soups, stews, and mayonnaise salads.

Musk yarrow *(Achillea moschata)* is also called iva and lady's rue; it is sacred to Mary. Woolly yellow yarrow *(Achillea tomentosa)* is a rare herb with hairy leaves; it blooms with bright yellow flowers. Fragrant yarrow *(Achillea fragrantissima)* is a woolly white perennial herb that blooms with scented white flowers. Fern-leaf yarrow *(Achillea filipendulina)* is also called golden yarrow, parkers, and cloth of gold.

The Magic of Vervain

by Eileen Holland

Vervain *(Verbena officinalis)*, the herb of enchantment, is a scentless perennial herb of the northern hemisphere. It is also called vervan, van van, ferfaen, verbein, verbena, verbinaca, dragon's claw, enchanter's plant, tears of Isis, Juno's tears, herba veneris (herb of Venus), persephonion, demetria, Mercury's moist blood, peristerium, sagmina, pigeon grass, pigeonwood, frog-foot, simpler's joy, columbine, altar plant, herba sacra, herbe sacrée, holy plant, herb of the cross, holy herb, and herb of grace. In the old language of flowers, vervain connoted enchantment.

Sacred Vervain

Vervain was considered a sacred plant in many ancient cultures. It was one of the sacred herbs of Greece, where it was used in sacrifices. Virgil called vervain "holy and rich." Jupiter's altars were sprinkled with vervain water, or swept with bundles of vervain, to purify them. Vervain was carried during peace negotiations in Rome, and used as an amulet by Germans when signing peace treaties. Vervain is associated with the planets Venus and Earth, the elements air and water, with female essence, with yin energy, and with the astrological signs Virgo and Libra. It has hot and dry qualities.

Vervain was a sacred herb of the Druids, who are said to have gathered it from shady places before sunrise—especially at the rising of the dog star. Druids are also said to have decorated their altars with vervain flowers, and to have used vervain water to purify their altars and sacred places. Female Druids are said to have worn crowns of vervain.

Vervain is sacred to the goddesses Aradia, Cerridwen, Demeter, Diana, Isis, Juno, and Venus; and to the gods Jupiter, Mars, Mercury, and Thor. There is an old Witches' saying that goes: "Vervain and dill lend aid to will." Vervain can be used in any spell to increase the power of the spellcaster. Conversely, there is an old belief that vervain can strip Witches of their powers. Vervain and dill were often used with trefoil to make magic hoops.

There is a theory of magic that says every magical act requires a sacrifice in order to be made manifest. This once meant actually sacrificing animals as burnt offerings to the gods—but no ethical practitioner in modern times would do such a thing. Sacrifice is now viewed as the time and effort you take to cast the spell, to gather the incense or candles or spell ingredients that are consumed by burning, and so forth. Vervain is an appropriate herb to burn in order to make a spell manifest, because of its ancient connection with sacrifice.

Vervain is generally used in magic for balance, anointing, centering, banishing, releasing, clearing, prosperity, peace, youth, visions, creativity, love, protection, divination, enchantment, inner power, healing, sleep, purification, immortality, invisibility, fertility, luck (especially for brides), justice, happiness, will power, prophesy, self-control, inner power, money, ritual cleansing, success in court, averting evil, blessing the home, creating harmony, enchanting locks, removing hexes, making children happy, giving children a love for learning, and for general defensive magic. Vervain is also considered a good purification incense.

Vervain is a charm for love, protection, safety, good fortune, and good eyesight. It is a charm against temptation, snake bites, insect bites, headaches, and the evil eye. As an herb of Thor, it averts lightning. Vervain can be woven into a wreath and placed on the front door of the house. It can also be hung above the bed or in a barn or stable, or it may be added to a mojo bag that is worn around the neck. Practitioners of black magic used vervain to empower the disgusting "hand of glory."

Vervain is an appropriate herb for the sabbats Imbolc, Ostara, Midsummer, and Lammas. It is considered an aphrodisiac and often used in sex magic. Vervain is said to give men firm erections, thereby enhancing love making. It is also used in making love potions, charms, talismans, and amulets—especially those meant to attract love. Vervain is sometimes called pigeon-wood or pigeon grass because doves and pigeons are attracted to it. In olden times, vervain was placed in dovecotes to attract birds. There was an old occult belief that when powdered and put in the Sun, vervain would make the Sun look blue.

Vervain averts incubi, succubi, demons, and other malevolent entities. Sorcerers are said to have worn crowns of vervain to protect themselves when they evoked demons. In an old ballad, a demon told a girl: "Gin you wish to leman mine, lay aside the St. John's wort and the vervain."

Vervain root is a charm for good luck, the fertility of trees and vines, and for calming your emotions. It is also a charm against epilepsy and the plague. Placed in the house, yard, or vineyard, a vervain root is said to bring a profit every year. Worn around the neck, a piece of vervain root is an amulet for good luck or an old charm against scrofulous and scorbutic conditions.

The essential oil of vervain is used for creativity, success in artistic careers, obtaining material benefits, and helping warriors escape from their enemies. It is said to increase the power of magical tools when used to anoint them.

Infusions of vervain, or sachets containing vervain, can be added to the bath for purification or for relaxation after heavy and difficult psychic work. Bathing in vervain every day for a week is said to draw money to you. An infusion of vervain can also be used as "blood of Mercury"—a potion useful for the invocation or worship of the God, and in spells that relate to him and his rulership. It can also be used as lustral water for consecration and ritual purification purposes. Sprinkle vervain water in the house to cast out malevolent spirits, and to protect the home from them.

Some practitioners of black magic believe that when placed in a home or between two lovers, powdered vervain root will cause anger, ill will, and arguments. This use of vervain makes little sense, however, given the overwhelmingly positive qualities of this herb. Sprinkle powdered vervain, or vervain water, around a home to attract peace and happiness to it. Sprinkle it around the rooms where guests will be entertained, and they will be assured a merry time. Sprinkle it in fields to ensure healthy crops. Add vervain to dream pillows to improve the quality of your dreams. Add it to a dream pillow or hang it above the bed to prevent nightmares.

Vervain Facts

Vervain has hairy leaves with toothed edges that are arranged in pairs and tough, erect stems that grow to two feet. Its roots are hairy and spindle-shaped. Vervain blooms from July to September with slender spikes of small blue, mauve, or purple flowers. Propagated by seeds, cuttings, or root division, it needs rich soil with good drainage. There was an old belief that if you planted vervain in fertile soil it would engender worms in eight weeks, and that a person who touched these worms would die.

Vervain is native to Europe. It grows wild on waste land, in pastures, near ruins, and beside roads. Its leaves, flowers, and roots can be used magically. Vervain leaves are best gathered before the flowers bloom, or at least before they are fully open. Midsummer is a traditional time for gathering vervain. It is said to provide the strongest protection when gathered with the left hand at the rise of Sirius, the dog star. Gathered while the Sun is in Aries, and combined with a grain of corn or a one-year-old penny, vervain was believed to heal epilepsy.

Recite this old charm while you gather vervain:

All-heal, thou holy herb, Vervain,
Growing on the ground;
Blessed is that place
Whereon thou art found.

According to Christian legend, vervain first grew on Mount Cavalry, where it was used to stop the bleeding of the wounds of the crucified Jesus. Christians crossed themselves and used this prayer while gathering vervain.

Hallowed be thou, vervain, as thou growest in the ground,
For in the Mount of Calvary thou wast found.
Thou healedst Christ our Saviour, and staunchedst His
bleeding wound.
In the name of Father, Son, and Holy Ghost, I take thee
from the ground.

There is an old Christian belief that vervain comes from the devil, but there is also a Christian belief that vervain averts the devil. In the Middle Ages, Swedes considered vervain a powerful charm against the devil.

Blue Vervain

Blue vervain *(Verbena hastata)* is also called wild hyssop, simpler's joy, erect vervain, pigeonwood, and herb of the cross. It is a tall, perennial, North American herb with squarish stems that grow to four feet. Blue vervain blooms from June to September with long spikes of small bluish-purple flowers. This herb can be found growing wild beside roads and in dry, grassy fields.

Use blue vervain in magic for evocation, spellwork, banishing, protection, love spells, and to attract wealth.

The Buckeye Nut

❧ by Robert Place ❧

The buckeye tree, *Aesculus glabra*, grows wild in the Midwest, especially in Ohio. It grows in the rich soil along the Mississippi and other rivers, and it can grow up to seventy feet tall and live for a hundred years. It has slender leaflets clustered in groups of five and ash-gray bark. In late spring, it produces red, white, or yellow flowers, and in summer large spiny fruit.

From this fruit emerges what many consider the buckeye tree's most valuable asset, a beautiful round, slightly irregular nut about one inch in diameter with a deep brown smooth surface and a tan oval spot on top. Because it looks like the eye of a deer, the Native Americans called the tree and the nut *hetuck*, which was translated by the first European settlers as "buckeye."

Characteristics of the Buckeye Nut

By most accounts, the buckeye nut is inedible. The nut contains a bitter-tasting toxin, aesculin, which can cause vomiting and paralysis if consumed. However, Native American tribes made it a standard part of their diet.

To accomplish this, they removed the inner and outer shell of the nuts and boiled off the toxin. Once the toxin was removed, the tribal peoples made a nutritious mash from the nutmeat.

Squirrels also seem to be able to dine on the tree without any ill effect. According to legend, this is because only half of a buckeye nut is poisonous. Squirrels are able to determine which half is safe to eat.

The Buckeye Tree

The bark of the buckeye tree has an unpleasant order. This accounts for its nickname "stinking buckeye." In general, wildlife does not tend to eat from the tree. Its nuts, twigs, and leaves are all potentially poisonous to livestock. As a result, the tree has few pests. Even bees are said to be poisoned by the nectar of its flowers.

Wood from the buckeye tree is light in weight and easy to carve. It also burns irregularly. The first settlers made use of it for carving troughs, platters, cradles, utensils, and toys. Also, the wood was planed into thin strips and woven into baskets and hats.

Before the invention of plastic, buckeye wood was used extensively for artificial limbs. Now, however, buckeye has very few commercial uses. Consequently, many farmers consider it a weed.

Still, despite the tree's bad smell, the nuts' unpleasant taste, and the plant's status as a weed, in 1953 Ohio chose the buckeye as its state tree. The buckeye is prevalent in Ohio, but even beyond its prevalence Ohioans have identified with the buckeye for much of their history. Traditionally, the residents of Ohio themselves have been referred to as Buckeyes. This odd nickname is usually traced to the presidential election of 1840, when General William Henry Harrison, of Ohio, was running for president. During the campaign, an opposition newspaper printed a disparaging article in which they described Harrison as unsuited for the White House, and more suited to live in a frontier cabin and dress in coonskins and strings of buckeyes.

Harrison seized on the label and used it to help him create an image of himself as a representative of the common man. He used buckeye nuts as campaign buttons. Of course, the fact that the newspaper used the buckeye to help create an image of a frontiersman shows that identification between the two existed before 1840. The first written record of the term being used as a nickname for an Ohio resident is from 1788. At that time, six-feet-four-inch tall Col. Ebenezer Sproat, who was the epitome of frontier pride, was part of the legal delegation at the first court session of the Northwest Territory. Sproat was given the nickname "buckeye" by the local Native Americans, and he accepted the name with pride.

The nickname was adopted by other frontiersmen as well. The hearty buckeye wards off disease and pests, grows wherever there is opportunity, and is nearly impossible to kill. With the buckeye name the frontiersmen were identifying themselves with the tenacity of the buckeye tree.

Ever since Harrison's victory in the 1840 presidential race, the word has been associated with Ohio in the national public imagination. Even the Ohio State football team, of all things, has gotten into the act—taking the Buckeye as its mascot for its sports teams in 1950.

Use of the Buckeye

The only medicinal use of the buckeye plant that I have read about is that an extract of the bark has been used in the treatment of diseases of the cerebro-spinal system.

As mentioned above, however, many consider the nut of the buckeye its most valuable asset. This is because it is used in magic. The buckeye is related to the European horse-chestnut. When the first settlers from Europe came to the Ohio region, they recognized the similarity between the two, and they believed that the buckeye had the same magical attributes that had been associated with the horse-chestnut in their homelands, (primarily Germany and the Netherlands).

Today, the buckeye nut is considered a powerful lucky token. Carrying a buckeye nut in your pocket is said to protect you from rheumatism, arthritis, and headaches. Some say that the buckeye nut can ward off any disease. Generally, it brings good luck, and it particularly brings good luck in sexual matters when carried by a man.

Buckeye as Sexual Token

This association with male sexuality brings us to the heart of the buckeye's symbolic power. According to the magical "doctrine of signatures," each herb displays its purpose by bearing a resemblance to the part of the body for which it is beneficial. The magical properties of the horse-chestnut stem from the fact that, in shape and size at least, it is similar to a man's testicle.

The horse-chestnut is narrow with a flat squared end. The full round nut of the American buckeye is a better match—which in theory would make it a more powerful magical tool than its Old World relative.

Don't misunderstand, however. Sexual symbolism is associated with fertility, but to ancient people fertility did not just mean the ability to have babies. Fertility of the land and of livestock created abundance and prosperity. Therefore, it is not surprising that the buckeye is also associated with good luck in matters of money.

The Buckeye in Hoodoo

We find that the use of the buckeye as a magical tool is most fully developed in the American Hoodoo tradition, where it is an important ingredient in a mojo for gamblers. Hoodoo refers to a system of folk magic indigenous to America. It stems from West-African traditions brought to America by slaves that have mixed with elements of Native American herb lore and European folk belief. Although Hoodoo is practiced primarily by African-Americans in the south, it has also had white practitioners from its beginning.

Often, Hoodoo is thought of as another name for Voudon, but author and Hoodoo practitioner Catherine Yronwode points out that they are not the same. Voudon is the name of an African-American religion practiced in Haiti and in New Orleans. It is related to other African-based religions such as African-Cuban Santeria and Palo, African-Brazilian Candomble and Umbanda, and African-Jamaican Obeah.

In these other forms, the traditional African deities or *orishas* are synthesized with Catholic saints. Hoodoo, which is also called rootwork, is not a religion. It is folk magic and herb lore that is practiced by predominately Protestant-Christian African-Americans in the United States.

One of the chief magical devices used in Hoodoo is the mojo. A mojo is a small flannel bag tied-up with magical ingredients inside. The name is possibly derived from the West-African word *mojuba*, which means "a prayer." It can also be called a hand, root bag, or many other names.

The most common form of mojo in the south is a red flannel bag that holds several ingredients that have been anointed with the proper oil. The ingredients can include roots and herbs and symbolic objects. Sometimes different colored bags are used. In that case, the color should match the magical purpose of the mojo—green is for attracting money, red for love, blue for peace, white for blessing, and so on.

A mojo made for an individual will be carried on that person so that it is out of sight. A man may carry it in his pocket. A woman may pin it in her bra or inside her skirt. Mojos used for protection may be hidden near a door. If someone other than its creator touches the mojo its power may be lost.

A traditional mojo used by gamblers to bring them luck while playing cards was made with a buckeye nut. In the past a gambler would take the buckeye nut and drill a hole in it. Then, he would pour quicksilver into the hole, and seal it with wax. After it was anointed with Fast Luck Oil, Van Van Oil, or another anointing oil, it was placed into the flannel bag and tied shut. This mojo was carried in your right front pant pocket while you gambled.

Quicksilver or mercury is used to make a connection with Mercury or Hermes, the god of luck and money. As quicksilver is toxic, it is not recommended for carrying in one's pocket. As a result, this particular charm has fallen out of favor. Instead of using quicksilver, most Hoodoo practitioners now tie the nut to a Mercury dime.

The Mercury dime was minted in the United States from 1916 to 1945. The profile on the coin is actually a head of Liberty wearing a winged Phrygian cap. All previous dimes had Liberty on them, but this was the first to give her wings. Because the winged cap reminds most people of Mercury, it is commonly called the Mercury dime. In Hoodoo, the Mercury dime is considered the most magical coin minted and is greatly prized. The most powerful dime to work with is one that bears the date of a leap year. This includes the 1916, 1920, 1924, 1928, 1932, 1936, 1940, and 1944 dimes.

The Buckeye Money Mojo

To make a money mojo, one should obtain a buckeye nut, a Mercury dime, a two-dollar bill, some anointing oil, and a red or green flannel bag. To set the right mood, light a green candle. Take the buckeye and the dime, and anoint them with the oil. Use Van Van, Money Drawing Oil, Fast Luck, or another oil sold by Hoodoo suppliers. If you prefer to make your own oil, simply soak the appropriate herbs in a good quality cooking oil. You can use lemongrass or other herbs that are associated with wealth or the god Mercury. Some Hoodoo workers rub the buckeye nut in the crevice between their nostril and cheek to anoint it with face oil. It is also considered powerful to anoint the entire bag when it is complete with the urine of one's lover. This is especially effective if it done during the intermission of a card game. You can, if you choose, use the bag when you return to the game.

But back to your Money Mojo: Take the anointed nut and dime, place them on the two-dollar bill, and then roll the bill up—with the dime and nut inside. Be careful to role the bill toward yourself. Fold the bill around its contents. You may prefer to tie it with a string.

Now, place the bundle in the mojo bag and tie it shut. Keep your Money Mojo in your right front pants pocket, or sew it under your skirt. Keep it out of sight and don't let anyone touch it, ever.

Putting the Money Mojo to the Test

In connection with writing this article, I decided to make my own Buckeye Money Mojo and test its efficacy. But first, a bit of background.

At present, I don't own any credit cards. I did at one time, but that is another story. Therefore, when I am traveling on business I like to have enough money on me to take care of emergencies. In the beginning of the summer, I had to travel from my home in the state of New York to a weekend Celtic Festival in Alexandria, Virginia, to sell some jewelry that I had designed.

Because of expenses from medical emergencies and the usual expenses associated with making a stock of silver and gold jewelry, we were particularly low on cash when it came time for me to attend the festival. I had only enough money to pay for the gas and tolls and one night in a hotel before I would run out. I figured that I could count on getting through the first day of the show and by then I would earn enough money to take care of any other expenses.

As I was relying on good fortune to get me through, this seemed like a good time to try out the mojo. Not only that, but I found that I actually had the right ingredients lying around my desk.

I had a buckeye nut that I had bought years ago on a whim in a *botanica*. I had a Mercury dime—not from a leap year, but still rare enough to be magical. I even had a two-dollar bill that I had saved when someone handed it to me as part of the payment for a silver pin. It was still crisp and new.

In my magical cabinet, I had a bottle of anointing oil. Furthermore, the bags that I put my jewelry in when I sell it are perfect for a mojo—three-inch by three-inch drawstring pouches made of green flannel.

To start my test, I lit a green candle. I anointed the ingredients, placed them on the two-dollar bill, and rolled the bill toward me. Then I tied it with a piece of string, put it in the drawstring pouch, and tied the pouch with a square knot. *(Note: In the ancient classical world, this knot was called the "Hercules knot," and it was considered the best knot for holding in magical power.)* I placed the pouch in the right front pocket of my jeans.

I left on a Friday with my pouch in my pocket. The trip to Virginia was uneventful except that on two occasions I was given the opportunity to help another motorist by jumpstarting their battery from mine. I keep good-quality heavy jumper cables in my van just for this purpose, but I had not had an occasion to use them in a few years. For it to happen twice in the same day was unusual. I figured at the time that I happened to be in the right place at the right time to be of service. I remember thinking how important it is for motorists to help one another. If we all can rely on each other, this is the best security that any traveler should ever need.

I arrived at the festival site on Friday evening and set up my tent and showcase. While I was working, a friend of mine who was also a crafts vendor at the festival gave me a coupon for a discount rate at a local motel chain. Naturally, that evening, I went to that motel.

As I pulled into the parking lot, the clutch pedal made an unusual sound, lost its tension, and fell to the floor. The cable that connected to the pedal had broken—it was useless. This would seem like a stroke of bad luck—after all, it is bad enough for one's car to break down while traveling, but not having enough money to fix the problem could make it seem like an insurmountable obstacle.

However, as I thought about it, I realized that the cable was worn out, and it could have broken anywhere while I was on the trip. It could have left me stranded in a rest stop on the way. Instead, it had allowed me to set up at the show and get to a comfortable place to stay for the evening before it broke. This was actually good fortune.

I left my van in the parking space and rented a room for the night. Then I realized that my friend who gave me the coupon would be staying in the same motel. This was another stroke of good fortune. I found his room number and called him on the house phone.

In the morning, he and his wife took my merchandise and luggage in their truck and brought it to the festival. I stayed with my van, and after some trial and error I found a dealer who was open on a Saturday and had him send a tow truck. As I did not have enough money to pay for the tow, I asked the driver to add his fee to the final bill, and he agreed.

After we dropped off the van, the tow truck driver said that his next call was near where I was going—so he could drive me to the festival. He let me out near the entrance, and I went to my booth and set out the merchandise. I was only about an hour late. Again, good fortune.

That day, I offered discounts to customers who paid in cash. In this way, I quickly I built up the money that I needed to take care of the situation.

I borrowed a cell phone to call my wife at home, and asked her to take care of the arrangements with the car dealer. That night when I called home, my wife informed me that her mother would pay the repair bill with her credit card. But the bad news was that the part necessary to complete the repair would not be available until the middle of the week.

This would seem like another stroke of bad luck, but she reminded me that my friend Rosemary, who was my partner on my first two tarot projects, lived near enough to come and pick me up. And I had been planning on visiting Rosemary after the show anyway. I called her up, and she quickly and eagerly agreed to come and get me.

That night I rode with the same friends who had helped me in the morning. We all were staying at the same motel, so they drove me back the next day.

When the festival was over, I packed up my tent and show-case into a neat pile, and secured the tent cover over it like a tarp. I had checked with the festival promoter first, and I knew that my display would be safe here until I could pick it up.

I put my merchandise in a separate pile and sat on it while I waited for Rosemary. Within minutes, Rosemary showed up in her Jeep, and I put the merchandise in the back. While I was at her house for the next couple of days, she lent me her laptop computer, and I was able to work on my book. The part came in on Tuesday, and Rosemary drove me to the dealers to pick up the van. The next morning I drove home. The trip was uneventful, and I returned from the show with a sharp profit.

The Moral of the Mojo

In looking back on the experience and asking myself if the buck-eye mojo worked, I realized that, although the van did break, and various other mishaps could have set me back, in general I was lucky. Always, the mishaps occurred where friends could help me, and not where I would have been stranded or without resources to deal with the problem.

This luck allowed me to be successful at the festival and to bring home the much-needed money. And of course, the greatest magic is what happens when friends help one another. All the mojo did is put me in the right place and time for friendship to be available.

The
Quarters and
Signs of the
Moon and
Moon
Tables

The Quarters and Signs
of the Moon

Everyone has seen the Moon wax and wane through a period of approximately twenty-nine and a half days. This circuit from New Moon to Full Moon and back again is called the lunation cycle. The cycle is divided into parts, called quarters or phases. There are several methods by which this can be done, and the system used in the *Herbal Almanac* may not correspond to those used in other almanacs.

The Quarters

First Quarter

The first quarter begins at the New Moon, when the Sun and Moon are in the same place, or conjunct. (This means that the Sun and Moon are in the same degree of the same sign.) The Moon is not visible at first, since it rises at the same time as the Sun. The New Moon is the time of new beginnings, beginnings of projects that favor growth, externalization of activities, and the growth of ideas. The first quarter is the time of germination, emergence, beginnings, and outwardly directed activity.

Second Quarter

The second quarter begins halfway between the New Moon and the Full Moon, when the Sun and Moon are at right angles, or a 90-degree square to each other. This half Moon rises around noon and sets around midnight, so it can be seen in the western sky during the first half of the night. The second quarter is the time of growth and articulation of things that already exist.

Third Quarter

The third quarter begins at the Full Moon, when the Sun and Moon are opposite one another and the full light of the Sun can shine on the full sphere of the Moon. The round Moon can be seen rising in the east at sunset, and then rising a little later each evening. The Full Moon stands for illumination, fulfillment, culmination, completion, drawing inward, unrest, emotional expressions, and hasty actions leading to failure. The third quarter is a time of maturity, fruition, and the assumption of the full form of expression.

Fourth Quarter

The fourth quarter begins about halfway between the Full Moon and New Moon, when the Sun and Moon are again at 90 degrees, or square. This decreasing Moon rises at midnight, and can be seen in the east during the last half of the night, reaching the overhead position just about as the Sun rises. The fourth quarter is a time of disintegration, drawing back for reorganization and reflection.

The Signs

Moon in Aries

Moon in Aries is good for starting things, but lacking in staying power. Things occur rapidly, but also quickly pass.

Moon in Taurus

With Moon in Taurus, things begun during this sign last the longest and tend to increase in value. Things begun now become habitual and hard to alter.

Moon in Gemini

Moon in Gemini is an inconsistent position for the Moon, characterized by a lot of talk. Things begun now are easily changed by outside influences.

Moon in Cancer

Moon in Cancer stimulates emotional rapport between people. It pinpoints need, and supports growth and nurturance.

Moon in Leo

Moon in Leo accents showmanship, being seen, drama, recreation, and happy pursuits. It may be concerned with praise and subject to flattery.

Moon in Virgo

Moon in Virgo favors accomplishment of details and commands from higher up while discouraging independent thinking.

Moon in Libra

Moon in Libra increases self-awareness. It favors self-examination and interaction with others, but discourages spontaneous initiative.

Moon in Scorpio

Moon in Scorpio increases awareness of psychic power. It precipitates psychic crises and ends connections thoroughly.

Moon in Sagittarius

Moon in Sagittarius encourages expansionary flights of imagination and confidence in the flow of life.

Moon in Capricorn

Moon in Capricorn increases awareness of the need for structure, discipline, and organization. Institutional activities are favored.

Moon in Aquarius

Moon in Aquarius favors activities that are unique and individualistic, concern for humanitarian needs, society as a whole, and improvements that can be made.

Moon in Pisces

During Moon in Pisces, energy withdraws from the surface of life, hibernates within, secretly reorganizing and realigning.

January Moon Table

Date	Sign	Element	Nature	Phase
1 Thu. 12:02 am	Taurus	Earth	Semi-fruitful	2nd
2 Fri.	Taurus	Earth	Semi-fruitful	2nd
3 Sat. 12:58 pm	Gemini	Air	Barren	2nd
4 Sun.	Gemini	Air	Barren	2nd
5 Mon.	Gemini	Air	Barren	2nd
6 Tue. 1:38 am	Cancer	Water	Fruitful	2nd
7 Wed.	Cancer	Water	Fruitful	Full 10:40 am
8 Thu. 12:38 pm	Leo	Fire	Barren	3rd
9 Fri.	Leo	Fire	Barren	3rd
10 Sat. 9:37 pm	Virgo	Earth	Barren	3rd
11 Sun.	Virgo	Earth	Barren	3rd
12 Mon.	Virgo	Earth	Barren	3rd
13 Tue. 4:38 am	Libra	Air	Semi-fruitful	3rd
14 Wed.	Libra	Air	Semi-fruitful	4th 11:46 pm
15 Thu. 9:33 am	Scorpio	Water	Fruitful	4th
16 Fri.	Scorpio	Water	Fruitful	4th
17 Sat. 12:18 pm	Sagittarius	Fire	Barren	4th
18 Sun.	Sagittarius	Fire	Barren	4th
19 Mon. 1:24 pm	Capricorn	Earth	Semi-fruitful	4th
20 Tue.	Capricorn	Earth	Semi-fruitful	4th
21 Wed. 2:11 pm	Aquarius	Air	Barren	New 4:05 pm
22 Thu.	Aquarius	Air	Barren	1st
23 Fri. 4:29 pm	Pisces	Water	Fruitful	1st
24 Sat.	Pisces	Water	Fruitful	1st
25 Sun. 10:06 pm	Aries	Fire	Barren	1st
26 Mon.	Aries	Fire	Barren	1st
27 Tue.	Aries	Fire	Barren	1st
28 Wed. 7:46 am	Taurus	Earth	Semi-fruitful	1st
29 Thu.	Taurus	Earth	Semi-fruitful	2nd 1:03 am
30 Fri. 8:18 pm	Gemini	Air	Barren	2nd
31 Sat.	Gemini	Air	Barren	2nd

February Moon Table

Date	Sign	Element	Nature	Phase
1 Sun.	Gemini	Air	Barren	2nd
2 Mon. 9:03 am	Cancer	Water	Fruitful	2nd
3 Tue.	Cancer	Water	Fruitful	2nd
4 Wed. 7:50 pm	Leo	Fire	Barren	2nd
5 Thu.	Leo	Fire	Barren	2nd
6 Fri.	Leo	Fire	Barren	Full 3:47 am
7 Sat. 4:03 am	Virgo	Earth	Barren	3rd
8 Sun.	Virgo	Earth	Barren	3rd
9 Mon. 10:12 am	Libra	Air	Semi-fruitful	3rd
10 Tue.	Libra	Air	Semi-fruitful	3rd
11 Wed. 2:58 pm	Scorpio	Water	Fruitful	3rd
12 Thu.	Scorpio	Water	Fruitful	3rd
13 Fri. 6:35 pm	Sagittarius	Fire	Barren	4th 8:39 am
14 Sat.	Sagittarius	Fire	Barren	4th
15 Sun. 9:14 pm	Capricorn	Earth	Semi-fruitful	4th
16 Mon.	Capricorn	Earth	Semi-fruitful	4th
17 Tue. 11:27 pm	Aquarius	Air	Barren	4th
18 Wed.	Aquarius	Air	Barren	4th
19 Thu.	Aquarius	Air	Barren	4th
20 Fri. 2:27 am	Pisces	Water	Fruitful	New 4:18 am
21 Sat.	Pisces	Water	Fruitful	1st
22 Sun. 7:45 am	Aries	Fire	Barren	1st
23 Mon.	Aries	Fire	Barren	1st
24 Tue. 4:30 pm	Taurus	Earth	Semi-fruitful	1st
25 Wed.	Taurus	Earth	Semi-fruitful	1st
26 Thu.	Taurus	Earth	Semi-fruitful	1st
27 Fri. 4:22 am	Gemini	Air	Barren	2nd 10:24 pm
28 Sat.	Gemini	Air	Barren	2nd
29 Sun. 5:12 pm	Cancer	Water	Fruitful	2nd

March Moon Table

Date	Sign	Element	Nature	Phase
1 Mon.	Cancer	Water	Fruitful	2nd
2 Tue.	Cancer	Water	Fruitful	2nd
3 Wed. 4:18 am	Leo	Fire	Barren	2nd
4 Thu.	Leo	Fire	Barren	2nd
5 Fri. 12:18 pm	Virgo	Earth	Barren	2nd
6 Sat.	Virgo	Earth	Barren	Full 6:14 pm
7 Sun. 5:31 pm	Libra	Air	Semi-fruitful	3rd
8 Mon.	Libra	Air	Semi-fruitful	3rd
9 Tue. 9:03 pm	Scorpio	Water	Fruitful	3rd
10 Wed.	Scorpio	Water	Fruitful	3rd
11 Thu. 11:57 pm	Sagittarius	Fire	Barren	3rd
12 Fri.	Sagittarius	Fire	Barren	3rd
13 Sat.	Sagittarius	Fire	Barren	4th 4:01 pm
14 Sun. 2:51 am	Capricorn	Earth	Semi-fruitful	4th
15 Mon.	Capricorn	Earth	Semi-fruitful	4th
16 Tue. 6:10 am	Aquarius	Air	Barren	4th
17 Wed.	Aquarius	Air	Barren	4th
18 Thu. 10:26 am	Pisces	Water	Fruitful	4th
19 Fri.	Pisces	Water	Fruitful	4th
20 Sat. 4:29 pm	Aries	Fire	Barren	New 5:41 pm
21 Sun.	Aries	Fire	Barren	1st
22 Mon.	Aries	Fire	Barren	1st
23 Tue. 1:10 am	Taurus	Earth	Semi-fruitful	1st
24 Wed.	Taurus	Earth	Semi-fruitful	1st
25 Thu. 12:35 pm	Gemini	Air	Barren	1st
26 Fri.	Gemini	Air	Barren	1st
27 Sat.	Gemini	Air	Barren	1st
28 Sun. 1:23 am	Cancer	Water	Fruitful	2nd 6:48 pm
29 Mon.	Cancer	Water	Fruitful	2nd
30 Tue. 1:07 pm	Leo	Fire	Barren	2nd
31 Wed.	Leo	Fire	Barren	2nd

April Moon Table

Date	Sign	Element	Nature	Phase
1 Thu. 9:45 pm	Virgo	Earth	Barren	2nd
2 Fri.	Virgo	Earth	Barren	2nd
3 Sat.	Virgo	Earth	Barren	2nd
4 Sun. 3:52 am	Libra	Air	Semi-fruitful	2nd
5 Mon.	Libra	Air	Semi-fruitful	Full 7:03 am
6 Tue. 6:24 am	Scorpio	Water	Fruitful	3rd
7 Wed.	Scorpio	Water	Fruitful	3rd
8 Thu. 7:50 am	Sagittarius	Fire	Barren	3rd
9 Fri.	Sagittarius	Fire	Barren	3rd
10 Sat. 9:33 am	Capricorn	Earth	Semi-fruitful	3rd
11 Sun.	Capricorn	Earth	Semi-fruitful	4th 11:46 pm
12 Mon. 12:33 pm	Aquarius	Air	Barren	4th
13 Tue.	Aquarius	Air	Barren	4th
14 Wed. 5:24 pm	Pisces	Water	Fruitful	4th
15 Thu.	Pisces	Water	Fruitful	4th
16 Fri.	Pisces	Water	Fruitful	4th
17 Sat. 12:24 am	Aries	Fire	Barren	4th
18 Sun.	Aries	Fire	Barren	4th
19 Mon. 9:43 am	Taurus	Earth	Semi-fruitful	New 9:21 am
20 Tue.	Taurus	Earth	Semi-fruitful	1st
21 Wed. 9:10 pm	Gemini	Air	Barren	1st
22 Thu.	Gemini	Air	Barren	1st
23 Fri.	Gemini	Air	Barren	1st
24 Sat. 9:56 am	Cancer	Water	Fruitful	1st
25 Sun.	Cancer	Water	Fruitful	1st
26 Mon. 10:14 pm	Leo	Fire	Barren	1st
27 Tue.	Leo	Fire	Barren	2nd 1:32 pm
28 Wed.	Leo	Fire	Barren	2nd
29 Thu. 8:00 am	Virgo	Earth	Barren	2nd
30 Fri.	Virgo	Earth	Barren	2nd

May Moon Table

Date	Sign	Element	Nature	Phase
1 Sat. 2:03 pm	Libra	Air	Semi-fruitful	2nd
2 Sun.	Libra	Air	Semi-fruitful	2nd
3 Mon. 4:38 pm	Scorpio	Water	Fruitful	2nd
4 Tue.	Scorpio	Water	Fruitful	Full 4:33 pm
5 Wed. 5:08 pm	Sagittarius	Fire	Barren	3rd
6 Thu.	Sagittarius	Fire	Barren	3rd
7 Fri. 5:17 pm	Capricorn	Earth	Semi-fruitful	3rd
8 Sat.	Capricorn	Earth	Semi-fruitful	3rd
9 Sun. 6:46 pm	Aquarius	Air	Barren	3rd
10 Mon.	Aquarius	Air	Barren	3rd
11 Tue. 10:52 pm	Pisces	Water	Fruitful	4th 7:04 am
12 Wed.	Pisces	Water	Fruitful	4th
13 Thu.	Pisces	Water	Fruitful	4th
14 Fri. 6:02 am	Aries	Fire	Barren	4th
15 Sat.	Aries	Fire	Barren	4th
16 Sun. 3:57 pm	Taurus	Earth	Semi-fruitful	4th
17 Mon.	Taurus	Earth	Semi-fruitful	4th
18 Tue.	Taurus	Earth	Semi-fruitful	4th
19 Wed. 3:47 am	Gemini	Air	Barren	New 12:52 am
20 Thu.	Gemini	Air	Barren	1st
21 Fri. 4:35 pm	Cancer	Water	Fruitful	1st
22 Sat.	Cancer	Water	Fruitful	1st
23 Sun.	Cancer	Water	Fruitful	1st
24 Mon. 5:07 am	Leo	Fire	Barren	1st
25 Tue.	Leo	Fire	Barren	1st
26 Wed. 3:52 pm	Virgo	Earth	Barren	1st
27 Thu.	Virgo	Earth	Barren	2nd 3:57 am
28 Fri. 11:22 pm	Libra	Air	Semi-fruitful	2nd
29 Sat.	Libra	Air	Semi-fruitful	2nd
30 Sun.	Libra	Air	Semi-fruitful	2nd
31 Mon. 3:08 am	Scorpio	Water	Fruitful	2nd

June Moon Table

Date	Sign	Element	Nature	Phase
1 Tue.	Scorpio	Water	Fruitful	2nd
2 Wed. 3:52 am	Sagittarius	Fire	Barren	2nd
3 Thu.	Sagittarius	Fire	Barren	Full 12:20 am
4 Fri. 3:12 am	Capricorn	Earth	Semi-fruitful	3rd
5 Sat.	Capricorn	Earth	Semi-fruitful	3rd
6 Sun. 3:10 am	Aquarius	Air	Barren	3rd
7 Mon.	Aquarius	Air	Barren	3rd
8 Tue. 5:38 am	Pisces	Water	Fruitful	3rd
9 Wed.	Pisces	Water	Fruitful	4th 4:02 pm
10 Thu. 11:49 am	Aries	Fire	Barren	4th
11 Fri.	Aries	Fire	Barren	4th
12 Sat. 9:37 pm	Taurus	Earth	Semi-fruitful	4th
13 Sun.	Taurus	Earth	Semi-fruitful	4th
14 Mon.	Taurus	Earth	Semi-fruitful	4th
15 Tue. 9:44 am	Gemini	Air	Barren	4th
16 Wed.	Gemini	Air	Barren	4th
17 Thu. 10:37 pm	Cancer	Water	Fruitful	New 4:27 pm
18 Fri.	Cancer	Water	Fruitful	1st
19 Sat.	Cancer	Water	Fruitful	1st
20 Sun. 11:05 am	Leo	Fire	Barren	1st
21 Mon.	Leo	Fire	Barren	1st
22 Tue. 10:10 pm	Virgo	Earth	Barren	1st
23 Wed.	Virgo	Earth	Barren	1st
24 Thu.	Virgo	Earth	Barren	1st
25 Fri. 6:50 am	Libra	Air	Semi-fruitful	2nd 3:08 pm
26 Sat.	Libra	Air	Semi-fruitful	2nd
27 Sun. 12:13 pm	Scorpio	Water	Fruitful	2nd
28 Mon.	Scorpio	Water	Fruitful	2nd
29 Tue. 2:15 pm	Sagittarius	Fire	Barren	2nd
30 Wed.	Sagittarius	Fire	Barren	2nd

July Moon Table

Date	Sign	Element	Nature	Phase
1 Thu. 2:01 pm	Capricorn	Earth	Semi-fruitful	2nd
2 Fri.	Capricorn	Earth	Semi-fruitful	Full 7:09 am
3 Sat. 1:22 pm	Aquarius	Air	Barren	3rd
4 Sun.	Aquarius	Air	Barren	3rd
5 Mon. 2:26 pm	Pisces	Water	Fruitful	3rd
6 Tue.	Pisces	Water	Fruitful	3rd
7 Wed. 7:03 pm	Aries	Fire	Barren	3rd
8 Thu.	Aries	Fire	Barren	3rd
9 Fri.	Aries	Fire	Barren	4th 3:34 am
10 Sat. 3:51 am	Taurus	Earth	Semi-fruitful	4th
11 Sun.	Taurus	Earth	Semi-fruitful	4th
12 Mon. 3:45 pm	Gemini	Air	Barren	4th
13 Tue.	Gemini	Air	Barren	4th
14 Wed.	Gemini	Air	Barren	4th
15 Thu. 4:40 am	Cancer	Water	Fruitful	4th
16 Fri.	Cancer	Water	Fruitful	4th
17 Sat. 4:56 pm	Leo	Fire	Barren	New 7:24 am
18 Sun.	Leo	Fire	Barren	1st
19 Mon.	Leo	Fire	Barren	1st
20 Tue. 3:44 am	Virgo	Earth	Barren	1st
21 Wed.	Virgo	Earth	Barren	1st
22 Thu. 12:39 pm	Libra	Air	Semi-fruitful	1st
23 Fri.	Libra	Air	Semi-fruitful	1st
24 Sat. 7:08 pm	Scorpio	Water	Fruitful	2nd 11:37 pm
25 Sun.	Scorpio	Water	Fruitful	2nd
26 Mon. 10:48 pm	Sagittarius	Fire	Barren	2nd
27 Tue.	Sagittarius	Fire	Barren	2nd
28 Wed. 11:57 pm	Capricorn	Earth	Semi-fruitful	2nd
29 Thu.	Capricorn	Earth	Semi-fruitful	2nd
30 Fri. 11:54 pm	Aquarius	Air	Barren	2nd
31 Sat.	Aquarius	Air	Barren	Full 2:05 pm

August Moon Table

Date	Sign	Element	Nature	Phase
1 Sun.	Aquarius	Air	Barren	3rd
2 Mon. 12:34 am	Pisces	Water	Fruitful	3rd
3 Tue.	Pisces	Water	Fruitful	3rd
4 Wed. 3:59 am	Aries	Fire	Barren	3rd
5 Thu.	Aries	Fire	Barren	3rd
6 Fri. 11:26 am	Taurus	Earth	Semi-fruitful	3rd
7 Sat.	Taurus	Earth	Semi-fruitful	4th 6:01 pm
8 Sun. 10:33 pm	Gemini	Air	Barren	4th
9 Mon.	Gemini	Air	Barren	4th
10 Tue.	Gemini	Air	Barren	4th
11 Wed. 11:20 am	Cancer	Water	Fruitful	4th
12 Thu.	Cancer	Water	Fruitful	4th
13 Fri. 11:30 pm	Leo	Fire	Barren	4th
14 Sat.	Leo	Fire	Barren	4th
15 Sun.	Leo	Fire	Barren	New 9:24 pm
16 Mon. 9:49 am	Virgo	Earth	Barren	1st
17 Tue.	Virgo	Earth	Barren	1st
18 Wed. 6:09 pm	Libra	Air	Semi-fruitful	1st
19 Thu.	Libra	Air	Semi-fruitful	1st
20 Fri.	Libra	Air	Semi-fruitful	1st
21 Sat. 12:37 am	Scorpio	Water	Fruitful	1st
22 Sun.	Scorpio	Water	Fruitful	1st
23 Mon. 5:08 am	Sagittarius	Fire	Barren	2nd 6:12 am
24 Tue.	Sagittarius	Fire	Barren	2nd
25 Wed. 7:46 am	Capricorn	Earth	Semi-fruitful	2nd
26 Thu.	Capricorn	Earth	Semi-fruitful	2nd
27 Fri. 9:08 am	Aquarius	Air	Barren	2nd
28 Sat.	Aquarius	Air	Barren	2nd
29 Sun. 10:33 am	Pisces	Water	Fruitful	Full 10:22 pm
30 Mon.	Pisces	Water	Fruitful	3rd
31 Tue. 1:46 pm	Aries	Fire	Barren	3rd

September Moon Table

Date	Sign	Element	Nature	Phase
1 Wed.	Aries	Fire	Barren	3rd
2 Thu. 8:16 pm	Taurus	Earth	Semi-fruitful	3rd
3 Fri.	Taurus	Earth	Semi-fruitful	3rd
4 Sat.	Taurus	Earth	Semi-fruitful	3rd
5 Sun. 6:24 am	Gemini	Air	Barren	3rd
6 Mon.	Gemini	Air	Barren	4th 11:10 am
7 Tue. 6:50 pm	Cancer	Water	Fruitful	4th
8 Wed.	Cancer	Water	Fruitful	4th
9 Thu.	Cancer	Water	Fruitful	4th
10 Fri. 7:06 am	Leo	Fire	Barren	4th
11 Sat.	Leo	Fire	Barren	4th
12 Sun. 5:16 pm	Virgo	Earth	Barren	4th
13 Mon.	Virgo	Earth	Barren	4th
14 Tue.	Virgo	Earth	Barren	New 10:29am
15 Wed. 12:54 am	Libra	Air	Semi-fruitful	1st
16 Thu.	Libra	Air	Semi-fruitful	1st
17 Fri. 6:25 am	Scorpio	Water	Fruitful	1st
18 Sat.	Scorpio	Water	Fruitful	1st
19 Sun. 10:30 am	Sagittarius	Fire	Barren	1st
20 Mon.	Sagittarius	Fire	Barren	1st
21 Tue. 1:35 pm	Capricorn	Earth	Semi-fruitful	2nd 11:54 am
22 Wed.	Capricorn	Earth	Semi-fruitful	2nd
23 Thu. 4:10 pm	Aquarius	Air	Barren	2nd
24 Fri.	Aquarius	Air	Barren	2nd
25 Sat. 6:55 pm	Pisces	Water	Fruitful	2nd
26 Sun.	Pisces	Water	Fruitful	2nd
27 Mon. 10:57 pm	Aries	Fire	Barren	2nd
28 Tue.	Aries	Fire	Barren	Full 9:09 am
29 Wed.	Aries	Fire	Barren	3rd
30 Thu. 5:24 am	Taurus	Earth	Semi-fruitful	3rd

October Moon Table

Date	Sign	Element	Nature	Phase
1 Fri.	Taurus	Earth	Semi-fruitful	3rd
2 Sat. 2:55 pm	Gemini	Air	Barren	3rd
3 Sun.	Gemini	Air	Barren	3rd
4 Mon.	Gemini	Air	Barren	3rd
5 Tue. 2:54 am	Cancer	Water	Fruitful	3rd
6 Wed.	Cancer	Water	Fruitful	4th 6:12 am
7 Thu. 3:23 pm	Leo	Fire	Barren	4th
8 Fri.	Leo	Fire	Barren	4th
9 Sat.	Leo	Fire	Barren	4th
10 Sun. 2:00 am	Virgo	Earth	Barren	4th
11 Mon.	Virgo	Earth	Barren	4th
12 Tue. 9:32 am	Libra	Air	Semi-fruitful	4th
13 Wed.	Libra	Air	Semi-fruitful	New 10:48 pm
14 Thu. 2:10 pm	Scorpio	Water	Fruitful	1st
15 Fri.	Scorpio	Water	Fruitful	1st
16 Sat. 4:58 pm	Sagittarius	Fire	Barren	1st
17 Sun.	Sagittarius	Fire	Barren	1st
18 Mon. 7:07 pm	Capricorn	Earth	Semi-fruitful	1st
19 Tue.	Capricorn	Earth	Semi-fruitful	1st
20 Wed. 9:38 pm	Aquarius	Air	Barren	2nd 5:59 pm
21 Thu.	Aquarius	Air	Barren	2nd
22 Fri.	Aquarius	Air	Barren	2nd
23 Sat. 1:13 am	Pisces	Water	Fruitful	2nd
24 Sun.	Pisces	Water	Fruitful	2nd
25 Mon. 6:24 am	Aries	Fire	Barren	2nd
26 Tue.	Aries	Fire	Barren	2nd
27 Wed. 1:37 pm	Taurus	Earth	Semi-fruitful	Full 11:07 pm
28 Thu.	Taurus	Earth	Semi-fruitful	3rd
29 Fri. 11:11 pm	Gemini	Air	Barren	3rd
30 Sat.	Gemini	Air	Barren	3rd
31 Sun.	Gemini	Air	Barren	3rd

November Moon Table

Date	Sign	Element	Nature	Phase
1 Mon. 9:53 am	Cancer	Water	Fruitful	3rd
2 Tue.	Cancer	Water	Fruitful	3rd
3 Wed. 10:32 pm	Leo	Fire	Barren	3rd
4 Thu.	Leo	Fire	Barren	3rd
5 Fri.	Leo	Fire	Barren	4th 12:53 am
6 Sat. 10:00 am	Virgo	Earth	Barren	4th
7 Sun.	Virgo	Earth	Barren	4th
8 Mon. 6:23 pm	Libra	Air	Semi-fruitful	4th
9 Tue.	Libra	Air	Semi-fruitful	4th
10 Wed. 11:05 pm	Scorpio	Water	Fruitful	4th
11 Thu.	Scorpio	Water	Fruitful	4th
12 Fri.	Scorpio	Water	Fruitful	New 9:27 am
13 Sat. 12:56 am	Sagittarius	Fire	Barren	1st
14 Sun.	Sagittarius	Fire	Barren	1st
15 Mon. 1:33 am	Capricorn	Earth	Semi-fruitful	1st
16 Tue.	Capricorn	Earth	Semi-fruitful	1st
17 Wed. 2:39 am	Aquarius	Air	Barren	1st
18 Thu.	Aquarius	Air	Barren	1st
19 Fri. 5:38 am	Pisces	Water	Fruitful	2nd 12:50 am
20 Sat.	Pisces	Water	Fruitful	2nd
21 Sun. 11:11 am	Aries	Fire	Barren	2nd
22 Mon.	Aries	Fire	Barren	2nd
23 Tue. 7:16 pm	Taurus	Earth	Semi-fruitful	2nd
24 Wed.	Taurus	Earth	Semi-fruitful	2nd
25 Thu.	Taurus	Earth	Semi-fruitful	2nd
26 Fri. 5:25 am	Gemini	Air	Barren	Full 3:07 pm
27 Sat.	Gemini	Air	Barren	3rd
28 Sun. 5:10 pm	Cancer	Water	Fruitful	3rd
29 Mon.	Cancer	Water	Fruitful	3rd
30 Tue.	Cancer	Water	Fruitful	3rd

December Moon Table

Date	Sign	Element	Nature	Phase
1 Wed. 5:50 am	Leo	Fire	Barren	3rd
2 Thu.	Leo	Fire	Barren	3rd
3 Fri. 6:00 pm	Virgo	Earth	Barren	3rd
4 Sat.	Virgo	Earth	Barren	4th 7:53 pm
5 Sun.	Virgo	Earth	Barren	4th
6 Mon. 3:46 am	Libra	Air	Semi-fruitful	4th
7 Tue.	Libra	Air	Semi-fruitful	4th
8 Wed. 9:43 am	Scorpio	Water	Fruitful	4th
9 Thu.	Scorpio	Water	Fruitful	4th
10 Fri. 11:54 am	Sagittarius	Fire	Barren	4th
11 Sat.	Sagittarius	Fire	Barren	New 8:29 pm
12 Sun. 11:42 am	Capricorn	Earth	Semi-fruitful	1st
13 Mon.	Capricorn	Earth	Semi-fruitful	1st
14 Tue. 11:10 am	Aquarius	Air	Barren	1st
15 Wed.	Aquarius	Air	Barren	1st
16 Thu. 12:24 pm	Pisces	Water	Fruitful	1st
17 Fri.	Pisces	Water	Fruitful	1st
18 Sat. 4:52 pm	Aries	Fire	Barren	2nd 11:40 am
19 Sun.	Aries	Fire	Barren	2nd
20 Mon.	Aries	Fire	Barren	2nd
21 Tue. 12:52 am	Taurus	Earth	Semi-fruitful	2nd
22 Wed.	Taurus	Earth	Semi-fruitful	2nd
23 Thu. 11:32 am	Gemini	Air	Barren	2nd
24 Fri.	Gemini	Air	Barren	2nd
25 Sat. 11:38 pm	Cancer	Water	Fruitful	2nd
26 Sun.	Cancer	Water	Fruitful	Full 10:06 am
27 Mon.	Cancer	Water	Fruitful	3rd
28 Tue. 12:14 pm	Leo	Fire	Barren	3rd
29 Wed.	Leo	Fire	Barren	3rd
30 Thu.	Leo	Fire	Barren	3rd
31 Fri. 12:33 am	Virgo	Earth	Barren	3rd

About the Authors

PEG ALOI, a teacher of film studies and a freelance film critic, is also the media coordinator for the Witches' Voice, Inc., which is located on the web at www.witchvox.com.

SCOTT APPELL has written four books. His latest book, *A Brave New World: The Sacred Herbs of Vodou, Santería and Candomblé*, is slated for completion in 2003. He is formerly director of education for the Horticultural Society of New York, and a past member of the publications committee of the Pennsylvania Horticultural Society. He is currently director of horticulture for the St. George Village Botanical Garden on St. Croix, in the U.S. Virgin Islands. He is also a board member of the American Violet Society.

VIVIAN ASHCRAFT lives in rural Ohio and has been gardening for more than twenty years. She discovered fairy gardening through research that began after she started to wonder about the spirits that her plants seemed to contain. Her other interests include writing, reading, and needlework.

ELIZABETH BARRETTE is the managing editor of *PanGaia* and assistant editor of *SageWoman*. She has been involved with the Pagan community for more than thirteen years and lives in central Illinois. Her other writing fields include speculative fiction and gender studies. Visit her website at: http://www.worthlink.net/~ysabet/index.html.

CHANDRA MOIRA BEAL is a writer living in Austin, Texas. She self-publishes books and has authored dozens of articles. In her day job, she is a massage therapist and reiki practitioner. She lives with a magical house rabbit named Maia. *Chandra* is Sanskrit for "the moon."

STEPHANIE ROSE BIRD is an artist, writer, herbalist, healer, mother, and companion. She studied art at the Tyler School of Art and at the University of California at San Diego, and she researched Australian Aboriginal art, ritual, and ceremonial practices as a Fulbright senior scholar. Currently, she leads herbcraft workshops at the Chicago Botanic Gardens. Her column "Ase! from the Crossroads" is featured in *SageWoman*. Her book *Sticks, Stones, Roots and Bones*, will be published by Llewellyn in 2004.

DALLAS JENNIFER COBB is a mother, partner, writer, and feminist. Determined to make a living doing what she loves, she writes and researches, grows organic vegetables and herbs, and produces natural body and health care products. In between, she plots and schemes to find novel ways to pay the bills while placing parenting at the top of her to-do list.

ELLEN DUGAN, also known as the Garden Witch, is a psychic-clairvoyant and a practicing Witch of more than seventeen years. Ellen is a master gardener, and she teaches classes on gardening and flower folklore at her local community college. A regular contributor to the Llewellyn's *Herbal Almanac* and *Magical Almanac*, she is also the author of *Garden Witchery* (Llewellyn, 2003). Ellen and her husband raise their three magical teenagers and tend to their enchanted gardens in Missouri.

EMBER follows a path of nature-centered spirituality that inspires her to write poetry and articles about nature and magic. Her writing has appeared in various literary journals and in several Llewellyn annuals. She lives in the Midwest with her husband and two feline companions.

EILEEN HOLLAND is a Wiccan priestess and a solitary eclectic Witch. She is the author of *The Wicca Handbook* (Weiser, 2000), and coauthor of *A Witch's Book of Answers* (RedWheel/Weiser,

2003). She is also the webmaster of Open, Sesame, a popular witchcraft site found at www.open-sesame.com.

FEATHER JONES has been a practicing herbalist, wildcrafter, and botanical instructor since 1982. She holds a certificate as a clinical herbalist from the Santa Fe College of Natural Medicine, and she has a part-time private practice. Feather is also founder and director of the Rocky Mountain Center for Botanical Studies, a state-certified herbal occupational school with one-, two-, and three-year programs of study in Western herbalism. She is an international lecturer, teacher, author, animal rights activist, and voice for wild plants.

RAVEN KALDERA is a Neopagan shaman, homesteader, activist, musician, astrologer, and wordsmith who did time in many cities before finally escaping. If you want to know more, do a web search on his name.

JAMES KAMBOS has had a lifelong interest in herbs and all forms of folk magic. He has authored many articles on these subjects and holds a degree in history. From his home in the Appalachian hills of southern Ohio, he writes, gardens, and paints.

JONATHAN KEYES lives in Portland, Oregon, where he likes to fiddle around in the garden and play with his cat. Jon works as an astrologer and herbalist and has written an astrological health book titled *Guide to Natural Health* (Llewellyn, 2002), as well as an herb book titled *A Traditional Herbal*. He is currently working on a book titled *Healers*, a series of interviews with various herbalists, *curanderos*, and medicine people from around the United States.

EDAIN MCCOY has practiced witchcraft for more than twenty years, during which time has studied many magical traditions—including Wicca, Jewitchery, Celtic and Appalachian traditions, and Curanderismo. She is listed in the reference books *Who's Who in America* and *Contemporary Authors*. She the author of seventeen books, including; *A Witch's Guide to Faery Folk* (Llewellyn, 1994), *Celtic Myth and Magick* (Llewellyn, 1995), *Inside a Witches'*

Coven (Llewellyn, 1997), *Celtic Women's Spirituality* (Llewellyn, 1998), *Entering the Summerland* (Llewellyn, 1996), *Bewitchments* (Llewellyn, 2000), *Enchantments* (Llewellyn, 2001), *Spellworking for Covens* (Llewellyn, 2002), and the forthcoming book *Advanced Witchcraft*.

CARRIE MOSS lives in Cheshire, England, and gets great pleasure from her own herb patch. She lectures in law and taxation at an agricultural college. In addition, she takes workshops in garden design, cooking, crafting, and generally enjoying herbs. She lives with her husband, two children, and a number of Hebridean sheep and rare breeds of hens.

LEEDA ALLEYN PACOTTI practices as a naturopathic physician, nutritional counselor, and master herbalist specializing in dream language, health astrology, and mind-body communication.

ROBERT PLACE is a visionary artist and illustrator whose award-winning paintings, sculpture, and jewelry have been displayed in galleries and museums in America, Europe, and Japan. He is the creator, and coauthor with Rosemary Ellen Guiley, of *The Alchemical Tarot* and *The Angels Tarot*, both published by HarperCollins, and he is the creator and author of *The Tarot of the Saints*, published by Llewellyn in 2001. The *Tarot of the Saints* appeared on the cover of Publisher's Weekly and won first runner up in interactive sidelines at the annual International New-Age Trade Show in Denver. He has completed his fourth Tarot deck and book set, *The Tarot of the Buddha*, which will be published by Llewellyn in 2003.

LAUREL REUFNER has been a solitary Pagan for some time now. She is active in the local CUUPS chapter, writing for their local publications and working on books, articles, and other bright, shiny objects too interesting to resist. Southeastern Ohio has always been her home. At the moment she lives in Athens County with her wonderful husband and two adorable little heathens, er, daughters.

LYNNE SMYTHE is a freelance writer living in Delray Beach, Florida, with her husband, son, and daughter. She spends too much time outside in the dirt, where her main gardening passions are attracting butterflies and growing organic herbs and vegetables. She is a member of the Evening Herb Society of West Palm Beach, and she writes a variety of articles for their newsletter.

TANNIN SCHWARTZSTEIN has dedicated a significant part of her life, both privately and professionally, to the pursuit of the spiritual arts. Tannin has studied diverse practices and paths such as chi gong, gnosticism, Afro-Caribbean religions, various shamanistic energy techniques, and even a pinch of ceremonial magic. She is the proprietor of Bones and Flowers, Worcester's only occult specialty store (www.bonesandflowers.com). And she is also a crafter in diverse media—such as acrylics, small sculpture, ceramic, bone, and wood—and a legally ordained Pagan minister.

S. Y. ZENITH is three-quarters Chinese, one tad Irish, and 100 percent lifelong solitary Pagan who has lived and traveled extensively in Asia over the past two decades. (These sojourns have included parts of India, Nepal, Malaysia, Thailand, Singapore, and Japan.) She is currently based in Sydney, Australia, where her time is divided between writing, experimenting with alternative remedies, herb crafts, and culinary delights. She is a member of the Australian Society of Authors.

Editor's Note

The contents of this book are not meant to diagnose, treat, prescribe, or substitute for consultation with a licensed heath care professional. Herbs, whether used internally or externally, should be introduced in small amounts to allow the body to adjust and to detect possible allergies. Please consult a standard reference source, or an expert herbalist, to learn more about the possible effects of certain herbs. Llewellyn Worldwide does not participate in, endorse, or have any authority or responsibility concerning private business transactions between its authors and the public.